Marital Communication
and
Decision Making

Marital Communication and
Decision Making

Analysis, Assessment, and Change

EDWIN J. THOMAS

THE FREE PRESS
A Division of Macmillan Publishing Co., Inc.
NEW YORK

Collier Macmillan Publishers
LONDON

The Free Press
A Division of Macmillan Publishing Co., Inc.
866 Third Avenue, New York, N.Y. 10022

Collier Macmillan Canada, Ltd.

Library of Congress Catalog Card Number: 75-41551

Printed in the United States of America

printing number

1 2 3 4 5 6 7 8 9 10

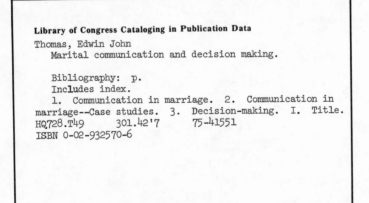

Library of Congress Cataloging in Publication Data
Thomas, Edwin John
    Marital communication and decision making.

    Bibliography: p.
    Includes index.
    1. Communication in marriage. 2. Communication in
marriage--Case studies. 3. Decision-making. I. Title.
HQ728.T49   301.42'7   75-41551
ISBN 0-02-932570-6

To the wives, husbands, and other intimates
who desire to improve their interpersonal relationships

Contents

Preface

COMMUNICATION AND decision making are basic in marital interaction. While success in these two areas is generally taken for granted, difficulties are by no means infrequent. Indeed, a significant number of couples seeking help for their marriages have some real limitations in these areas, which may threaten the very existence of the marriages.

Analysis and assessment of verbal behavior in communication and decision making can be intricate and complex. Until recently there have been virtually no systematic techniques that would help reduce the complexity to manageable proportions and isolate the behavioral components involved. Also there has been a dearth of procedures available for remediation of problems in these aspects of verbal behavior.

The purpose of this book is to present concepts and procedures for the analysis, appraisal, and modification of difficulties in marital communication and decision making. The role of social learning is emphasized, and a variety of new methods of assessment and remediation are presented. The approach to social learning is systematic—through detailed, step-by-step practice procedures, case examples, and verbatim transcripts of verbal behavior. Although written primarily for those who work with couples and families who have problems in communicating and in making decisions, this book should also be useful to students, marital partners, and others who wish to learn more about marriage and the family.

For the past five years, my colleagues and I have carried out behavioral assessments and modification programs with dozens of couples and families referred to our research project for assistance. A number of single-case experiments were conducted to examine the feasibility and efficacy of selected procedures of assessment and remediation. Several new techniques were developed, implemented, and evaluated in the research and also in my own individual consultations with marital partners. (Selected portions of this research have been reported in professional journals in recent years, and additional technical reports for researchers are currently being written.) This book, however, is not a technical report of research findings, but rather a distillation of selected information relevant to practitioners, garnered on several projects and from individual consultations.

Although the book was conceived as an entity and written so as to provide an orderly, integrated, and coherent exposition, the chapters can be grouped for special purposes into components for separate study. Chapters 1–4 deal with marital communication, Chapters 5–7 with marital decision making. Chapters 3 and 4, on the assessment and modification of marital communication, and Chapters 6 and 7, on the assessment and change of marital decision making, comprise, along with the related appendixes, something of a practice manual on these areas of behavior. Chapters 1, 2, and 5 are more theoretical and analytic in that they deal with social-learning factors in marital communication and decision making. Selected chapters and appendixes may also serve to sharpen the practitioner's skills in some of the procedures presented.

Acknowledgments

I WISH TO ACKNOWLEDGE the support provided for the initial research for this book by the Social and Rehabilitation Administration, U.S. Department of Health, Education and Welfare in the form of grants SRS-CRD-425-8-286, CRD-529-0, and SRS-10-P 56023/5-02. Much of the manuscript was prepared while I was on sabbatical leave from the University of Michigan in the fall term, 1974. My sincere thanks go to Dr. Phillip Fellin, Dean of the University of Michigan School of Social Work, and Ms. Ann Fowler, Administrative Assistant of the school, for facilitating the completion of this work. I particularly wish to acknowledge the stimulation provided by my recent colleagues in research, Dr. Claude Walter, Dr. Kevin O'Flaherty, Dr. Robert C. Carter, and Ms. Joyce Borkin, all of whom participated in selected aspects of earlier research and with whom I have written technical research reports and journal articles on particular portions of the work. I also benefited from having collaborated at various earlier points with Dr. David Birch, Dr. William Butterfield, Mr. Roland Etcheverry, Dr. Arthur Frankel, Dr. Eileen Gambrill, and Mr. Robert Hodnefield, with some of whom I have also written articles or technical reports. Special mention should be made of Ms. Ann Commorato and Ms. Judith Brieger, who undertook a field test of a few of the assessment and modification procedures in the Family Service of Genesee County, Flint, Michigan. I also wish to mention my valuable association at various times on the project with Nancy Addison, Jean Anmuth, Jack Butler, Judith Doersch, Harriet Fusfeld, Walter McDonald, Gerald Miller, William D. Miller, Gretchen Murray, David Riddle, Mary Sarason, Susan Stern, and Eugene Talsma. I greatly appreciate the competent secretarial assistance provided in manuscript preparation by Vivian A. Thomas.

Marital Communication
and
Decision Making

CHAPTER ONE

Couple Communication and Verbal Behavior

TALKING IS ONE OF the primary activities marital partners engage in together and most couples spend enormous amounts of time talking to each other. Communication between marital partners is vitally important for individual wellbeing and mutual harmony. It reflects difficulties and strengths in the marriage and in other areas of life, and sets the stage for future marital satisfaction or discord (Lederer and Jackson, 1969; Levenger and Senn, 1967; Navran, 1967; and Raush, Barry, Hertel, and Swain, 1974).

Communication difficulties are probably the most common type of problem encountered in couples who seek assistance to improve their interpersonal relationships. Among the frequently heard complaints are that partners argue, quarrel, nag, insult, or put each other down; that they talk past each other, don't say what they mean, mislead, talk out of both sides of their mouths, or lie; that they can't or won't understand what is said, or ignore each other; that they talk too much, too little, too softly, or too loudly; that they never offer praise or acknowledgment for doing a good job; that there is too much gloomy talk and too little that is pleasant.

Practitioners whose job it is to assess and alter verbal behavior of marital communication will find their work much easier if they have a conception of the behavioral events that comprise marital communication and some of its principal characteristics. This chapter therefore presents a social-learning analysis of verbal behavior in marital communication, intended to provide a framework for the practical work of assessment and remediation.

1

Verbal Behavior as Operant Behavior

There have been many approaches to communication. Some have regarded the spoken word as somehow incidental or secondary to non-verbal behavior, such as motor action. Other approaches have viewed words largely as signs of the speaker's internal state, his intentions, motives, ideas, or attitudes. In the approach adopted here, couple communication is specified as the verbal behavior of marital partners. Verbal behavior, consisting mainly of overt vocal responding, can be unequivocally observed and, when appropriate, recorded and objectively measured.[1] Although verbal behavior is often related to non-verbal behavior and may also provide clues about the speaker's internal state, it is first and foremost important in its own right. Verbal behavior is a direct indicator of what is generally meant by communication. The verbal responses themselves may be functional or dysfunctional for the marital relationship, and, if they are made accessible to the practitioner, they may be specified directly, acted upon, and modified in the interests of an improved marriage.

In the production of speech, verbal behavior is operant behavior inasmuch as it directly implicates the skeletal-muscular system (Skinner, 1957). This type of behavior involves the striated muscles of the skeletal system as opposed to the glands and smooth muscles involved in respondent behavior. Like other forms of operant behavior, verbal behavior has the following properties:

1. Verbal behavior is under the control of its consequences. That is, stimuli occurring immediately following classes of verbal behavior can serve to accelerate or diminish the future rate of responding for these response classes, depending on whether the stimuli are reinforcing or punishing. Many studies have indicated that selected aspects of verbal behavior may be accelerated or decelerated through the presentation of particular stimuli following the verbal behavior.[2] If proper consequences can be found in modification efforts, desirable verbal behavior may be increased and undesirable verbal behavior can be decreased.

2. Response characteristics of verbal behavior may be treated as

[1] This view is narrower than that of Skinner (1957), who defined verbal behavior as "behavior reinforced through the mediation of other persons" (p. 14).

[2] Reviews of research and reports of findings in this area have been prepared by such writers as Holz and Azrin (1966), Kanfer (1968), Krasner (1958), and Matarazzo and Wiens (1972).

rates, durations, magnitudes, or latencies, depending upon the particular response properties of interest. Thus, one may be interested in the frequency of a husband's positive talk (rate per minute or per hour); the entire amount of time during which couple verbal interchange occurs (duration); the intensity of verbal tantrums (rated, for example, on a scale of judged intensity); or the interval between the end of one mate's speech and the beginning of the other's (measured as a latency of time between speakers).

3. Verbal behavior may be cued by the presentation of such discriminative stimuli as verbal instructions. Discriminative stimuli serve as stimulus occasions upon which a given response, if emitted, will produce reinforcement. Under appropriate conditions, instructions, signals, and gestures can all serve as cues in the presence of which given verbal responses may be emitted and others not. If stimuli do not function properly as discriminative cues for given verbal behavior, discrimination training can be undertaken in order to establish the cues as proper occasioning stimuli for the behavior.

4. Although there is some evidence that verbal behavior may be somewhat easier to change than nonverbal behavior (Dulany and O'Connell, 1963; Salzinger, Portnoy, and Feldman, 1964), it is perhaps prudent to take the conservative view now that, until shown to the contrary, changes in verbal behavior will be no easier to achieve than are changes in nonverbal operant repertoires.

5. It is probably safe to assume that when such changes occur, they will be highly specific situationally, unless generalization is programmed (O'Leary and Drabman, 1971; Kazdin and Bootzin, 1972; and Walker and Buckley, 1972).

6. The verbal repertoire, like other operant repertoires, has a particular response topography. What is relevant here is that human speech is probably the largest, most complex, and most finely honed operant repertoire of all. Not only are there many thousands of individual speech elements, but they are complexly interrelated and may be combined in seemingly unlimited ways. Marital interaction involves especially great complexity because there are two response repertoires, each combined in particular ways in the rapid back-and-forth verbal exchanges of the partners.

In addition to its great size and complexity, there are other relevant characteristics of verbal repertoire. There are relatively few descriptive labels in the language to characterize the behavioral components. A verbal interchange called an argument, for example, may or may not consist of such behaviors as overgeneralization, disagreement, faulting, illogical talk, screaming, and irrelevant talk. Without behavioral specification and analysis, the components of verbal behavior cannot be described precisely, and the formal distinctions of such specialized fields as syntax and logic simply do not capture the significant behavioral components.

Still another characteristic of the verbal repertoire is that the response classes for verbal behavior may be very uncertain. That is, it is not at all clear, short of careful empirical study, what verbal responses cohere as identifiable, unitary groups of responses. This has posed difficulties in carrying out research on verbal behavior, as emphasized by Holz and Azrin (1966) and Salzinger (1967). At one extreme, speech itself may be a response class inasmuch as it would appear to consitute a functional class for some psychotics (Sherman, 1963; Thomson, Fraser, and McDougall, 1974). At the other extreme, it is possible that under given circumstances verbal elements as small as a sound or a given grammatical unit may constitute functional classes. Practitioners must often proceed to specify responses, select elements of verbal behavior for modification, and evaluate effects of modification efforts without being sure that the target responses constitute a simple, functional response class.[3]

Verbal Behavior as Stimuli in Interaction

The verbal behavior of the speaker consists of stimuli for the listener. There is no basis for assuming that verbal stimuli operate differently from other stimuli in affecting behavior, and there is considerable evidence that verbal behavior may control behavior by means of several well-known stimulus functions. Five of those functions will be discussed here—reinforcement, punishment, extinction, discriminative control, and the operation of eliciting stimuli.

The reinforcing function of verbal behavior is perhaps the most familiar. What person B says following the speech of person A may increase person A's future rate of responding in that area of speech. What person B said may thus be regarded as having been reinforcing. For example, speaker B may say, "Yes, that's good," following what A said on topic X, with the consequence that responses on topic X are more frequently emitted by A in the future. Saying "yes," "good,"

---

[3] For details concerning other aspects of verbal behavior and language not directly relevant here, the reader is referred to such writers as Mowrer (1960), Salzinger (1967), Skinner (1957), and Staats (1968).

"mn-hm," "I approve," "right on," "neat," "correct" may serve as verbal reinforcement in an interchange.

Verbal behavior may also be punishing inasmuch as what is said following a given response serves to suppress the future rate of responding for that response. For example, if speaker B says, "I disagree," following speaker A's expression of opinion, with the consequence that speaker A thereafter reduces the rate of expressing these opinions, this would illustrate the diminution in the rate of responding following a stimulus presentation that behavior analysts refer to as punishment. Other verbal responses that may have a punishing consequence are "no," "you're wrong," "uh-uh," "incorrect," "really!" "you're crazy," "you must be kidding!" and "I don't believe you."

Verbal behavior previously sustained by verbal reinforcement or punishment may also be extinguished. The extinction of a verbal response previously sustained by reinforcement consists of withholding the previously reinforcing verbal stimuli, with the consequence that the response previously reinforced is greatly reduced or eliminated. For instance, the verbal response to be reduced might be a husband's tendency to scream "What time is it?" in the expectation that his wife will answer, no matter where she is in the house or what else she is doing. If, instead of replying "7:45" or whatever the time is, the wife steadfastly fails to reply and no one else in the home answers instead, this behavior of the husband should ultimately be eliminated. To be successful, extinction requires that there be no accidental or periodic reinforcement; the withholding of reinforcement should be continuous, with no exception.

Extinction also applies to punishment. That is, responses previously sustained by verbal punishment often can be restored to their prepunished level when the punishing response is withheld in an extinction procedure.

Verbal stimuli may be discriminative inasmuch as they set the occasion for, and provide some control over, emitting certain verbal responses. For example, a husband might say, "I like talking with you about what happened on your job today," with the consequence that the wife would proceed immediately to discuss happenings of the day at work and, in consequence, receive the husband's commendation. In this example, the husband's comments served as a discriminative stimulus (S^D), which is a stimulus that provides the occasion for producing a given response that, in turn, is likely to be reinforced. S^Ds exercise varying degrees of stimulus control over particular responses, ranging from a modest amount to near-perfect control. Thus, following the presentation of a discriminative stimulus, the occasioned response may occur with a given degree of probability and, when it does occur, it may be reinforced with a given degree of probability. Reinforcement of responses produced by S^Ds, like reinforcement of other responses, occurs on a reinforcement schedule which may or may not be continuous. Indeed, most real-life reinforcement schedules are intermittent. Common forms of verbal discriminative stimuli are requests, instructions, and demands, but almost anything that is said may have the function of an S^D.

A related stimulus that is important in discrimination is the S^Δ (S-delta). The S^Δ is the stimulus that provides the occasion for a response which, if produced, will not lead to reinforcement. If at bedtime the wife says, "I am not in the mood," and the husband makes sexual advances anyway, with no payoff, the wife's comment would illustrate an S^Δ for sexual advances by the husband.

Discriminative control of speaker responding is probably pervasive in verbal interaction. This is very clear in the case of responding to questions of fact. For example, a person may ask another, "What is two times two?" "What's your name?" or "How old are you?" In such cases, a very definite response is under the control of the question and, over time in most cases, only the correct response would be reinforced. Verbal responses such as these, which are controlled by a particular object, event, or property of an object or event, Skinner (1957) called "tacts." Analogous factual questions relating to family life might be the following: "What did it cost?" "Where did you go?" or "What's the best way to get to the shoe store?" Many questions involve matters of objective or subjective fact that are reportorial but are also to some extent discretionary. For example, the wife might ask, "What did you do today?" and the husband could reply in detail by reporting factually more or less precisely what he did. There is discretion, however, inasmuch as he may elect to emphasize certain things and mute or even omit others. Analogous questions are as follows: "How do you feel?" or "What do you think of this?" Discriminative control also operates where there are no matters of fact involved. For example, the husband might say to his wife that the meal was very nice and the wife might respond with, "Thanks, I hoped you would like it." The latter response might be the wife's characteristic reply to a compliment of the type bestowed by the husband. Or, the husband might say "I love you," and the wife, predictably, might reply, "I love you, too."

In addition, the speaker's response itself can serve as a discriminative stimulus to produce still other responses. That is, dicriminative control over responding may be exercised not only by what others say but by what one says oneself. In response to her husband's query, "What did you do today?" the wife might report on what she did, and her words may trigger additional lines of response not relating directly to her day's activities. Thus, the wife might say that she worked in the morning without event, went shopping in the afternoon, went to the library, where she obtained a new novel, and then, might launch into a discussion of interesting books that a friend had recently recommended; and, while discussing these books, she might be reminded of the English literature class she took in college and how inspiring the lectures had been.[4]

An eliciting stimulus is one that produces respondent behavior, such as anxiety, sexual arousal, elation, or anger. These behaviors, sometimes called emotional responses, involve the glands and smooth muscles. Stimuli that have the capability of eliciting respondent behaviors do so automatically and in reflexlike manner. The stimuli, if they have been conditioned, were once neutral, and, through the processes of classical conditioning, in which an unconditioned stimulus is paired with a neutral stimulus, have taken on the capability of producing the conditioned responses. Thus, a husband may say to his wife, "I love you," with the consequence that the wife becomes aroused sexually. The words "I love you" are conditioned emotional stimuli, originally neutral but now capable of producing intense emotional responses because of particular conditioning experiences. A less happy example involves the husband saying "I hate you," with the consequence that the wife responds with intense anxiety. Actually, all words have the capability of producing emotional reactions in the listener, depending upon his or her particular conditioning history for those words. There is reason to believe that many of the words and phrases we hear do, in fact, frequently produce conditioned emotional reactions (Staats, 1968).

Furthermore, as Staats (1968) has emphasized, words can be conditioned by higher-order processes by the way they are paired, and the objects to which the words relate reacted to accordingly. For instance, if the wife says, "Your son was a thief yesterday," the negative conditioned emotional reactions associated with "thief" may become connected with "son," and the father is likely to react negatively to his son.[5]

---

[4] Analyses of these and other intraverbal connections may be found in Skinner (1957) and Staats (1968), among others.

[5] These and other behavioral explanations of the complex processes involv-

In all the above examples, true functional relationships of the stimuli and the responses were assumed. From such examples, when true functional relationships were assumed, it is easy to presume that functional relationships can readily be inferred from the content of what is said. Not so. The descriptive meaning of what is said should not be confused with the possible functional properties of the verbal behavior. For example, a husband might say, "I like it when you say things like that" in response to his wife's flattery, with the consequence that the wife flatters her husband less rather than more in the future. In this example, the descriptive content of the message was rewarding in the popular sense of that word, but the functional consequence was punishing inasmuch as there was a consequent diminution in the rate of responding. What is intended to be reinforcing may not be in fact. Likewise, what is intended to be punishing in fact may be reinforcing. In response to a controversial opinion about politics, for instance, the husband may say, "I disagree," and this, in turn, could produce more rather than less subsequent discussion of the subject by the wife.[6] These examples illustrate what Browning and Stover (1971) have called the reversed polarity of reinforcers; that is, the expected outcome of a stimulus operation is the opposite of what in fact happens. The importance of the difference between descriptive and functional relationships cannot be stressed too strongly. What determines a functional relationship is not always what it appears to be on the basis of speaker intent or descriptive content but rather what actually ensues in speaker response. True functional relationships must be determined empirically either from careful observation in natural situations or with experimental methods.

When a given stimulus function has been provisionally identified, it is also possible that the stimulus may have one or more additional functions as well. For example, a wife's remark, "I think that's nice," may function as a reinforcing stimulus for her husband's behavior at that point and also as an eliciting stimulus for a respondent, such as his sexual arousal. Many stimuli that are punishing also elicit anxiety. For instance, a husband may insult his wife in response to which the wife says, "Don't you ever do that again"; in addition to suppressing the future frequency of such insults, the statement also may arouse anxiety in the husband. Most reinforcing and punishing

---

ing the learning of meaning and the relationship of language and emotion are discussed in detail in Das (1969), Mowrer (1960), Staats and Staats (1963), and Staats (1968).

[6] Such a comment as "I disagree" might also have discriminative properties for the listener; this topic will be discussed more fully in connection with multiple stimulus functions.

stimuli are also discriminative. A reinforcing stimulus in verbal interchange, for example, not only increases the rate of responding for behavior thus reinforced but may also serve as an S^D for this class of responses. Multiple stimulus functions of the type indicated above are probably more commonly encountered than single functions with the verbal stimuli in verbal interchanges. Analyses of verbal behaviors that restrict possible stimulus functions to only one are probably oversimple.

The verbal stimulus has meaning that is combined with vocal inflection and nonverbal cues, such as facial expression, gesture, and body position. Verbal stimuli are thus multichanneled. The semantic component involves the meaning of the words; the vocal part relates to the tone of voice and inflection with which the words are expressed; and the nonverbal feature embraces other stimuli, such as those conveyed by the face, limbs, and torso. Studies have suggested that each of these components may convey separately its own information (e.g., Mehrabian and Ferris, 1967). These channels of information may be consistent or inconsistent. Where there are inconsistencies, such as in a compliment given semantically combined with indifferent or negative vocal inflection, the response of the listener is likely to be considerably less positive than were the compliment given with a more pleasant inflection. Where possible, couple communication should be examined for vocal and nonverbal as well as semantic components.

There are two features of group interaction particularly relevant here. One is that marital and family interaction involves more than one target for verbal stimuli. When a mother speaks to a child in the presence of others in the family, the father and other children may be affected as well. When speaking to his wife in couple interaction, the husband influences his own behavior as well as that of his wife. Each person is of course part of his own behavior-controlling environment, and he is very likely to be influenced by what he himself says. That is, the speech of the speaker produces response-generated cues for himself that may affect not only what he is about to say but what he may say in the more remote future. The effects produced for the speaker himself may differ from the effects produced for others. Thus, the speaker may be reinforced by his own talking whereas the listener may find the talking aversive; or the speaker may find his own talking aversive whereas the listener may find it reinforcing.

A second feature is that verbal behavior of marital partners in interaction involves rapidly shifting speakers so that the effect of the verbal behavior of any speaker at any time may be subtle and difficult to discern. Furthermore, the effects for the partners may be different with each interchange. To the extent that each individual serves as a source of contingencies for the speaking of the other, the rapid shifting of speakers provides for many possible changing contingencies for each partner. These contingencies may or may not be consistent and may constitute, altogether, very complex controlling conditions for verbal behavior.

Among the practical implications of these characteristics of interaction is that, if the objective of analysis is to appraise the antecedent-consequent relationships for verbal interchanges, very careful tracking of the interaction must be carried out; and modification of verbal behavior, when undertaken during ongoing couple or family interactions, requires precise, pinpointed intervention.

Dual Functions of Verbal Behavior

There are essentially two functions of verbal behavior in communication—message sending and behavioral guidance.[7] The objective of message sending is to inform the listener. To accomplish this, sufficient, clear, and accurate information needs to be given. Message sending requires an adequate medium, which, in the case of verbal communication, consists largely of the voice channel. Among the vocal features prerequisite to good message sending are speaking at a rate that will allow for careful listening, speaking neither too quickly nor too slowly following the termination of the partner's speech, speaking long enough, loudly enough, and fluently enough to be understood, and not employing excessively affective speech.

The function of behavioral guidance embraces a variety of possible consequences for the listener. At a minimal level, these involve holding the attention of the listener, having him track adequately what the speaker says, sustaining appropriate amounts of speech when the listener talks, and maintaining necessary continuity of the themes of content covered in the interchanges. It is generally necessary, in addition, to have a reasonably equitable speaker-listener interchange, with essentially one speaker talking at any given time. More specific objectives may involve giving information on a particular topic, conveying information in a given way, producing verbal

---

[7] Many writers have made this distinction. Jackson (1965), for example, differentiated between the report and command components; see also Watzlawick, Beavin, and Jackson (1967).

or nonverbal reinforcement from the listener, or persuading the listener to change his behavior.

The functions of message sending and behavioral guidance may fail to be accomplished properly because of the verbal behavior of the speaker, which may create in the listener the wrong impression, dislike of the speaker, loss of attention, the feeling of being deceived, mistrust, or such inappropriate emotional responses as fear or anxiety. It may also generate avoidance of the speaker, including termination of contact; the exchange of ambiguous, incomplete or incorrect information; needless and aversive repetition of verbal behavior; loss of thematic continuity of the verbal interchange; escalation of disagreement; needless interpersonal conflict; failure to solve problems and make decisions, where verbal behavior relates to these activities; suppression of the expression of ideas and feelings; and unpleasant emotional conditions that interfere with other activities such as eating, sex, and sleeping.

Any of these difficulties may adversely affect the couple relationship, causing reduced satisfaction of the partners, increased unhappiness, and interpersonal conflict along with greater likelihood of estrangement and dissolution of the relationship.

Analytic Dimensions for Verbal Behavior in Communication

Most verbal behavior may be analyzed in at least five relevant ways. Four of these dimensions relate to the message-sending function: content, representational accuracy, information, and vocal properties. The other dimension of analysis is behavioral guidance, the same term that we used above to refer to the second function of communication.

CONTENT

The content of verbal behavior consists essentially of what is said. For example, the content of the statement "I like you very much" has to do with the speaker's approval of the person to whom the statement is addressed. Marital communication can pertain to almost any area of content. However, the most common referent areas in marital communication appear to involve money, sex, affection, work, attention shown to family members, behavioral control, member privacy, child management, relationships with relatives, social activities outside the home, the handling of alcohol and drugs, religion, politics, allocation of time together, division of labor of family members, family decision making, and communication among family members. Discussion involving any area of content generally yields valuable information about how content is typically handled by the couple and about the referent area itself. For example, there may be problems of thematic continuity indicated by excessive dwelling on given subjects or avoidance of important topics. Discussion about the referent area itself indicates possible strengths or limitations of marital behavior in that area and also whether possible difficulties in that area might directly affect marital communication.

REPRESENTATIONAL ACCURACY

The content of verbal behavior involving referents, such as events, people, or objects of the world, is represented in the language of the verbal behavior. The real-world referents may be depicted accurately or inaccurately. For instance, the husband may assert that his wife is angry when she is not. Misrepresentations may also be indicated by lack of speech specificity, overgeneralization, or other representational inaccuracies.

INFORMATION

Verbal behavior also conveys information inasmuch as it reduces uncertainty for the listener. Among verbal behavior difficulties involving information are the conveying of too much or too little information or the provision of overly redundant or insufficiently redundant information.

VOCAL PROPERTIES

The vocal feature of verbal behavior embraces the sound of the talk, including its volume and pleasant or unpleasant qualities. Excessive loudness or softness and aversive sound are among the vocal difficulties of marital verbal behavior.

BEHAVIORAL GUIDANCE

Guidance of the listener's behavior is provided by the speaker's verbal behavior through such stimulus functions as response elicitation, reinforcement, punishment, extinction, or stimulus control achieved through the presentation of S^Ds and S^As. Among the possible difficulties of behavioral guidance in marital interaction are excessive control, inappropriate control, and ineffective control.

Some Interaction Patterns

Despite the intricacies and complexities of verbal interchanges, the behavior of individuals in dyadic interaction displays important stabilities and regularities. For example, Matarazzo and Weins (1972) found high correlations between measures of selected formal characteristics of the interviewee's speech by two different interviewers. For example, the correlation for the duration of utterance was .77, and analogous correlations in the 60's and the 70's were found for the duration of silences, percentage of initiatives, and number of interruptions. Similar findings were reported by Jaffe and Feldstein (1970) in their examination of formal characteristics of speech in dyadic conversation. In regard to stability, they concluded:

> In summary, the results of the three experiments suggest that the time patterns of an individual's conversational style—the duration of his pauses, his switching pauses, his vocalizations, and his contribution to the frequency of speaker switches in conversation— remain remarkably stable during the course of a conversation and consistent from one conversation to another with the same partner regardless of the time lapse between them, or whether the topical focus or some other condition of the conversation changes [pp. 38–39].

These authors also present evidence to suggest that the duration of vocalizations is the most stable characteristic of those examined. Even so, it seems that talk time is very much modifiable when subjected to experimental interventions intended to systematically increase or decrease this speech characteristic. Thus, Matarazzo and Weins (1972) found that interviewee speech duration could be readily increased in response to interview "mn-hm mn-hms" and head nodding.

Selected characteristics of the content of verbal behavior also appear to be relatively stable. In their study of twenty-four members of five families during baselines of two weeks, Patterson and Reid (1970) calculated stability coefficients for a number of interaction variables derived from systematic family observation. Reliability estimates for the odd- and even-numbered five-minute blocks of data yielded coefficients of .73 for number of initiations, .65 for number of interactions, .70 for number of positive reinforcers, and .70 for number of negative consequences.

Despite such stabilities, there are interdependences between interacting partners. The stabilities referred to above, for example, are less when individuals interact over periods of time with different conversational partners as compared with the same partners (Jaffe and Feldstein, 1970). Each partner must somehow adjust his speech to that of the other. This mutual adjustment is a type of pattern matching, as has been shown dramatically in the research of Matarazzo and Weins (1972). They found that, in an interview, the duration of the interviewee's speech was markedly influenced by the duration of the interviewer's speech. When the interviewers planfully spoke for longer periods of time, so did the interviewees; likewise, when the interviewers spoke systematically for shorter periods of time, so did their subjects. Another example of interdependency in dyadic interaction is the relationship of reaction times of speakers. In their study of client reaction time in interviews with a counselor, Lauver, Kelley, and Froehle (1971) found that there was a direct relationship between client and therapist speech latencies; longer client latencies led directly to longer therapist latencies.

Another interdependency involves act-to-act patterns in marital communication, as discovered by Raush, Barry, Hertel, and Swain (1974) in their analysis of communication of marital partners who discussed various assigned topics involving conflict situations. The conclusions of these researchers in regard to what they called behavioral reciprocity are directly relevant here. There appears to be an interaction version of tit for tat, as follows:

> [A]lthough there is a modal tendency to respond to any act (interchange) with a cognitively oriented response, cognitive acts by one partner elicit a higher than expected proportion of cognitive responses from the other; approaches to resolution draw similar approaches from the partner; and attempts at emotional reconciliation receive responses in kind; so, too, do coercive acts and personal attacks receive reciprocal responses. . . . Rejecting acts tend to elicit either emotional appeals or coercive tactics [p. 198].

The idea of reciprocity, as proposed by Rausch and his associates, is that like tends to beget like in regard to messages of communication. Working with different concepts and measures, Patterson and his associates have proposed a similar conception of marital interaction. They suggest that coercive acts lead to further coercion and that positive behaviors tend to be reciprocated in kind. There is generally an equity in the exchange of observable aversive stimuli (Patterson and Hops, 1972). For example, in their analysis of family interactions, they found a median correlation of 0.65 between the proportions of aversive interaction "given" and "received." In this instance, coercion tended to be associated with coercion. In their review of studies such as those of Wills, Weiss, and Patterson (1974) and Birchler (1972), Jacobson and Martin (1976) concluded that at this time there was evidence for reciprocity on the average across couples inasmuch as positives correlated with positives and negatives with negatives, but that it appeared that there was greater reciprocity for the positives than for the negatives.

In a study of maritally distressed couples and nondistressed spouse-and-stranger dyads, Birchler, Weiss, and Vincent (1975) studied the social-reinforcement exchange. Among the relevant findings were that the distressed dyads in contrast to their nondistressed counterparts produced less positive and more negative social reinforcement, and fewer pleases and more displeases and conflicts. However, the married individuals from distressed couples interacted much more favorably when they had discussions with strangers, emitting about twice as many negative and about one third fewer positive statements to spouses than when interacting with strangers. These findings suggest that although partners in distressed marriages in general evidenced more negatives and fewer positives than did non-distressed spouses, the negatives they exchanged may be a pattern characteristic of the particular spouse-spouse interactive relationship and social-learning history of the partners and that such partners may have the response capability to interact much more competently if given proper conditions for doing so.

The results of a study by Wills, Weiss, and Patterson (1974) are particularly relevant here because these researchers studied the relationships of pleasurable and displeasurable behaviors within spouse dyads, not merely across couples. The study involved seven non-distressed married couples from whom detailed data were collected for fourteen consecutive days, with focus on the pleasurable and dis-pleasurable behavior of the spouses in relationship to marital satis-faction. One finding was that displeasurable behaviors, taken to-gether, accounted for 65 percent of the explained variance of marital satisfaction ratings whereas pleasurable behaviors accounted for only 25 percent of this variance. Another finding was that, in a within-couple analysis, in contrast to the across-couple results reported earlier, there was a much greater tendency for spouses to reciprocate displeasurable than pleasurable behaviors. The study also indicated that the pleasurable and displeasurable dimensions of marital satisfaction were independent, thus implying that changing the partners' behavior on one dimension may have no effect on their behavior on the other. Because of this independence and the disproportionate influence of displeasurable behaviors on marital satisfaction, these authors concluded in regard to intervention approaches that their findings argued for developing modification programs to decrease the rate of displeasurable behavior rather than to focus only on increasing the rate of pleasurable behaviors, as stressed in some approaches (e.g., Stuart, 1969; Weiss et al., 1973).

Social Structure of Family Verbal Behavior

Analysis of family verbal behavior discloses that it differs in a number of ways from communication carried on in most work situations and in other instrumental activities of life. Social-structural factors influencing family communication are listed below.

1. Conventional stimulus control over the topics to be discussed by given family members is relatively lacking. In most families, most topics can be discussed at almost any time. Such freedom and flexibility to communicate have advantages for family members, to be sure, but the relative lack of structure provides an opportunity for communication difficulties to germinate and grow into patterns.

Generally there are no set times for family members to talk on given subjects and not on others. Thus, most families do not have protected, regular times to take up problem solving, decision making, pleasant talk, reports concerning what family members have done, or family administrative matters. This allows the family talk to be controlled more easily by highly diverse, nonpatterned stimuli, such as what someone happened to say, what one happened to read in the paper, the casual sight of something, fatigue, anger, or other emotional or physical conditions of the body. In consequence, inappropriate stimulus control can readily be established over given topics of conversation. Mealtime can become the occasion for airing family difficulties, quarreling, and fighting; the time for sexual activities can be associated with talk about the day's events, with the result that amorous inclinations diminish; television viewing may be a time during which parents endeavor to plan and administer family matters.

Such inappropriate stimulus control is fostered also by the fact that unless special times are set aside for the verbal behavior in question, almost all family communication is concurrent with other behaviors such as eating, driving in the automobile, getting dressed, watching television, or sex. Because each of these nonverbal activities has its own controlling conditions, regularly combining particular verbal behavior with these activities allows the verbal behavior to come under the control of conditions that guide the concurrent behaviors as well as the concurrent behaviors themselves. Thus, if arguments have been allowed to go along with meals, arguing may come to be controlled by the conditions, such as hunger, that control eating at meals and the eating itself also may actually come to cue and reinforce the arguing.

2. Decision-making issues in the family tend to spill over into general family communication and, if family decision making is not accomplished at a specific time, decision matters may infuse virtually all talking of family members. One reason is that most families lack a regular pattern of problem solving and decision making that serves to take care of family business, thereby relieving other discussions of this burden. Another reason is that many particular decision issues recur only rarely, and some are unique, one-time issues. For example, one day the decision might be how to handle unexcused absences at school for the fifteen-year-old under special circumstances. The next day it might be whether the children should go to their great-grandfather's funeral. The next day it might be what to do about the husband's car accident. What is decided in each of these cases need not apply again even if the same problem comes up on another occasion.

3. Family communication involves a small, limited audience such that any given member's verbal behavior is vulnerable to the deficiencies of the partner's verbal behavior. For instance, a nonresponsive listener can eventually diminish the amount of his partner's verbal behavior; or an especially avid listener, who positively reinforces the partner, can greatly accelerate the amount of the partner's speech, thereby possibly producing a problem of partner overtalk. Because of the smallness of the audience and the possibly exaggerated impact of any given person, family communication is particularly vulnerable to the influence of deviant family members.

Also relevant is that reinforcement outside the family may be meager and uncertain. To the extent that it is, the remaining sources within the family take on greatly exaggerated significance. Many individuals work at ungratifying jobs, have few outside interests or pleasures, and experience a sense of isolation and alienation from society. All too many persons live in urban blight and feel a sense of rootlessness, and almost everyone is affected by the rapid changes occurring in social life and societal institutions. To the extent that couples are highly dependent upon internal sources of reinforcement rather than upon those deriving from outside the family, the members are acutely vulnerable to variations and deficits of reinforcement within the relationship. Under these conditions, very small reductions in reinforcement arising from partners can produce exaggerated reactions and changes in verbal and nonverbal behavior. Men and women in exclusive, closed relationships or marriages are especially vulnerable to internal alterations and deficiencies of reinforcement as are housewives who obtain little gratification outside the family, and men and women whose jobs are unsatisfactory and who derive little pleasure from other outside activities.

4. The family, being nuclear and relatively isolated, tends to be detached from most external corrective influences. There is virtually no important external control placed upon the internal workings of most families. This makes it possible for exceedingly unusual patterns of verbal behavior to develop and be sustained without any external detection or alteration. Individual members may abuse one another verbally, persons may brutally dominate others in their verbal behavior, and some individuals may find their speaking behavior virtually extinguished without anyone else's knowing of it unless, perhaps, someone goes to seek help from an outside source. Even then, efforts to change family verbal behavior may be offset or even nullified by lack of cooperation of family members.

5. Even though it is relatively isolated from external corrective influences, the family is in large measure an open system inasmuch as virtually any disruptive input may be brought back into the family by any member. Thus, the husband or wife may have had a very bad day at work and may bring his or her troubles home, berate others, and make everyone else upset; or the children may have had a difficult day at school, come home angry and tired, say things they would not ordinarily say, and initiate family arguments. Unless special efforts are made to cope with such external input, these disruptive influences will not be adequately contained and kept from needlessly affecting others.

Given these characteristics of family verbal behavior, it is understandable how readily the members may develop dysfunctional patterns of communication. Many such difficulties relate directly or indirectly to one or another of the social-structural conditions mentioned above. Thus, there may be failure of members to engage in the relevant verbal behavior required in problem solving or decision making; there may be a confounding of nonverbal activities with inappropriate verbal behavior, such as arguing while watching TV; there may be failure of given members to control the topics of conversation; there may be inconclusive arguments and efforts to make decisions; there may be too much unpleasant talk and too little reporting of member behavior and gratifying talk for listeners as well as speakers; and individuals may overreact with arguments and conflict to minor reductions in reinforcement from their partner.

Social-structural conditions such as those identified above provide a social context that allows and, in some cases, predisposes family members to develop communication difficulties. As important as they are, however, the particular sources of difficulty for particular couples may derive rather directly from these general sociological conditions (called structural deficits for couple communication) or they may be much less directly related (e.g., shortcomings of partner interaction). It is in the context of these social-structural conditions that family members develop particular communication strength and difficulties.

Sources of Difficulty in Verbal Behavior

Analysis of the sources of difficulty in verbal behavior relevant to intervention should be focused on contemporary, precipitating, and sustaining conditions rather than on the originating conditions, which, unless they continue to affect behavior, are not accessible to remediation. Contemporary sources of difficulty, however, are operative here and now and may be directly altered or at least weakened by countervailing remediation.

There are at least five sources of verbal behavior difficulty: repertoire deficit, referent conditions, setting events, structural deficits, and partner interaction. Procedures relating to the assessment of these sources are discussed in Chapter 3. Chapter 4 discusses modification procedures.

REPERTOIRE DEFICIT

A deficit in a partner's verbal repertoire based on prior learning in contexts other than the couple relationship may cause difficulties. For example, an individual may never have learned to let others talk and, in consequence, talks incessantly when in the presence of his partner. Another example might be the wife who never learned in her early years to talk about anything but herself and therefore bores her husband with excessive egocentric talk. Because of the essentially idiosyncratic nature of social learning in communication, individuals may have repertoire deficits in virtually any area of communication upon entering a couple relationship. Difficulties of verbal behavior arising from repertoire deficits may be remedied most readily by providing training for the partner to accelerate specific responses.

REFERENT CONDITIONS

Particular conditions in the life situation of the partners that do not embrace communication proper may coexist with and give rise to disordered verbal behavior. Consider, for example, serious financial problems. Money troubles in the family may generate arguments which would not have occurred had there been no financial difficulties and might not recur if these difficulties were resolved. In this example, the verbal behavior of the quarrels is presumed to be under the control of the financial difficulties to which they relate. Solution of the financial difficulties would then eliminate the necessity to quarrel.

Quarreling, of course, is only one type of verbal behavior that may be related to a referent condition. Problematic verbal behavior may be controlled by referent conditions that involve sex, affection, attention, behavioral control, work, child management, social activities outside the home, relatives, alcohol or drugs, religion, politics, time together, division of labor, member privacy, or family decision making. Communication difficulties that may be traced directly to referent conditions generally require that attention be given first to the remediation of the referent condition.

SETTING EVENTS

Bijou and Baer (1966) have described the "setting factor or event" as a large class of stimulus operations pertinent to both operant and respondent behavior for which the term "motivation" has heretofore been widely, loosely and diversely applied. Kantor (1959) has said:

> Such setting factors as the hungry or satiated condition of the organism, its age, hygienic or toxic condition, as well as the presence or absence of certain environing objects, clearly influence the occurrence or non-occurrence of interbehavior or facilitate the occurrence of the activities in question in varying degrees [p. 95, as quoted in Bijou and Baer, 1966, p. 778].

Bijou and Baer review the effects on reinforcement operations of such setting events as deprivation, satiation, and sex-membership and indicate that education, socialization, injury, and medication are other possible setting events.

In this context, setting events (or, less precisely, event setters) refer to states of the organism that affect how the individual reacts to stimuli that relate to his verbal behavior. Common setting events for verbal behavior are sex deprivation, anxiety, anger, fatigue, sickness, and drug taking. These conditions generally set the events unfavorably for communication, making it likely that marital partners will have more communication difficulties than would otherwise be the case. For instance, if a couple were to endeavor to discuss a serious matter when both were exceedingly fatigued, it is very possible that they would have disagreements and the disagreements would be escalated. Discussion of most issues when one or both partners is extremely angry is clearly risky. When dealing with setting events that are temporary and easily remediable, one generally postpones work on communication to a time when these unfavorable conditions are not operative. In those special cases where the setting events are long-term and have adverse effects on couple communication, attention in modification should be directed first to these conditions rather than to the communication itself.

STRUCTURAL DEFICITS

Deficits of structure consist of the absence of stimulus conditions that, if present, would occasion desirable verbal behavior. For example, the partners may rarely speak with each other, not because it is aversive to do so or because they lack the capability to communicate, but because their lives are scheduled so that neither partner has time for such communication. The deficit consists of specific stimuli of time and place to produce talking rather than other behavior. When the response capability exists, deficits of structure may be remedied by establishing stimulus conditions of time, place, and opportunity so that the desirable verbal behavior will be produced.

PARTNER INTERACTION

The verbal behavior of a partner may precipitate or sustain particular problematic surfeits or deficits of partner verbal responding.

For any particular surfeit of verbal response, the following partner verbal behaviors may be controlling conditions.

1. *Verbal reinforcement of a response surfeit*. For example, the husband's pessimistic talk may be attended to and commented on favorably by the wife, which sustains or increases such talk. This would be an example of positive reinforcement by the partner.

In the case of negative reinforcement, the excessive faulting of a husband could be reinforced negatively by the occasional but reliable behavior change of the wife. Thus the husband could complain frequently and seemingly without consequence concerning the housekeeping habits of the wife, and the wife could reply negatively; however, occasionally she also cleans the house and consequently reinforces negatively the husband's complaints by removing the noxiousness for him of the dirty house. This illustrates what Patterson and Reid (1970) have called coercive control. Such control, these authors contend, serves as a basis for negative interaction in families. There is no question that a great deal of the negative interaction in families may take this form and be sustained by the negative reinforcement (i.e., removal of aversiveness) provided by the eventual compliance of the person whose behavior is complained about. However, it is essential to note that whenever there is negative talk, such as excessive faulting, there is also almost always a very high degree of immediate negative response, such as counterfaulting or disagreement, and these responses may in fact serve as *positive* reinforcement for the negative talk. That is, the faulting of partner A may be sustained more by the disagreements and counterfaults of partner B, where these serve as positive reinforcers for the faulting of partner A, than by the occasional behavior change of partner B so as to remove the aversive condition giving rise to the fault. This example recalls the earlier discussion (p. 8) of functional relationships and the importance of distinguishing between the descriptive meaning of the stimulus (e.g., "negative" talk) and the way it in fact functions in relationship to responses.

Another example of negative reinforcement involves excessive talking. In this instance, partner A speaks frequently and abundantly to escape and avoid the aversive speech of partner B. That is, partner A's talking is reinforced negatively by averting partner B's talking. Research by Weiss, Lombardo, Warren, and Kelley (1971) on the reinforcing effects of speaking in reply suggests not only that opportunity to speak is a reinforcer but, more important, that speaking in response to the expression of controversial opinions is controlled essentially by being able to turn off these opinions.

2. *Verbal stimulus control of a response surfeit*. Whenever partner A inappropriately cues partner B to speak on a controversial subject,

with the result that partner B speaks excessively on this subject, this type of stimulus control is illustrated. Such cueing may take the form of asking the partner his opinion on a controversial subject at an inopportune time, such as during a meal, during a television program that they both want to view, or just before starting sex. Surfeits can also be controlled by any one of a number of words and phrases that have "red flag" properties tending to trigger inappropriate and excessive responding of the partner. For instance, the mate may say nothing more than "I disagree," and this could generate a tirade of inappropriate partner response.

3. *Verbal eliciting control of response surfeit.* If one spouse says, "I think you're crazy," and this makes the other angry and the anger in turn generates a verbal tantrum, it illustrates how the first response may serve as an eliciting stimulus for the respondent behavior of anger that then generates a flood of verbal responding that otherwise would not have occurred.

Turning now to response deficits, there can be at least the following controlling conditions exercised by the verbal behavior of the partner.

1. *Weakness of verbal reinforcement.* If a mate consistently fails to reinforce positive talk of the partner, the strength of responses involving positive talk may be low. Any class of verbal response that is reinforced only rarely or not at all, with support from no other sustaining conditions, will be weakened and low.

2. *Verbal punishment by the partner.* Deficits consisting of undertalk and underresponsiveness may have been produced by partner verbal punishment and sustained by periodic punishment when higher levels of talk and responsiveness happen to be generated.

3. *Lack of verbal stimulus control.* The positive talk of a mate may be in the repertoire but rarely evidenced because the spouse fails to cue it. For instance, the wife may rarely if ever commend the husband for his fine handiwork around the house; however, were he to say, for example, "What do you think of that job?" the wife might readily respond with, "That's very good; I like that."

Difficulties of partner interaction generally involve long-term and recurring communication habits and patterns and call for alteration of the verbal behavior of one or both partners.

CHAPTER TWO

Verbal Strengths and Problems

DESIRABLE VERBAL behavior facilitates adequate message sending and appropriate behavioral guidance of the marital partners. In regard to message sending, the messages should be sent clearly, accurately, and efficiently and provide the appropriate amount of information. The vocal features of speech should not interfere with information transmission. Thus, the rate of speaking should not be too fast or too slow, the time delay in responding to the speaker should not be too long or too short, and the speaker should speak fluently enough, long enough, loudly enough, and without inappropriate affect.

There are likewise several criteria of appropriate behavioral guidance. The speaker should hold the listener's attention, speak so that most or all of what he says can be followed, allow the listener his say and, in general, achieve a more or less equitable balance of speaker-listener interchange. Furthermore, appropriate control consists of maintaining the necessary continuity of theme, speaking so as to provide an adequate amount of positive feedback and reinforcement for the partner, and, when appropriate, engaging in efforts to persuade or to change the behavior of the listener.

Although it is possible to indicate generally what the desirable characteristics of marital communication are, it is more difficult to specify the categories of verbal response that would in fact be judged as desirable or undesirable for particular marital partners. There are important individual and couple differences in response to given verbal stimuli. What is appropriate behavioral guidance for one couple may be aversive for another; what is a clear message for one marital partner may be nonsense for another. Furthermore, what is acceptable verbal behavior to both marital partners may be unacceptable from the point of view of a professional helper. The partners, for example, may regard their frequent arguing as the price they must pay to resolve problems whereas the practitioner may see the arguing as a relatively aimless, inconclusive, and needless ordeal for both mates. It is consequently impossible to specify given verbal responses as being uniformly desirable or undesirable in marital interchange. Ideal specification consists of an individualized identification. Short of that, it is possible only to indicate the verbal responses that are likely to be desirable or undesirable for most mates.

The objective of this chapter is to suggest response categories of readily identifiable verbal behavior that may be indicative of strength or difficulty in the marital interchange. Although the response categories presented here are not necessarily exhaustive or inclusive, they illustrate the variety and range of marital verbal behavior. They cover a large number of behavioral particulars likely to be encountered in professional work with problems of marital communication. The response categories necessarily involve descriptive, not functional, response classes.[1] However, the response categories relate to particular surfeits or deficits of verbal responding that have behaviorally definable referents, can be measured objectively, and require a minimum of inference on the part of an outside judge.

The categories of response are organized around the five dimensions of verbal behavior identified in the first chapter: content, representational accuracy, information, vocal properties, and behavioral guidance. For each dimension, specifications of possibly functional and dysfunctional verbal behavior are given. The specifications of possibly dysfunctional response categories are taken in the main from the response categories of the Verbal Problem Checklist developed to assess strengths and problems of couple verbal behavior (Thomas, Walter, and O'Flaherty, 1974a). The examples provided of verbal problems are necessarily brief; the reader should understand that analysis of many verbal interchanges, not just one instance, would be required in order to make reasonably accurate judgments about the extent to which partner verbal behavior falls into the response categories. The objective here is to present and illustrate response categories, not to describe assessment procedures, which will be taken up in Chapter 3.

---

[1] It is difficult enough to endeavor to isolate true functional response classes in research (Salzinger, 1967; Holz and Azrin, 1966), let alone in clinical work, where time and tools are generally less adequate.

Representation of Referents

Verbal behavior that represents events and objects of the world is generally most desirable when that representation is accurate. Accuracy applies to the representation of objects and events outside the person as well as to private states, such as the individual's own emotions, beliefs, and attitudes. Several important ways in which referents may be misrepresented in verbal behavior are discussed below.

In *overgeneralization,* the interactant misrepresents real-world referents (behaviors or other phenomena) by under- or overstating such characteristics as their amount, importance, or quality. For example, overgeneralization of amount may involve the use of the word "always" when an event occurs sometimes; likewise, there may be overgeneralization in using the word "never" for events that sometimes do occur. Overgeneralization may take many forms, including making dogmatic statements in which the overstatement is combined with strong expression of opinion. A particularly common type of overgeneralization is what Albert Ellis (1962) calls "catastrophizing" and Goodman and Maultsby (1974) call "awfulizing." In this type, the individual grossly and irrationally exaggerates the seriousness of a given life situation or difficulty.

The following dialogue is an example of overgeneralization for the husband, who has just arrived home from work.

> **W:** The house is a little messy tonight; please excuse it because it's unusual, as you know. [*It truly is, because she is a competent and conscientious homemaker.*]
> **H:** You never seem to have the house clean and in order.
> **W:** I said this is an exception. I hope you'll understand. You know, you're getting me mad.
> **W:** You always laze around, not getting things done. You're lazy, a goof-off.
> **H:** I try to do a good job. Let's forget it now.
> **H:** You never let *me* forget things, do you?

In *poor referent specification,* an interactant fails to speak concretely and specifically in regard to the referent; instead, his speech tends to be general and abstract. This next example of poor referent specification for the wife is drawn from a conversation about what happened at a party the night before, where the husband drank too much, said things he shouldn't have said and took several minor liberties with one of the woman guests.

H: What's bothering you about last night?
W: I didn't have a good time.
H: What do you mean?
W: You know, it wasn't really a fun party.
H: I guess I had a good time.
W: Well, I didn't.
H: So?
W: You made a fool of yourself.
H: I did? How did I do that?
W: Oh, you know. You sure did have a good time, and, believe me, I didn't.

Presumptive attribution is misrepresenting the meanings, motivation, feelings, or thought of others by incorrectly attributing non-obvious characteristics to them ("mind reading," "second-guessing"). The following example involves presumptive attribution of the husband in discussing what bothered his wife at the party the night before. In this example, we assume again that what really bothered the wife was that the husband drank too much, said things he shouldn't have said and engaged in minor improprieties with another man's wife.

H: What's bothering you about last night?
W: I didn't have a good time.
H: What do you mean? You had a good time.
W: You know, it really wasn't a fun party.
H: I guess I know what's bothering you; it's because George and Mary [*the host and hostess*] didn't pay much attention to you and, furthermore, it's one week before your period and you're always bitchy at this time.
W: You made a fool of yourself.
H: I think that when you get bitchy you blame things on others when you shouldn't. What really ticked you off was that they didn't pay much attention to you and you were in a bad mood.

In *incorrect autoclitic*[2] an interactant misrepresents real events by making incorrect remarks regarding what he is about to say. For instance, a speaker might say that what he is about to say is true and then proceed to speak an untruth, or he may announce that he is about to tell a very funny joke and then tell a story that is not funny at all. Incorrect autoclitics are, in effect, incorrect editorializing and metacommunication concerning the speaker's own verbal behavior.

---

[2] The term "autoclitic" refers to verbal responses of the speaker that pertain to the speaker's verbal behavior and that have an effect on the listener (Skinner, 1957).

In the following example, the wife has strong feelings of anger and dislike for her husband, combined with only modest affection.

W: I'm going to tell you how I really feel about you.
H: How do you feel?
W: I really love you and have no bad feelings. It's pure love. I don't really harbor any ill feelings at all.

Misrepresentation of fact or evaluation is when an interactant incorrectly represents facts, such as real-world events, or evaluations of others, such as their preferences and interests. This category is something of a catchall for inaccuracies that do not fall into the prior categories. What is often called lying is generally illustrative here. An example for the husband:

W: Where did you go last night?
H: Oh, I had a business meeting. [*In fact, he had gone to a motel with a lover.*]
W: You stayed out awfully late.
H: It was a long meeting and afterwards we went out for a drink and talked a while.

Content

A large number of relevant verbal categories pertain to the content of the speaker's verbal behavior. The specifications below have been divided into two main areas, thematic continuity and a larger, more diverse grouping called content handling, for want of better description.

THEMATIC CONTINUITY

Suppose the wife says to her husband, "What happened in your appointment with the doctor today?" If the husband replies by reporting what happened, adequately and fully, this would indicate thematic continuity with regard to what his wife asked him about. Thematic continuity would also be illustrated in this instance if the husband and wife carried on additional interchange on the same topic, providing new information, observations, and evaluation. In some cases, continuity is demonstrated in a single response, whereas in others a number of speaker-interchanges would be required to make a judgment.

There are many ways in which lack of thematic continuity may be evidenced. Thus, rather than staying on a topic long enough to address it, there may be too little responding, quibbling over minor details, premature shifting to another topic, sudden introduction of irrelevancies, or avoidance of the subject altogether. Thematic continuity can also be violated by persisting excessively or overresponding on a given subject, such as a relevant but minor topic within a larger theme. Categories relevant here are described below.

In *content avoidance,* an interactant clearly and openly averts the opportunity to talk about a given subject or subjects. The topic may be clear, as indicated by a speaker asking questions about it or by what the previous speaker has said, it may be implicit or, in some cases, may be an assigned topic used for purposes of practitioner assessment. An example for the husband:

W: What happened at the doctor's office today?
H: Nothing.
W: You mean to say he told you nothing about your health?
H: I don't wish to talk about it. [*And, in fact, he does not discuss the topic further.*]

Content shifting is defined as an interactant prematurely introducing a different topic from what is currently being discussed. The example again involves the husband:

W: What happened at the doctor's office today?
H: I've been wondering how Joe did in school today? Did he get his test back in mathematics?

In *underresponsiveness,* an interactant says too little in relation to what a previous question or comment appears to call for. (This applies to speeches as distinguished from undertalk, to be presented later.) This next example involves a women who has been having pains in her legs, has suspected phlebitis, and has a heart condition and arthritis.

H: What happened at the doctor's office today?
W: Not much. He looked at my leg and ankle.
H: Is that all?
W: He took my blood pressure.

Quibbling involves an interactant endeavoring to clarify or dispute a tangential and irrelevant detail. In the example following, both get involved in the quibbling.

W: What happened at the doctor's office today?
H: I didn't go to the doctor's office today.
W: You did too.

H: No, I went yesterday.
W: I thought it was today.
H: No.
W: Are you sure?
H: Positive.

A *detached utterance* consists of an interactant talking on a subject whose relationship to the immediate focus of the discussion is not clear. The talk may involve irrelevant examples, ideas, or hypothetical situations. In the example below the italicized part for the husband is illustrative.

W: What happened at the doctor's office today?
H: Yes, I went to the doctor today. He said my blood pressure was a little high. *I had a good lunch, turkey and stuffing. Gravy was not too good, though.* My heart is okay. Says I'm too fat. Need more exercise.

Topic content persistence consists of an interactant speaking excessively on a given topic. The following example presumes lengthy prior discussion of the football game by the husband, with the wife already having indicated that she was familiar with the game and was finished with the subject.

H: That was some pass to Jones in the end zone. He was wide open. No one around. What a play!
W: Yes, I saw it, you know?
H: The pass was overthrown slightly but that guy Jones got it anyway. Good hands—and he runs fast. A very crucial play.
W: (*Silence.*)
H: It was fourth down, too, just fifteen seconds left before the half . . . [*Etc., etc.*]

Overresponsiveness involves an interactant speaking too long, with what is said going beyond what is called for in response to the partner's talk. (Overresponsiveness relates to speeches of the speaker in response to what is requested or suggested by the others whereas overtalk, to be given later, applies to speaking more than one's partner, or others, in the interaction, considering the entire period of verbal interchange.) The example below involves overresponsiveness of the husband.[3]

W: Harry, how do I recognize the Smiths' house when I get to Pine Street?

[3] This example and several of the others here are revisions of examples of verbal categories suggested initially by Robert Hodnefield and Harriet Fusfeld.

H: Well, it's halfway down the first block, on the left side; I think the drive is on the right, with a walk made out of bricks. Yes, it's painted dark green and has a mailbox in front with their name on it.

W: Are there other green houses on the street?

H: No, just that one.

W: Oh, that's all I needed to know.

In *temporal remoteness,* an interactant dwells excessively on referents pertaining to the past or the hypothetical future. This next example involves past talk of the wife in the context of faulting her husband, a common form of temporal remoteness. The couple have been married twelve years.

W: When you took me out after I first got pregnant, you didn't open doors for me, you weren't nice to me and ignored me a lot.

H: Oh, I am not sure I remember.

W: You know, you used to ignore me when we visited my family too. I remember one Sunday just after we got married when you didn't speak to me all afternoon, even when riding home afterwards.

H: Do I ignore you now?

W: When I gave birth to Esther, you came to see me once in the hospital—only once, mind you. Even then, you acted bored and distracted by other things.

Illogical talk consists of an interactant making a statement that is illogical from the perspective of what he or others have said. The following example involves the wife.

H: I have real questions about the way you're raising the children. You can't seem to discipline them properly, and I wish you would be tougher with them.

W: All right, if that's the way you feel about it, I won't have anything more to do with them; I won't even talk to them.

The wife's illogical response to the husband was made in the context of his faulting her child management. The wife's response was an instance of irrelevant conclusion, which is one of several types of idiosyncrasies of relevance. Other types of logical difficulties, as explicated by Shneidman (1969), are idiosyncrasies of meaning, enthymematic idiosyncrasies, idiosyncrasies of logical structure, and idiosyncrasies of logical interrelations.

Illogical talk may affect more than the topical flow of conversation. It affects most problem solving and decision making, for example.

Some of the difficulties described above are more important threats to thematic continuity than others. Content avoidance, for example, involves not addressing the content at all and hence may be much more serious than a brief, detached utterance. Any of these verbal problems may have other, possibly more serious, consequences than the disruption of topical flow. Thus, quibbling may be escalated into an intense argument involving mutual faulting, and both parties may become very angry; overresponsiveness of one partner may be boring and unrewarding for the other; illogical talk of both partners may make for hopelessly confused discourse and decision making; and past talk may involve vindictiveness over past injustices and prevent problem solving in the present. There are other verbal behaviors that may adversely affect thematic continuity. For example, excessive disagreement may draw partners off topic, as may too many obstrusions or an excess of partner faulting.

HANDLING OF CONTENT

In general, content is handled well when the speaker avoids excessive negative talk, expression of opinion, disagreement, and pedantry while also engaging in a goodly amount of acknowledgment and positive talk so as to sustain a reasonable level of verbal behavior of the partner. Details involving each of these are given below.

In *negative talk surfeit* an interactant expresses excessively frequent or lengthy negative evaluations of others, events, or other aspects of his surroundings. When these negative evaluations are applied to the behavior of others with whom he is interacting, they are referred to as *faulting;* when these negative evaluations are not tied directly to the behavior of others, they are referred to as *pessimistic talk*. Negative talk surfeit may take the form of sarcasm, recrimination, nagging, and bad-name calling. In their analysis of marital fighting, Bach and Wyden (1969) used colorful expressions to depict different forms of verbal abuse and negative talk in marital fights. Thus, they speak of gunnysacking, scapegoating, the Virginia Woolf (a ritualized exchange of insults), and the Vesuvius outburst (a kind of verbal tantrum in which there is great venting of emotion, but which is nonfunctional). Readers may be interested to know, incidentally, that the "ragiolic" is a person who engages in a chronic, one-way, growling rage.

An example of faulting by both partners:

> **H:** I do think you have not been a very good mother to our children.
> **W:** Well, you haven't been a good father; and you're not much of a husband, either.

H: You should talk; you're a lousy housekeeper—you leave things all over, don't clean up, leave the house dirty.

W: I'm sick of you. You're just a loser. Hear that, a loser!

An example of pessimistic talk by the husband:

W: We seem to be getting along fairly well now, what with you having a steady job and now that we have some savings again.

H: I am worried about expenses, though, money for our health and money for our old age.

W: But we have some insurance for those things, don't we?

H: Yes, but I still worry. My health may go bad, even though it's okay now, I guess. I worry about everything—how dull things are, no fun, the children.

In *positive talk deficit,* an interactant fails to compliment or say nice things about the other as a person or about what the other says or does. An example of positive talk deficit for the husband:

W: I guess I'm not the world's best housekeeper, but I would like to have a compliment occasionally.

H: You know how I feel about the way you do things.

W: No, how do you feel about that?

H: You do your job like you're supposed to and like other women do.

W: But how is that as it applies to me?

H: Oh, I don't know.

In *positive talk surfeit* an interactant excessively compliments or says nice things about the other person or about what the other says or does. An example for the husband:

H: You're a super housekeeper. [*Actually, the wife isn't at all and she knows it.*]

W: I do a fair job, but I'm not that good.

H: You really are fantastic; you make great meals; keep the house spotless and make everyone happy; and you're also a very good mother and a wonderful wife.

W: You exaggerate; I don't deserve such compliments.

H: I like everything about you—the way you walk, talk, sit, everything.

W: You're overdoing it. I do some things well but not everything like that.

Acknowledgment deficit is failing to admit or give credit when the other is correct in a statement or failing to express recognition of the other's point of view or assertion. An example for the wife:

H: I like you, yet I sometimes have strong negative feelings. I guess I'm confused and I'm not sure what to do about it.

W: (*Silence.*)

H: What I'm trying to say is that I have mixed feelings about you that I finally realized I have. This is very important for me because it upsets me a lot and I don't know what to do about it.

W: So that's how you feel about it?

H: I'm not sure I think clearly but I know that my feelings are mixed. It's a very uncomfortable situation and I wish that I could get this over to you so that you understood.

W: Are you sure that's your point of view?

Acknowledgment surfeit is giving excessive credit to the correctness of the other's statement or expressing excessive recognition of the other's point of view or assertion. An example for the wife:

H: I like you, yet I sometimes have strong negative feelings.

W: I understand; I know how you must feel.

H: Actually, there are times when I hate you, I really dislike you.

W: Yes, I see; I understand and I know how you must feel.

H: Sometimes I want to get away from you, to leave altogether.

W: Yes, dear, I understand.

H: Never see you again. I want to marry someone else.

W: Yes, I agree you must feel awful.

H: What I am trying to say is that I don't really love you any more.

W: I understand how you must feel; I see.

Opinion deficit is failure to express a preference or an opinion regarding referents when the discussion seems to call for some evaluation.

H: Let's take a vacation in Mexico.

W: So?

H: It would be fun. We could eat Mexican food, go hear the bands, and travel around the countryside.

W: What else could we do?

H: We could go to the bull fight, take special sightseeing trips, and take some tours to out-of-the-way places. What do you think?

W: I don't know what to think.

The lack of opinion on a given subject at a given moment is not particularly indicative of an opinion deficit but the repeated failure to express an opinion on different subjects or the same subject for a long period of time would be indicative of lack of opinion.

Opinion surfeit is expressing more opinions regarding the referents than the interaction seems to require. In the conversation below, the husband and wife are dressing to go to a special event on Saturday night. The example of opinion surfeit involves the husband.

W: How does my hair look?

H: I like your hair in front, but it is too close in back. Your dress is a little short and it is too loose. I like your shoes, although they could have higher heels. Your makeup is fine. Oh, don't take that silver-colored purse. I don't like it at all.

In *excessive disagreement* the interactant repeatedly disagrees with the other's statements. An instance involving the husband:

H: In order to put more money aside for our savings, you should help me save more.

W: Could I give you one hundred dollars a month out of my pay?

H: No, I don't like that.

W: Then maybe I should look for a better job.

H: I'm not sure about that because you've been on this one for several years and it's a reliable job situation.

W: Maybe I should look around but not give up this job.

H: That's very time consuming: you have other things to do.

W: We could save more around the house—not buy certain luxuries.

H: No, I don't like that either.

W: How about you working more overtime?

H: That's not good either.

In *excessive agreement* the interactant repeatedly agrees with the statements of others. In this next example the husband, who is and has been a thoroughgoing atheist and isn't really about to be converted to religion, agrees excessively with his wife's religious views.

W: You should believe in God, as I do.

H: Yes, I agree.

W: He will make you strong and strengthen your life.

H: I agree.

W: You should also worship Him.

H: I agree.

W: Belief in God is important in your life and you should recognize it.

H: Yes, I agree.

Excessive threatening is stating repeatedly that if given partner behavior does not occur, the interactant will arrange for the loss of rewards for him or if certain behaviors are engaged in by the partner, the interactant will arrange for certain aversive conditions to occur. The threats generally are not converted into reality by the person issuing them. An instance for a wife:

H: We certainly argue a lot.

W: We argue all the time. If you don't stop disagreeing with me, I'll get you—really.

H: (*Silence.*) Well, we don't argue all the time, though.

W: If you don't stop fighting with me all the time, I will do something to hurt you.

H: Perhaps we should see someone about this—someone who is trained to help people with marital problems like those we have.

W: If we don't, I think I'll leave you—just walk out. If you don't stop arguing, I'll stop talking to you.

In *pedantry* an interactant uses big, unfamiliar words where simple, better-known words would be suitable (e.g., saying "trepidation" for "fear" or "vicissitude" for "change"). For example: "I think the problem with your communication is that you habitually employ a lot of redundancy around the principal theme you are expostulating and expounding."

Several other categories might be mentioned briefly. These are *negative talk deficit,* in which the interactant fails to express negative evaluations, especially in situations in which they would be warranted; *excessive promises,* in which a needlessly large number of promises are made, generally with little likelihood of follow-through; *excessive use of abstractions;* and *dogmatic statement,* in which an interactant makes a statement in a categorical, unqualified, all-or-none, "black-or-white" manner.

Information

Message sending is most functional when the information is conveyed clearly, accurately, efficiently, and in sufficient amount. Speakers should avoid providing too little or too much information, redundant information, or ambiguous messages.

When *too little information is given* the interactant fails to provide sufficient information considering what might be reasonably expected at that point in the discussion:

H: How much are you spending for groceries every week?

W: Not too much; not too little either.

When *too much information is given* the interactant provides an excessive amount of information concerning a subject compared with what is necessary. For example:

H: How much are you spending for groceries every week?

W: This week I spent about $15 for meat, about $10 for produce, $7 for paper and cleaning supplies, around $5 for bakery goods, $8 for dairy, and I guess around another $7 for extras—close to $50.

> And last week it was a little more because we had company—
> your relatives. It was then about $67.

When *redundant information is given* an interactant excessively
repeats information already given or known. In the following example, the husband is needlessly redundant.

> **W:** What are we going to do about the old car?
> **H:** Have it fixed. It will cost $100–200 to get it running right for the
> winter.
> **W:** We sure need to get it going; we need two cars now.
> **H:** It'll cost $100–200 to fix it; that's what they tell me, $100–200.
> **W:** I heard you—$100–200.
> **H:** Yes, it's $100–200—$100–200.

With an *ambiguous message* an interactant conveys a message
that has vague meaning, is puzzling, or a paradox. The "double-
bind" message, as discussed, for example, by Bateson, Jackson, Haley,
and Weakland (1956) and Watzlavick, Beavin, and Jackson (1967),
may be one consequence of the frequent use of ambiguous messages in
family interaction.

> **H:** If I ask you, "What's wrong," you will tell me, okay?
> **W:** I'll try, but you'll get angry, you won't understand.

Here is another example, again of the wife giving an ambiguous
message:

> **H:** I want to pay off the bills by dividing them up half and half, an
> equal amount each month to each.
> **W:** It's a good idea but we won't do it.

Conversational Guidance in Behavioral Control

Each partner in verbal interchange with a mate guides the conversation by how long he or she talks and whether he or she interrupts, asks a lot of questions, or directs the other in regard to what he
or she should say. Appropriate conversational guidance generally
consists of each partner's allowing the other to speak in a reasonably
equitable exchange without either disrupting the speaking of the
other too much or exercising too much control over the other, such
as by asking questions or cueing the other too frequently. Several
verbal categories relate directly to conversational guidance.

An interactant makes *obtrusions* if he frequently makes utterances
while another is speaking. Such attempted intrusions become inter-

ruptions if they produce immediate and apparently premature termination of the speech by the other. An example for the husband:

> **W:** I'd like to tell you something important about how I feel about you. It's that . . .
> **H:** (*Interjecting.*) Let me tell you something. I went to the shopping mall today and bought a sweater for myself. It looks good. Want to see it?
> **W:** What I want to say is . . .
> **H:** (*Interjecting.*) It's green and yellow. Nice, huh? Oh, I also bought some socks.
> **W:** It's that I'm increasingly upset about . . .
> **H:** (*Interjecting again.*) The socks are better looking than . . . [*Etc., etc.*]

With *excessive question asking* an interactant asks too many questions. An example for the wife:

> **W:** Tell me about how it was before we got married?
> **H:** I didn't date much, but I had a few affairs.
> **W:** What do you mean, affairs?
> **H:** Well . . .
> **W:** Were they sexy? Did you do it?
> **H:** I went with this one girl, Esther, who . . .
> **W:** Was she pretty? What happened with her?

In *excessive cueing* an interactant employs more verbal cues than are necessary, asking too many questions or making too many requests, directives, commands, or suggestions. An example for the husband:

> **H:** Tell me what you and Mary talked about yesterday. Tell me what she said.
> **W:** She told me about the party.
> **H:** Tell me what happened at the party.
> **W:** Mary said that people had a good time . . .
> **H:** Who had such a good time?
> **W:** Joe and Phyllis had real fun; they even danced together.
> **H:** Tell me what else happened. [*Etc., etc.*]

The above categories involve verbal behavior that clearly relates to conversational guidance. Many of the other verbal categories pertaining to other dimensions of verbal behavior, taken up elsewhere in this chapter, also may affect the control of speaking in the verbal interchange. For example, if one partner talks too much, he can of course dominate the floor; fast talking of one partner can produce vocal pattern matching in the other; avoidance of content by one partner may constrain the other to speak more; a high degree of acknowledgment may reinforce certain behaviors whereas lack of acknowledgment may diminish talking on given subjects. Actually, any verbal response may serve to guide the speaking of the partner, exercising some behavioral control of partner responding.

Vocal Properties

Desirable vocal properties of verbal behavior consist of speaking at an adequate rate, for an appropriate length of time, and with appropriate latency following the talk of the partner. Other desirable vocal properties involve speaking loudly and fluently enough to be understood and with appropriate affective expression. Among the difficulties involving vocal properties are *fast talk, slow talk, rapid latency, slow latency, overtalk, undertalk, loud talk, quiet talk, singsong speech, monotone speech,* and *dysfluent talk* (e.g., stuttering). In addition, there is *affective talk,* as in expressing too much emotional vocal behavior (e.g., crying, whining, screaming), considering the content of what is said, and *unaffective talk,* as in expressing too little emotion vocally, given the content of what is said. Because these vocal features cannot be illustrated with the written word, there are no examples here. Readers interested in applying these categories to examples of verbal behavior should turn to the transcripts in Appendixes A and E, the analysis presented in Appendix B, and the training procedures suggested in Appendix G.

Some Characteristics of the Verbal Response Categories

Consider the following example, in which possible verbal response categories are indicated in brackets.

H: Lately you've been suggesting that I overdefine what I was saying. [*Fault, given knowledge of what was said before.*]

W: Um-hm. Not overdefining it, just defining it. [*Disagreement and beginning of quibbling.*]

H: All right—unnecessarily defining. [*Misrepresentation.*] In other words, instead of saying it as a nice . . .

W: Now you're doing it. [*Obtrusion, minor fault.*]

H: I'm explaining myself, in other words, saying what I am defining. [*Quibbling.*] My complaint is I'm asked to comment on a meaty topic on which I can expound at considerable length and when I get into the meaty topic about three or four minutes, then I'm told

I'm overdefining it or I'm unnecessarily going into detail or that she doesn't agree. [*Faulting, pedantic talk, overresponsiveness.*]

Several characteristics of the verbal response categories are illustrated above. First, the units of response for a given response category are units of meaning rather than given grammatical segments. For instance, quibbling could be manifested by what one partner says in response to the other or in a long series of partner interchanges. A fault could be expressed in a single word or by a very long speech. Second, a given verbal response may contain indications of more than one response category. For instance, in the last speech of the husband we have at least a fault, pedantry, and overresponsiveness. The categories can be viewed as overlapping with at least some others.

Patterns and Interdependencies

Consider the following example:

H: You don't keep the house very clean. [*Fault.*]
W: I clean it every day. [*Disagreement.*]
H: Every day? [*Disagreement.*]
W: Every day. I sure do clean it. [*Disagreement.*]
H: You haven't done it this week. [*Disagreement.*]
W: What do you mean this week? [*Disagreement.*]
H: Which rooms?
W: I've done the living room and kids' room. The babysitter runs the vacuum cleaner every other day and I do it at night, but you're not there to notice. [*Disagreement.*]

Here we have an interchange that begins with a fault and then generates a series of disagreements. The fault-disagreement interplay was repeated in this instance for other areas involving the wife's presumed inefficiencies in the management of the house, such as in putting away the ironing board and vacuuming floors. Repetition of the same type of partner-partner interchange in many areas of the interaction is what is here identified as a pattern.

The fault-disagreement pattern, initiated by the husband, was also found throughout the interaction for the wife, as illustrated below:

W: I think I'd appreciate it more if you didn't take six months to mow the lawn. [*Fault.*]
H: It's been mowed. Otherwise it would be above your knees. [*Disagreement.*]
W: It *was* above my knees. [*Disagreement.*]

H: One section of it. Not the front where people can see it. [*Disagreement.*]

W: Why not mow the whole thing?

H: I don't do everything I could.

In addition to the pattern of fault-disagreement, another common one involves the pattern of fault-fault, in which a fault is followed by a counterfault and this in turn is followed by another fault. Practical work with many couples suggests that this may be the most frequent pattern. Once initiated, this pattern tends to persist without resolution and generally leads to escalation of the disagreement and generation of anger or anxiety. Despite the commonness of these particular patterns, however, there is great variety and individuality in the patterning and interdependencies of couple verbal interchange. The search for relevant patterns for particular couples requires careful examination of verbal interchanges and consideration of the many possible functions and dysfunctions that such interchanges may perform.

Themes and Profiles

One way to characterize the verbal exchanges of marital partners is in terms of themes that apply to what one or both say. For example, a theme for one couple was most simply expressed as "It's not a problem." The husband complained mainly about what he alleged to be the wife's weak and ineffective child management. His continuing and extended criticism of the way she disciplined the children was bitter and humiliating and painful for her. This generated continuing disagreements and countercomplaining. The wife complained chiefly that the husband spoke too much to others in public and too little to her in private. Each partner refused to recognize the validity of the complaints of the other; for both, the complaints constituted no problem. (Transcript 1 for couple E in Appendix A provides some information consistent with this theme.) In addition to "It's not a problem," other common themes are "You're wrong, I'm right," "It's your fault," and "It's a catastrophe."

Thematic characterizations of couple interchange often embrace a great deal of information and serve to focus attention on a central issue rather than on a variety of minor details. When backed up by observation and good data, a correct thematic characterization can be valuable. It is rare, however, that verbal interchanges between marital partners can be so simply and cogently characterized as displaying a single theme. In addition, thematic characterizations can easily exaggerate some features at the expense of other, valid elements, downplay or gloss over important strengths, and foster all-too-easy labeling of repertoires in contrast to careful response specification.

Because of their complexity and diversity, verbal interchanges of marital partners may best be characterized as profiles of particular strengths and limitations. Analysis might reveal, for instance, that among the wife's strengths are logical talk, accuracy in representation, specificity, and some positive talk along with the limitations of frequent faulting and excessive disagreement. The husband's strengths might consist of frequent acknowledgment of the wife and some positive talk combined with the limitations of overtalking, faulting and overgeneralization. Marital partners generally have a variety of particular strengths combined with several specific verbal problems.

In a study of the verbal behavior of marital partners referred for assistance with communication difficulties, ratings of amount were made for forty-nine categories of verbal response (Thomas, Walter, and O'Flaherty, 1974a), such as those response categories referred to in this chapter. It was found that out of a possible forty-nine areas that could have been rated as problematic, an average of only four were rated as problematic for the husbands and three for wives. Categories that in general were rated high for both husband and wife were negative talk surfeit (mainly faulting), excessive disagreement, positive talk deficit, overgeneralization, poor referent specification, content shifting, content persistence, acknowledgment deficit, and obtrusions. These categories were rated in the upper third of amount ratings for both husbands and wives. Possible communication strengths are suggested by the verbal problem categories rated in the lower third of the distribution for couples. Low ratings were given in this study for fast talk, slow talk, singsong speech, monotonic speech, pedantry, incorrect autoclitic, detached utterance, positive talk surfeit, acknowledgment surfeit, excessive agreement, dysfluent talk, redundant information given, too much information given, negative talk deficit, and illogical talk.

Is is helpful to be familiar with response categories, such as those covered in this chapter, when endeavoring to specify the strengths and limitations of given couple's communication. However, to carry out a behavioral analysis and assessment for purposes of planning intervention, the practitioner should also be familiar with relevant approaches to assessment, including systematic procedures for collecting and evaluating assessment information. These are the topics taken up in the next chapter.

CHAPTER THREE

Assessment of Marital Communication

IN COLLECTING AND evaluating information to plan for the modification of marital communication, practitioners have been handicapped by the lack of relevant guidelines and procedures. Although marital communication involves no unique tasks of assessment, as compared with other areas of behavior, there are several special challenges. The practitioner must determine whether communication should be worked on instead of other possibly related behavior, specify the behavioral components involved in the communication, determine possible controlling conditions for the target verbal behaviors, and select what particular verbal behaviors are to be the targets of intervention. Assessment in this area also involves adaptation of procedures developed more fully for other areas of behavior. This chapter addresses these aspects of assessment, first presenting the larger context of remediation, then the basic and optional steps of assessment, and finally the specialized procedures.

Communication Problems in Perspective

Our emphasis upon marital communication should not obscure the larger context in which assessment and remediation are most generally undertaken. Communication is only one aspect of the lives of marital partners, and the procedures to be taken up here are relatively specialized. Family members have concerns other than those involving communication, and couple verbal behavior should be placed in proper perspective with these other concerns. The practitioner may often work with nonverbal problems prior to handling problems of marital communication; sometimes these nonverbal problems may be dealt with concurrently with those of marital communication; and sometimes the practitioner takes up nonverbal concerns of the couple following successful remediation of communication. To consider these other concerns of family members, the helper will have to employ a more general practice procedure than that which is suitable for marital communication. In addition, whatever his orientation and general procedure, the practitioner's primary commitment should be to the wellbeing of the individuals with whom he works. Adherence to humanitarian values, the ethical principles of the practitioner's profession, and the goal of competent service will greatly facilitate the realization of this commitment.

The Tasks of Assessment

The approach to assessment recommended here presupposes that assessment will be carried out before modification is attempted. This means that during assessment there will be no intervention undertaken unless there is an exceptional circumstance, such as a crisis in some area of the client's life, that merits immediate attention.

Assessment involves the collection of several classes of relevant information and, as compared with many other approaches, it is relatively comprehensive. Procedures to gather and process information are carried out to try to minimize bias; the assessment process may therefore be characterized as behaviorally neutral. A major exception to behavioral neutrality involves the warm personal relationship between practitioner and marital partners and other "positively biased" practitioner influences intended to facilitate such objectives as the production of relevant information and cooperation with the intervention regimen.

After the practitioner and the marital partners have decided provisionally to work in the area of communication, the collection and appraisal of information are directed mainly toward helping the practitioner answer these four questions:

1. Is there a problem of marital communication that warrants intervention?
2. If so, what are the specific verbal behaviors that define the problem operationally?
3. What are the probable sources of the communication difficulty?
4. What should be the behavioral objectives of intervention?

The assessment procedures outlined in this chapter are directed toward facilitating the gathering and appraisal of information relating to these questions.

Basic Steps

There are a number of activities that should be carried out in any relatively complete assessment. By way of overview, these activities are listed in outline form:

Preliminary Steps
1. Inventory of problem areas
2. Selection of and contract for target area
3. Commitment to cooperate

Steps in Assessment of Marital Communication
4&5. Response specification and identification of probable sources of difficulty
   a. Objectives and general approach
   b. Initial inquiry
   c. Response display procedure
      (1) Topic selection
      (2) Discussion of topic
      (3) Scanning
      (4) Postdiscussion inquiry
      (5) Other procedures of display
   d. Response specification procedures
   e. Data types for possible sources of difficulty
6. Assessment of behavioral and environmental resources
7. Specification of behavioral objectives
8. Respecification of contract for target area

Assessment of communication cannot be undertaken until several preliminary activities have been completed. The practitioner must become familiar with the marital partners and their major concerns, there should be some initial understanding between the partners and the helping person that marital communication is the area to be worked on, and the partners should be willing to cooperate in the work (Steps 1–3). Response specification and identification of probable sources of difficulty (Steps 4 and 5) initiate detailed assessment of marital communication, and Steps 6 to 8 carry forward guidelines and procedures relevant to couple communication.[1] Other steps and specialized procedures are set forth in later sections of this chapter.

INVENTORY OF PROBLEM AREAS (STEP 1)

The objective of the initial inventory is to identify the spectrum of concerns as seen by the marital partners. This serves to provide the mates and the practitioner with an early profile of possible areas of focal behavior so that they can arrive at some decision as to which target area deserves attention first. The practitioner generally obtains each spouse's description of presenting problems and general behavioral objectives while preparing his own list of the more conspicuous problems he detects. Rather than being a history or detailed specification, the information at this point consists mainly of the ready labels that the marital partners are willing to apply to their primary concerns. Couple communication is generally mentioned as a concern at this point.

SELECTION OF AND CONTRACT FOR THE TARGET AREA (STEP 2)

The goal of this step is to obtain the oral or written agreement of the marital partners and the practitioner concerning which area of behavior is most in need of attention first. Their agreement should facilitate rapid assessment and early movement into remediation.

It is, of course, frequently the case that marital communication is the contracted area. However, nonverbal problems are almost always identified as well. The agreement at this point to work on marital communication is based on available information and the judgment of all parties. The choice can of course be changed when more information has been gathered.

The practitioner should affirm at this point that, at least for the present, the couple intend to work on improving the marriage and are not about to dissolve the union. There is ordinarily little point in entering into a contract to try to remedy disordered communication

[1] Although these procedural steps are very much adapted to the area of marital communication, they are patterned generally after those of PAMBOS (Procedure for the Assessment and Modification of Behavior in Open Settings), developed to facilitate the collection of information and change of behavior with the variety of behavioral difficulties encountered in the open community agency (Thomas, Carter, and Gambrill, 1970; Gambrill, Thomas, and Carter, 1971; and Thomas and Walter, 1973).

if the marriage is about to be dissolved. A couple at the point of possible marital dissolution generally face other, more critical issues, they may part at any time, and there may be too much turbulence and conflict to permit sustained, orderly work on an area such as marital communication.

COMMITMENT TO COOPERATE (STEP 3)

To increase the likelihood of full cooperation, the marital partners are asked to agree to cooperate fully in those activities integral to the procedure, such as in giving complete and accurate information during assessment, complying with requests and recommendations made during remediation, and maintaining regular contact at the appointed times. If the partners agree as indicated, the practitioner moves on to the more specific steps given below. If the partners do not agree to cooperate, however, and further discussion fails to resolve the issues, work may be stopped altogether.

The steps detailed above serve to provide preliminary justification for focusing on couple communication and for obtaining additional information relating to this area of behavior. Subsequent steps of the procedure are intended mainly to yield information about the particular behavioral components of the communication difficulty, the possible controlling conditions, and what behavioral elements involving marital communication would appear to deserve primary emphasis.

RESPONSE SPECIFICATION AND IDENTIFICATION OF PROBABLE SOURCES OF DIFFICULTY (STEPS 4 AND 5)

Although they relate to different information, Steps 4 and 5 are discussed together because the procedures yield information pertaining to both steps.

Objectives and General Approach

Response specification involves the precise identification of the behavioral components of the couple communication so that subsequent modification can be pinpointed. The behavioral components consist of particular surfeits or deficits of verbal behavior, such as those described in Chapter 2 and identified in Appendix A. Specification of verbal behavior also provides information about possible difficulties of decision making. Together, the response particulars help the practitioner to decide whether marital communication merits intervention.

Identification of probable sources of difficulty[2] involves isolating the likely contemporaneous causes of the verbal behavior of interest. These sources generally consist of either precipitating or maintaining conditions for the focal verbal behavior. Any response deficit or surfeit may be accounted for by one or more of such sources of difficulty. These are important because knowledge of the source of difficulty directs the practitioner to the appropriate interventions. For instance, if a referent condition, such as poor child management, is found to be the primary factor leading to disordered verbal behavior, the remediation would focus first on child management. Intervention directed toward alteration of a source of communication difficulty serves a dual purpose; it improves not only the communication difficulty but the problem giving rise to it.

Repertoire deficits are not uncommon in many areas of behavior, but they may be less common in communicative verbal behavior because of the extensive experience and opportunity to speak afforded in daily living for most individuals. Birchler, Weiss, and Vincent (1975) found that the maritally distressed spouses they studied were able to respond more favorably when given different partners to interact with than they did when they interacted together. Even so, peculiarities of social-learning history do occur and may produce idiosyncratic repertoire deficits for individuals. Deficits of this type might involve accuracy of representation, logical talk, thematic continuity, positive talk, and acknowledgment, among others. The true repertoire deficit, in which responses essentially were never learned, may of course be confused with deficits due to other sources, such as long-term failure of the partner to cue and reinforce selected responses. Although practical experience suggests that the latter is a much more likely source of response deficit than the former, the practitioner should nonetheless be vigilant to discern true repertoire deficits. Repertoire deficits call for somewhat different training for partners than deficits arising from partner interaction.

As was indicated in Chapter 1, many referent conditions may give rise to problems in marital communication. Financial difficulties may involve too little money, too much money, or conflict involving allocation of funds. Sexual hangups may consist of frigidity, psychological

---

[2] The five sources of difficulty—repertoire deficits, referent conditions, setting events, structural deficits, and partner interaction—are discussed in Chapter 1, pp. 19–23. Familiarity with this earlier section is presupposed in what follows.

impotence, infidelity, or too few or too many sexual encounters considering partner preferences. Affection and attention may be excessive, inadequate, or inappropriate. Problems of behavioral control may consist of such difficulties as domination or exploitation by a partner or unilateral action or decision making on what should be joint matters in the marriage. Among the child-management conditions are misbehavior of the children, lack of proper parental guidance and control, or inability to get along satisfactorily with one or more of the offspring. The partners may have different interests in regard to social and recreational activities. Relationships with relatives may include inability to get along with them, excessive demands, and maintenance of proper distance and intimacy. Problems with drugs and alcohol include overuse and addiction as well as disagreements over how and whether they are used. Whether or not the partners are of the same religion, there may be important differences in philosophy, moral conviction, religious belief, and practice. Time is a valued resource that partners often share too little or too much with each other. Difficulties in the division of labor include disagreements about who does what under what conditions as well as the failure of one or both partners to engage in given marital, household, or occupational activities affecting their mutual wellbeing. Any or all of these referent conditions may generate problems in partner communication, such as disagreement, faulting, and overgeneralization.

Communication difficulties having their source in referent conditions tend to be restricted to that area of content. However, a major unresolved difficulty in a referent area may also occasion widespread verbal behavior difficulties, as might the existence of several different referent conditions.

A large variety of events may set up unfavorable conditions for marital communication. For example, an externally caused depression for one or both partners may adversely affect verbal behavior; sexual deprivation may lead to arguments; anxiety about or pressure of work may lead to disagreements; anger of one or both spouses may lead to needless faulting; fatigue may eventuate in overgeneralizations; and the use of drugs or alcohol may cause people to say things they would not say otherwise. Such setting events as sex deprivation, anxiety, anger, fatigue, sickness, and the effects of drugs occur fairly frequently in the lives of most couples and, to the extent that they do, are likely to be controlling conditions for difficulties of verbal behavior.

This is an appropriate place to mention the special condition, based upon some blend of referent and setting-event conditions, that might best be identified as the "restricted" marriage. The restricted marriage is important here because it may have the effect of setting events unfavorably for marital communication and exaggerating the unpleasantness for the partners if any marital communication difficulties do come up. In the restricted marriage, the potential for satisfaction, pleasure, and fulfilling experience are especially limited for both husband and wife. Restricted marriages generally involve few activities outside the marriage; few outings of the partners together or alone; frequent overwork by the husband or the wife or both; little variety or novelty in the marriage; few friends or a group of only several old friends or acquaintances, with no newcomers; low frequency of marital sex or inhibited, unimaginative, boring, and unliberated sex; few special meals or special pleasure-producing activities at home; and, if there are children, few activities with them that provide new experience, pleasure, and growth for all involved. Each individual may or may not be "adjusted" otherwise, and in no sense is a restricted marriage synonymous with what some might call a "neurotic" or "pathological" marriage. There may or may not be marital incompatibility in the restricted marriage.

The restricted marriage can generally be detected in two principal ways. First, there are unrealized potentialities for fun, pleasure, novelty, and enriching experience, as indicated above. In extreme cases it might best be called a "locked-in" marriage. Second, one or both of the mates feels a sense of being closed in, limited, disinterested, bored, or unhappy. "Housewife fever" and a sense of personal unfulfillment are sometimes indications of a restricted marriage for the wife. Disinterest in the home and a sense of restriction combined with an unfulfilled desire to do things outside the home are sometimes special indicators for the husband. If communication difficulties can be traced directly to such a marital situation, modification should first be directed to unlocking the restricted arrangements.

Deficits of structure presume a response capability of the partners such that, given the proper stimulus conditions of time, place, and opportunity, the desired verbal behavior will have a good likelihood of being emitted. Absence of these stimulus conditions combined with evidence of partner response capability are the main clues to structural deficit.

Partner interaction, the fifth and last source of difficulty, involves the verbal behavior of the partner that precipitates or sustains particular verbal behaviors of the spouse. Thus, any particular surfeit of verbal response may be traced to partner reinforcement, partner cueing, or eliciting properties of the partner's verbal behavior; and any given response deficit may be accounted for by weakness in the verbal reinforcement of the partner, verbal punishment by the partner, or lack of verbal stimulus control by the partner. Partner interaction difficulties such as these are very common with couples who have disordered communication and may coexist with other sources of difficulty in verbal behavior.

Throughout both assessment and modification, the practitioner must be alert to the ever-present possibility that, despite the agreement of the clients and the practitioner to work on couple communication, there is a more important concern that should be addressed before or instead of marital communication. There is always a chance, remote as it is, that a very important problem having little or nothing to do with couple communication will surface and become clear to the practitioner in the course of work on marital communication. Examples might be serious drug abuse of a partner, alcoholism, or psychosis. These are called *Alpha* problems to distinguish them from referent conditions that are noncommunication difficulties which give rise to communication problems. Almost any problem, if it is serious enough, could be an *Alpha* problem, deserving of priority over marital communication.

Further, couple decision making may be much more problematic than the communication difficulty, thus requiring priority consideration. Decision difficulties of couples generally have more adverse consequences for other areas of living than most communication problems have by themselves. Also, couple decision-making difficulties often give rise to communication problems, which mask the basic decision-making difficulties. These are some of the reasons why work on couple decision making, if it is defective, generally takes precedence over work on marital communication. The practitioner must therefore be alert throughout assessment to the possibility that decision making is a problem and deserves attention first.

Initial Inquiry

Initial interviews with the partners are intended to elicit information on these four topics:

1. *The strengths and difficulties of marital communication.* These data provide a basis for specification of the behavioral components of communication.
2. *The subjects the partners have difficulty communicating about.* Information concerning the content areas of communication

difficulties may shed light on the pervasiveness of the difficulties and the possible role of referent conditions.

3. *Stimulus conditions associated with communication difficulties and strengths.* By identifying the immediately preceding stimulus conditions for given communication difficulties, the practitioner learns about the role of referent conditions, unfavorable setting events, structural deficits, and partner interaction as possible sources of the difficulties. In addition, information about the stimulus conditions that may give rise to communication strengths often provides clues to facilitative conditions that can be accelerated in the intervention.

4. *Possible difficulties in marital decision making.* To rule out marital decision making as a possible area of difficulty, brief inquiry is directed to such topics as how well the couple makes decisions together and whether there are any significant disagreements, dissatisfactions, or unresolved issues associated with the making of decisions.

If the inquiry affirms that the main difficulties involve communication, further questioning involving decision making is stopped and assessment of communication is continued. However, if the main difficulty turns out to be decision making, whether or not there are also communication difficulties, the practitioner should work on decision making first, using procedures such as those described in Chapter 6.

Initial inquiry, which generally takes fifteen to thirty minutes, need not be exhaustive or elaborate to yield important leads; subsequent assessment activities are generally better sources of extensive and pinpointed information.

Response Display Procedure

Response display of verbal behavior initiates work on communication in detail. The primary objective is to obtain a sample of verbal responses of the marital partners for purposes of specification and for possible use in measurement and subsequent evaluation. Actual behavioral samples of the verbal responses are almost always superior to self-report alone. With few exceptions, marital partners cannot report precisely and accurately what the actual behavioral components are and how they may be patterned and interrelated. The response display also provides an opportunity to learn more about possible sources of the communication difficulties through what the partners say about the content discussed. The Response Display Procedure, described below, consists of topic selection, topic discussion, scanning, postdiscussion inquiry, and response specification proper.

Topic Selection. The response display consists of having the marital partners discuss particular topics chosen by the practitioner to enhance the likelihood of obtaining a relevant sample of their verbal behavior and yield additional information concerning possible referent problems in that area. Only one topic is discussed at a time. General topics that are good to start with are the strengths and problems in the marriage or the expectations each partner has of the other. These topics usually provide additional data about possible referent problems that may be related to communication or decision-making difficulties. Somewhat more specific topics suitable for discussion next are the communication strengths and problems, or how decision making is handled in the marriage. Each of these topics may provide valuable information concerning communication or decision making as carried out at home, in addition to serving as the basis for the display of verbal responses then and there. There are, of course, many more specific topics that may be selected to provide information expressly about a given referent area. Thus, partners may be requested to discuss how such matters as affection, sex, money, who has control over what, child management, relatives, the use of drugs or alcohol, attention shown to family members, privacy, or recreation are handled in the marriage and the effect on the marriage. One to four discussion topics are generally enough to obtain an adequate sample. Suggested topics for the assessment of decision making are given in Chapter 6.

Discussion of Topic. Topics are assigned to marital partners for discussion in the office setting or in the home if the office sample proves inadequate. During the discussion in the office, the therapist sits inconspicuously to one side or withdraws from the room. Discussions are tape-recorded, with the couple's permission, for subsequent analysis. Each topic is generally discussed fifteen to twenty minutes. Partners should usually be seated facing each other, thus allowing nonverbal cues to enter directly into the communication.[3] Appendixes A and E present discussions on different topics.

[3] In special cases, such as for research purposes, a barrier may be erected between the partners or they may be seated back to back, so that facial and body cues are screened out. The former provides a better and purer sample of the verbal behavior per se whereas the latter is more complex and lifelike. There are advantages and disadvantages to each method.

Scanning. The practitioner should listen to the discussion as it transpires to note strengths and difficulties of verbal behavior, possible concerns in the area of decision making, the role that referent conditions and unfavorable event setters may play in communication problems, and look for relevant aspects of nonverbal behavior. The critical feature of scanning is that the practitioner is already familiar with the relevant information on these topics and tracks the discussion for significant data that may be relevant.

The following topics should be scanned for:

1. Significant communication strengths or difficulties (see Table 3-1).
2. Selected referent conditions that may affect the marital communication (see Table 3-2).
3. Selected setting events that may affect marital communication adversely (see Table 3-3).
4. Significant difficulties of nonverbal behavior (see Table 3-4). These include in particular any excessive indications of dissent, such as shaking the head, laughing inappropriately or mockingly, not tracking by not maintaining eye contact, and turn offs, such as grimaces, exasperated sighs, and rolling of the eyes upward.[4]
5. Decision-making difficulties that may generate discord or themselves be significant problems. Continuing disagreement concerning allocation of money in the family, unilateral action taken by one partner, failure to make proper decisions, failure to complete the relevant steps in decision-making are all clues suggesting decision-making difficulties (see Chapters 5 and 6).

In contrast to coding and systematic measurement, scanning aids the observer in detecting any major factors falling into these categories. There will almost always be some or even many uncertainties remaining after such scanning. This is no problem because information to be obtained in subsequent steps will generally resolve these uncertainties.

Postdiscussion Inquiry. One objective of postdiscussion inquiry is to determine the adequacy of the sample of verbal behavior yielded

---

[4] Additional information on nonverbal categories such as these, and their use in coding nonverbal behavior, may be found in Patterson and Hops (1972) and Weiss, Hops, and Patterson (1973).

TABLE 3-1. Selected Strengths and Difficulties of Marital Verbal Behavior*

Representation of Referents	Information
Incorrect autoclitic	Ambiguous message
Overgeneralization	Redundant information given
Presumptive attribution	Too little information given
Poor referent specification	Too much information given
Content (Thematic Continuity)	Conversational Guidance and
Content avoidance	Control
Content shifting	Excessive cueing
Detached utterance	Excessive question asking
Illogical talk	Obtrusions
Overresponsiveness	Vocal Properties
Quibbling	Affective talk
Temporal remoteness	Disfluent talk
Topic content persistence	Fast talk
Underresponsiveness	Loud talk
Content (Handling)	Monotone speech
Acknowledgment deficit	Overtalk
Acknowledgment surfeit	Quiet talk
Excessive agreement	Rapid latency
Excessive disagreement	Sing-song speech
Excessive expression of threat	Slow latency
Negative talk surfeit	Slow talk
Opinion deficit	Unaffective talk
Opinion surfeit	Undertalk
Pedantry	
Positive talk deficit	
Positive talk surfeit	

* See Chapter 2 for definitions, and examples and minor categories.

TABLE 3-2. Selected Referent Conditions That May Affect Marital Verbal Behavior*

Affection between partners	Political differences
Attention to partners or others	Privacy of members
Behavioral control of partner	Relationships with relatives
Child management	Religion
Division of labor in the home	Social activities and recreation
Use of drugs or alcohol	Sex
Family or marital decision making	Work
Money	

* See Chapter 1 and text for details.

TABLE 3-3. Selected Setting Events That May Affect Marital Verbal Behavior*

Anger
Anxiety
Depression
Effects of drugs, alcohol, and medication
Fatigue
Illness, injury
Sex deprivation

* See Chapter 1 and text for details.

TABLE 3-4. Selected Categories of Nonverbal Behavior*

Assent
Attention
Dissent
Laugh
Negative physical contact
Not tracking
Positive physical contact
Turn off

* Adapted from the Marital Interaction Coding System of Hops et al. (1972), Document 01234, ASIS National Auxiliary Publications Service, c/o CCM Information Sciences, Inc., 909 Third Avenue, New York, New York 10022.

in the discussion. To this end, marital partners are queried about what was typical or atypical in their communication. This is ordinarily sufficient to get a general idea about the representativeness of their verbal responses, but if it is not the practitioner may replay the tape, stopping periodically to ask the couple how typical the conversational segment is. The verbal sample should also be compared for consistency with what is already known about the verbal behavior of the partners.

Although the topics assigned in the discussion generally yield relevant content, it has been found that the samples of verbal responses of the same partners produced by different topics, reckoned in terms of ratings of categories on the Verbal Problem Checklist, are remarkably similar (Thomas, Walter, and O'Flaherty, 1974a). For instance, although a couple might discuss different things when talking about child management than when discussing marital role expectations, they might fault each other to the same extent in both discussions. In the author's clinical work, atypical response displays are the exception rather than the rule. However, the practitioner should always be alert to the possibility of unrepresentative samples of verbal responses.

There are at least two noteworthy types of atypical sample. One is the "false positive," in which the response display yields a better sample than usual. For example, one wife was found to be considerably less abrasive and to use many fewer faults in the office discussion than she did at home. This is something of a "company manners" effect. A not uncommon false positive involves obtaining a fully adequate amount of talk during the response display for a partner who is alleged to talk too little at home. The second type is the "false negative," in which the sample obtained during the response display is worse than the one usually yielded at home. Thus, there may be a suppressed amount of talking, as in deliberately not talking much during the response display. There may be an excessive amount of faulting compared with the usual amount—something of a "sanctuary effect," in which the partner is free to be negative in the presence of the therapist but is unable to express such negative comments when alone with the mate.

An atypical sample can often be handled by obtaining one or more additional response displays after partners have become more accustomed to the situation. This failing, it is then best to obtain samples of verbal interaction at home.

A second objective of the postdiscussion inquiry is to follow up leads suggesting the existence of an *Alpha* problem more important than communication or that decision making is an important difficulty.

A third objective of this inquiry, and the major one concerning marital communication, is to pursue clues to the sources of the communication difficulty provided by the discussion. For instance, if it appears that most disagreements are related to drinking of the partners and to discussions held when they are very tired, the extent to which the communication difficulties may be attributed to such unfavorable setting events as fatigue and alcohol-induced irritability should be explored further. If the arguing appears to be about sex and there are some sexual difficulties, the possible effect of the sexual problem in generating the communication difficulty should be pursued. If the partners communicate adequately but often don't talk at home, the possible role of structural deficits should be looked into.

The total time required to complete an inquiry generally runs from five to thirty minutes. Again, detailed inquiry is not required unless there are many fruitful leads or a lead yields critical new information. Uncertainties can be pursued further with the assignment of additional discussion topics, in subsequent postdiscussion inquiry, or by subsequent procedures. Generally, topic discussion and postsession inquiry should be repeated if uncertainties continue to exist.

Other Procedures of Display. In addition to the discussion of topics in an office setting, discussions tape-recorded at home for subsequent analysis may be useful. These home discussions should generally be structured by time, place, and topic so as to yield the desired information. If response displays consisting of office discussions are found to be suitable, there is little reason to obtain a home sample unless the helper wishes to be especially certain of the adequacy of the sample. In situations where home recording is unlikely to yield good or representative data, it may be possible to obtain written records from clients of the significant aspects of the verbal behavior. Although verbal behavior is often very difficult to record accurately in this way, salient discrete events, such as whether or not someone talked or faulted, can ordinarily be recorded with sufficient accuracy if the recording is done soon after the events occur. Major disagreements and arguments, of course, are typically easy to remember and, hence, to record. If written records cannot be kept by the marital partners, a last resort is to endeavor to obtain the needed information by interview alone. Although this is very much second best, it is often the only remaining available means. In the interview, concrete examples should be solicited, quotations obtained where possible and paraphrased if they cannot be recalled exactly. Partner reactions, where relevant, should also be obtained.

Response Specification Procedures

After adequate data have been obtained by means of the Response Display Procedure or some alternative to it, response specification itself should be undertaken. The four procedures of specification given here are alternatives, each with advantages and disadvantages.

1. *Informal appraisal.* If the practitioner is very familiar with response categories, such as those of the Verbal Problem Checklist described below, it is not necessary to use a rating schedule in order to complete specification. Specification can be done informally simply by writing down the major communication difficulties and strengths after response display. However, in such instances the practitioner should be very familiar with specific verbal response strengths and limitations and experienced in their identification. It is recommended that most practitioners use the Verbal Problem Checklist or some other list of verbal strengths and problems to increase the comprehensiveness and accuracy of identification. Informal appraisal is the most rapid but least objective and systematic procedure.

2. *Postdiscussion rating.* The behavioral elements in partner communication can be specified readily by means of rating after discussions have been listened to or after tape replay or response display discussions. A useful instrument to facilitate such specification is the Verbal Problem Checklist (Thomas, Walter, and O'Flaherty, 1974a). This is a rating schedule consisting of a set of forty-nine inductively derived categories of potentially problematic areas of verbal responding (see Appendix C for sample schedule). Each marital partner is rated on each of the forty-nine categories of verbal response immediately after the practitioner listens to a response display. After the categories have been rated, the therapist records any patterns he has discerned. This rating schedule has been shown to be rapid, accurate, relatively reliable, and valid, given the validity criteria examined. Details concerning the Verbal Problem Checklist are presented later in this chapter in the section on Specialized Procedures.

3. *Postdiscussion coding.* Responses may also be specified by means of postdiscussion coding. This is probably the most accurate procedure, given the present level of measurement sophistication, but it generally entails large investments of time and effort, especially if tailormade, individualized specification is what is desired. Coding procedures are described more fully later in this chapter and in Appendix D.

4. *On-line coding.* Coding of responses for purposes of specification can be carried out as the responses occur ("on-line"), provided that coders have been properly trained to code reliably and that there is suitable electromechanical equipment or other means of recording. On-line coding, in principle, is probably the most efficient and rapid way to specify responses (as well as to baseline and monitor them), but it ordinarily requires considerable investment in training and technical tool-up. Signal and electromechanical systems suitable for these purposes, including a computerized apparatus, are described later in this chapter.

Nonverbal behavior may be specified also in those cases where it is judged to be a problem. At present, there is no clinical instrument for specifying and measuring nonverbal behavior. For this reason, specification here can consist simply of careful description of the behavioral components of the partner's problematic nonverbal responses. The observer will be aided in specification by knowing the categories of nonverbal behavior presented in Table 3-4 or with a larger set of the Marital Interaction Coding System.[5]

Data Types for Possible Sources of Difficulty

Unlike the other sources of difficulty, partner interaction involves analysis of the verbal interchanges of the partners as these occur or afterward in appraisal of taped records. Thus, in seeking possible controlling conditions having locus in partner verbal behavior, one scans the data of the response displays for consistent association between a mate's verbal behavior and characteristic responses of the partner. For example, if there is noteworthy undertalk and under-responsiveness of the wife combined with a high degree of verbal abuse of the husband every time she does speak, one may speculate that in addition to other possible controlling conditions, the wife's speaking has been suppressed by the punishment of the husband's responses. After formulating provisional functional hypotheses, the practitioner looks for corroborating data, such as consistencies in the associations of partner-partner responses across the response displays. In some instances, a hypothesis may be supported or refuted by obtaining more information from partners concerning the characteristic patterns of their verbal interchange. In special cases where the outcome merits the effort, coding of selected aspects of speaker-speaker interchange or special electromechanical devices may be employed to discern more precisely the role of partner responding in controlling the mate's target responses.

Considering the other sources of communication difficulty, information provided by the initial inquiry, the topic discussions, post-discussion inquiry, and response specification is generally sufficient for arriving at an operational "source hypothesis" concerning the probable controlling conditions for the difficulties of verbal behavior. (An example of how source hypotheses can be formulated from such data is provided in the analysis in Appendix C.) Again, when the above-mentioned information still leaves uncertainties, additional procedures, such as one of those discussed below, may be required.

[5] Hops, Wills, Patterson, and Weiss (1972) developed the coding system for research purposes to be used in connection with coding from videotapes. Document 01234, ASIS National Auxiliary Publications Service, c/o CCM Information Sciences, Inc., 909 Third Ave., New York, N.Y. 10022.

Appendixes A, C, and E provide response displays and assessment appraisals that illustrate aspects of response specification and identification of possible sources of difficulty as presented above.

ASSESSMENT OF BEHAVIORAL AND ENVIRONMENTAL RESOURCES (STEP 6)

Appraisal of behavioral and environmental resources provides critical information concerning the feasibility of alternative modification approaches. Without the requisite resources, the practitioner will be limited in what may be accomplished. Behavioral resources include the availability of suitable relatives or other mediating persons to participate in a modification program. The marital partners themselves may (or may not) possess critical behavioral resources. For example, the strengths of one partner, such as being behaviorally specific, not overgeneralizing, and using abundant positive talk, often may be used directly to accelerate given desirable responses of the other. Communication strengths of partners greatly increase their value as mediators.

In the case of verbal behavior, environmental resources consist largely of equipment that the practitioner may make use of in the implementation and modification plan. For example, portable tape recorders, counters, cueing devices, timers and electromechanical devices, such as the light signaling system to be described later, may all be employed in special situations to assist in monitoring and modification. The more behavioral and environmental resources available to the practitioner, the more options he has in putting together a suitable modification program.

SPECIFICATION OF BEHAVIORAL OBJECTIVES (STEP 7)

Even though provisional and general behavioral objectives are established from the early stages of assessment, the final specification of behavioral objectives is undertaken at the end of assessment, when information deriving from prior steps has been collected and evaluated. Operational behavioral objectives cannot be specified without appraisal of information relating to response specification, possible controlling conditions and behavioral resources.

Altogether, the assessment will have yielded information relating to possible *Alpha* problems, decision-making difficulties, surfeits and deficits of partner verbal behavior, and sources of the communication difficulties. Many diverse profiles of difficulty for partners can be anticipated. For example, there may be *Alpha* problems and no others; there may be decision-making difficulties along with communication difficulties; there may be mainly communication difficulties, but with variation in the extent to which the different sources of difficulty are operative (e.g., referent and partner interaction may be sources, with minimal involvement of the others). In the face of such diversity, it is helpful to have general priorities to serve as a basis for determining the behavioral objectives.

If there is an *Alpha* problem, such as chronic alcoholism of one or both partners, work on this problem should be the first priority. If there are significant decision-making difficulties, they should be remediated first, postponing work on the communication difficulties for later, if they still persist after the decision-making has been improved.

If communication difficulties are the main problem, as is often the case when a couple has sought out and agreed to work on marital communication, the first priority would be to address any clearly evident sources of communication difficulty involving referent conditions, setting events, the "restricted marriage," or structural deficits before working on partner verbal behavior. Remediation of these sources, if they are truly the maintaining conditions for the communication difficulty, will of course make it unnecessary to work on the communication behavior itself. However, if communication difficulties persist, they will need to be addressed directly. Difficulties in marital verbal behavior also deserve priority attention if they derive from repertoire deficit or partner interaction without any significant involvement of other sources of difficulty.

The main target responses for intervention generally turn out to be those problems of verbal behavior having locus in partner interaction. For planful intervention, particular classes of verbal response must then be selected as the targets of intervention. There will ordinarily be three or four clear-cut problematic response categories for each partner, with a range of one or two to about ten. If a rating schedule is used, such as the Verbal Problem Checklist, the categories receiving the highest ratings are of course those that generally would be selected for modification. Given several response categories that are roughly equal in rating, those judged to be the most serious, pervasive in effect, or capable of improving the marriage if successfully changed would be selected as the immediate targets of intervention. For instance, if faulting and affective talk are judged (by whatever means) to be about equal in amount, faulting would easily take precedence over affective talk because it so often generates counterfaulting, disagreements, escalation of conflict, and negative interaction, without any constructive outcome. Affective talk, although it could result in such adverse effects, is typically not followed by so much negative interaction.

Deficits in desirable verbal behavior suggest goals that emphasize acquisition, strengthening, or maintainence. Most assessments of marital communication reveal a large number of response categories in which there is no real difficulty and a few for which there is clear evidence of strength. In regard to the acceleration of desirable verbal responses, one must select particular responses to be increased and not assume that other desirable responses will automatically be elevated at the same time. Each one of the several desirable responses that needs to be accelerated must be identified and acted on directly.

There will almost always be some verbal responses that should be done away with. One cannot anticipate, however, that a given problematic response will be automatically decreased by increasing something else. For example, one cannot expect a decrease in faulting to accompany an increase in positive talk. It is possible to engage in considerably more positive talk than before and still fault a great deal —even as much as before. Likewise, an increase in desirable responding in one area has relatively little if anything to do with a decrease in negative responding in another. One would not anticipate any necessary decrease in illogical talk, for instance, if there were an increase in content specificity. In only very restricted areas of responding will an increase in a given area be associated with a possible decrease for its counterpart. For example, an increase in response specificity has a good chance of occurring at the expense of overgeneralization. Even so, however, it is still possible to have a high level of response specificity with some overgeneralization remaining. Therefore, objectives to decelerate given verbal responses will almost always be required, as is also true of particular acceleration objectives. In most cases this would consist of the companion objectives of increasing one response and of decreasing its opposite. Thus, one would endeavor to increase positive talk and decrease negative talk, to increase specificity and decrease overgeneralization, to increase logical talk and decrease illogical talk.

This dual-focus approach to intervention objectives is entirely consistent with the research results of Wills, Weiss, and Patterson (1974), who found that the pleasurable and displeasurable dimensions of marital satisfaction were independent and that displeasurable behaviors exercised a disproportionate influence on marital satisfaction. These authors concluded that intervention programs should try to decrease the rate of displeasurable behavior as well as increase the rate of pleasurable behavior.

Although these comments pertain to verbal behavior, they are equally relevant to nonverbal behavior. Nonverbal behavior is an aspect of partner interaction that may be defective, in which case it can be considered along with any verbal behavior in formulating targets of intervention.

RESPECIFICATION OF PROBLEM CONTRACT (STEP 8)

The problem contract to work in the area of communication agreed to in the early stages of assessment is generally not specific in regard to particular aspects of communication. Once the behavioral objectives have been specified, therefore, it will be necessary to respecify the contract accordingly. The respecification consists of agreeing to work on the particular area or areas of behavior identified as the behavioral objectives in the assessment. This agreement serves to guide subsequent work in remediation.

Other Steps

In addition to the basic steps outlined above, a full assessment may draw on such other steps as baselining, the assessment probe, and assessment feedback. These steps are essential, optional, or unnecessary, depending upon one's objectives and available resources.

BASELINING

Following specification, it is often desirable to obtain a preintervention estimate of the level of the target behavior. This information provides the practitioner with a quantitative basis for judging the seriousness of the problem. Sometimes the baseline indicates that the behavior occurs too infrequently to justify intervention. In rare instances it reveals that the target behavior is much more in need of intervention than was originally anticipated. Base rates also provide an important standard against which the success of the intervention may subsequently be evaluated.

The baseline should be quantitatively expressed and carefully measured for an appropriate period of time prior to intervention. The quantitative expression may be in terms of frequency (such as the number of positive statements), duration (e.g., the length of arguments), magnitude (such as rated amounts of given behaviors using a checklist), or latencies (e.g., the time a mate takes to reply to

what the partner says). Specialized procedures for obtaining baselines, among them the Verbal Problem Checklist, content coding,
and electromechanical devices, are discussed later in this chapter.
Ideally, the recording required to obtain baselines should be simple,
accurate, systematic, and unobtrusive.

Most baselines of verbal behavior can be obtained in a relatively
short period of time, especially when response displays are used as a
source of data. Assuming that an adequate sample of couple verbal
behavior has been obtained in the display, it is ordinarily the case
that one or two typical response displays, each lasting for twenty
minutes or so, yields an adequate estimate of the preintervention
level of the target behavior. When the assessment is done at home,
baselines generally take longer, especially if written records are kept
by the marital partners.

There are occasions, however, when no baselines need to be
taken. Thus, baselines are not ordinarily obtained for infrequent
or episodic events. If a couple has an argument once every two
months, no matter how violent, this would ordinarily not be baselined. Deficits of verbal response, like other behavioral deficits, are
likewise ordinarily not baselined. When baselines are not sought, it
is especially important to obtain an estimate of the premodification
level of the target behavior. If arguments are the focus of modification,
for example, the practitioner should get the couple's estimate of how
often such arguments have occurred over a period—say, the previous
six months.

Baselines are often essential when carrying out clinical research
and outcome evaluation. However, unless a rating schedule is used
for purposes of specification and baselining, the quantification required for determining base rates can be costly in time and effort.
Unfortunately, in routine clinical practice, baselines are all too easily
omitted if the practitioner is not familiar with rapid baselining procedures or if his approach to intervention places little emphasis
upon the determination of outcome success. Although it can be said
in general that the determination of baselines is highly desirable, the
above factors have to be taken into consideration in deciding whether
the effort is worth the return in clinical practice.

THE ASSESSMENT PROBE

The assessment probe is a miniature experiment in which the
practitioner intervenes in the couple's life situation before beginning
intervention proper to obtain assessment information that would not

be readily available otherwise. Ordinarily the probe takes the form of a request that the couple engage in behavior relating to communication which would not be asked for during assessment. The information thus yielded is carefully appraised and is considered along with other assessment data in formulating an intervention plan before embarking upon modification (Thomas, 1975).

I recently saw one couple in their mid-twenties who complained that their main problem was communication. Early assessment information indicated that they had very few difficulties, although both talked very little at home, especially the husband. To test the hypothesis that the couple could carry on mutually rewarding conversations if only they would take the time to sit down and discuss things with each other, an assessment probe was undertaken in the form of a request that the couple set aside a half hour each evening to discuss personal matters. This was a highly successful experiment in that the couple was able to have productive and satisfying conversations, provided that such talk was anticipated and scheduled. The results of the probe suggested that appropriate verbal behavior of the partners could be evoked by the appropriate external stimuli, such as appointed times. (If the couple failed to have the conversation or had particular communication problems when they did, these results would also have been very informative in the assessment.) After the other parts of assessment were completed, scheduled conversations were added to the modification program and continued into the period of maintenance.

ASSESSMENT FEEDBACK

It is valuable to provide feedback concerning the results of the assessment just prior to specification of behavioral objectives and formulation of the modification program. The purpose of assessment feedback is to convey the essential results to the couple, including the facts turned up in the assessment as well as the practitioner's appraisal of their relative importance. The feedback facilitates establishing realistic behavioral objectives.

There are essentially five areas on which assessment information may be provided: (1) possible decision-making difficulties; (2) the referent conditions that may be worth working on in their own right or may give rise to communication difficulties; (3) setting events that may adversely affect couple verbal behavior; (4) restricting conditions of the marriage that may give rise to communication difficulties; and (5) the behavioral components that specify the main strengths and limitations of couple communication. Positive information is given first, and then other information relating to problematic features. It is essential that the negatives be restricted to a few of the very most important ones, avoiding at all costs conveying excessively detailed negative feedback. Assessment feedback differs from corrective feedback and instruction, which is feedback augmented with a discussion of the dysfunctions of the problem behavior and instructions concerning how to behave differently. Corrective feedback and instruction are only given as part of a modification program. Chapter 4 provides further details on corrective feedback and instruction.

Specialized Procedures

There are several specialized procedures that facilitate carrying out the assessment steps described above. Without using such procedures, assessment is not likely to be sufficiently precise, accurate, or systematic. Each of the methods that follows is relevant to the monitoring of behavior during modification as well as to assessment.

THE VERBAL PROBLEM CHECKLIST

The Verbal Problem Checklist (VPC) is a schedule used clinically to rate potentially problematic categories of verbal responding. The VPC was developed primarily for specification of the behavioral components of couple communication, but it may also be used, where appropriate, for baselining before modification and for monitoring during and after intervention. Although it may easily be employed along with other procedures, the VPC is a valuable alternative to postsession coding of verbal responses from taped records or transcripts and to the use of electromechanical devices.

In the research report on this schedule (Thomas, Walter, and O'Flaherty, 1974a), reliabilities for raters and categories were disclosed to be moderate to very high (median gammas were .69 for husbands and .66 for wives). Commorato and Brieger (1973) also reported very satisfactory reliabilities in the use of the instrument in connection with an agency application of selected procedures. Evidence of the validity of selected ratings was reported for two validation criteria (Thomas, Walter, and O'Flaherty, 1974a). In this study, the VPC was found to narrow the number of possible problem areas from a maximum of forty-nine to an average of four for husbands and three for wives—about seven per couple. The use of the VPC to rate areas of verbal responding after marital partners discussed assigned topics was found to be a relatively rapid and simple technique of response specification. With experience and practice, ratings of both partners can be completed for all categories in approximately five minutes. The VPC was found in this study and in subsequent use to be a viable method to follow in the specification of potential problems of verbal responding.

The categories of the VPC were given in Chapter 2, where strengths and limitations of verbal behavior were discussed. The response categories apply to the verbal behavior of the speaker and involve verbal responding of a surfeit or deficit nature that may be potentially problematic. The categories refer to objectively definable referents that may be concretely measured and require a minimum of inference on the part of the rater. The categories were inductively derived in connection with over four years of research on family verbal behavior in which target behaviors for modification were selected on the basis of individualized assessment. Many of the verbal behaviors to which the categories refer have now been quantified in connection with baselining and modification in single-couple experiments. The categories are intended to facilitate specification of the particular verbal strengths and limitations of marital partners. In the VPC, each marital partner is rated immediately after the discussion on each of the forty-nine categories of verbal response.[6] The ratings range from 0 (not at all) to 3 (a large amount). After all the categories have been rated for each partner, the rater then indicates any patterning he has observed. Finally, he recommends areas for modification, if these have been evident. (Illustrative ratings with the VPC are given in Appendix C, based upon the transcript of couple verbal behavior presented in Appendix A. Training procedures for rating verbal behavior are given in Appendix G.)

---

[6] The categories are as follows: overtalk, undertalk, fast talk, slow talk, loud talk, quiet talk, singsong speech, monotone speech, rapid latency, slow latency, affective talk, unaffective talk, obtrusions, quibbling, overresponsiveness, underresponsiveness, excessive question asking, pedantry, dogmatic statement, overgeneralization, undergeneralization, excessive cueing, incorrect autoclitic, presumptive attribution, misrepresentation of fact or evaluation, topic content avoidance, other content avoidance, topic content shifting, other content shifting, topic content persistence, other content persistence, poor referent specification, temporal remoteness, detached utterance, positive talk deficit, positive talk surfeit, acknowledgment deficit, acknowledgment surfeit, opinion deficit, opinion surfeit, excessive agreement, excessive disagreement, dysfluent talk, too little information given, redundant information given, too much information given, negative talk surfeit, negative talk deficit, and illogical talk.

CODING

The objective of coding is to classify units of verbal behavior for purposes of specification, baselining, monitoring, or other factors that may relate to outcome evaluation. Coding can be especially useful when dealing with unusual, idiosyncratic, and individualized characteristics of verbal response for which fixed-response categories might not be appropriate. Coding is very often essential to achieve appropriate quantification of verbal behavior in carrying out clinical research, systematic outcome evaluation, and studies of new clinical procedures.

Bijou et al. (1969) have distinguished between specific and general response codes. In the former, response categories particular to the events to be classified are specially created. There are highly predictable stages in the development of a specific response code. The first stage typically entails the collection of response units that are possible exemplars of response categories. Following this there is the provisional definition of response categories and the coding of taped records or typed transcripts of couple interaction to test out the code categories. The final code consists of the refined and revised categories, which then are employed with a different segment of data to determine reliability. When reliability has been established as satisfactory, the coding is undertaken in earnest for purposes of classifying data for research findings. During coding proper, it is generally desirable to have additional checks on reliability because of possible drifts of reliability and shifting meaning of code categories.

An example of a specific response code is that for content specificity developed to capture the particular elements of denotative specificity in a case application of the efficacy of SAM, an electrical-mechanical light-signaling apparatus (Carter and Thomas, 1973a). Using transcripts of discussions of the couple's financial problems and a coding scheme developed for this purpose, content specificity was coded before and after modification. The verbal unit of analysis that was coded was a self-contained segment of speech with its own subject and predicate. To be coded as specific, any given verbal unit had to refer to recent events, not those in the remote past or the hypothetical future, and it had to denote discrete stimulus events, including behaviors, or affective events, such as feelings or opinions, that described concrete stimulus events. The inter-rater reliability for two independent coders was .85. To provide a quantification of content specificity on a minute-by-minute basis, the statistical analysis called, first, for counting the number of words contained within verbal units coded as specific and then converting those numbers to percentages for each minute interval by dividing them by the total number of words in that interval. The percentages were then plotted and subjected to a trend analysis.[7] By this means, it was possible to show that the intervention, which in this case was corrective feedback and instruction combined with periodic light feedback, was associated with an increase in the mean percentage of words in specific coded units from 18, in baseline, to 58, in modification.

A general response code consists of one or more response categories that may be employed to code almost any unit of behavior. An example of a general code for marital interaction is the Marital Interaction Coding System (MICS) of Hops, Wills, Patterson and Weiss (1972), described in research reports of Patterson and Hops (1972) and of Weiss, Hops and Patterson (1973). In this system there are verbal categories such as agree, approval, accept responsibility, command, compliance, criticize, and compromise and nonverbal categories such as assent, attention, compliance, laugh, noncompliance, normative, smile, and turn off.

One or more categories of the VPC, described above, could constitute a general response code. Thus, the practitioner might find it valuable to employ a general response code for coding faulting (see Appendix D). The advantage of a general response code is that once the practitioner is familiar with it, it may be readily employed with many different couples and, if suitable, permits systematic comparison of these couples.

Content coding becomes practical for routine assessment and modification to the extent that it may be made rapid, reliable, and accurate. To these ends, it helps to employ a general rather than a specific response code, to use trained and reliable coders, and to carry out the coding on the spot rather than after sessions. These favorable conditions were all present in research conducted to examine the adequacy of on-line baselining and modification (Thomas, Walter, and O'Flaherty, 1971; Thomas, Walter, and O'Flaherty, 1974b).

The series of subjects involved six couples who engaged in very high rates of faulting and low amounts of positive talk. For each couple, there were two before-after single-couple experiments to reduce faulting and one to increase positive talk. Findings were reported for one typical couple. Let us consider only faulting, so as to illustrate some details more simply.

The intervention consisted of corrective feedback and instruction

---

[7] See Figure 5 of Carter and Thomas (1973a).

to reduce the faulting combined with red-light feedback to the speaker whenever faulting occurred, to indicate therapist disapproval. Faulting was defined as any criticism, complaint, or negative evaluation of the partner's behavior by the speaker. In the on-line coding, the coding task was divided between two therapist-experimenters, one of whom coded for the husband and the other for the wife. Endeavoring to signal as rapidly as possible, the therapist signaled the onset of a coded event by pushing one button and the offset by pushing another button. The signals were sent to a computer that recorded each fault, without the partners being aware of it, during baseline; during intervention, the same recording of faulting was undertaken, but now, each time the therapist coded a fault, the signal also illuminated a red light before the offending partner to indicate therapist disapproval. The couple discussed communication difficulties in their marriage, first during baseline and again during modification. Each session lasted twelve minutes, and all coded faults were recorded immediately by the computer.

To check the reliability of the on-line coding, taped records of the discussion periods were replayed and coded independently again by the two coders using the computer-assisted signaling apparatus. To determine reliability, computer printouts of the on-line coding were then compared with the printouts for post-session coding. The formula for determining reliability was the number of agreeing signal judgments divided by the total number of signal judgments. Total reliability for on-line coding of faulting was .69 for coder 1, .63 for coder 2, and .58 for three-way agreement for both coders with on-line coding. (Post-session coding yielded higher reliabilities, as might have been anticipated, the grand index over all periods for three experiments being .81.) Altogether, these on-line reliabilities were considered to be fully adequate, considering the difficulty of the coding. Delays in on-line coding obviously reduced reliability. It was found that errors of omission due to slow reaction time accounted for most of the disagreements and that there were very few errors of commission.

Equally important is the fact that on-line coding was found in subsequent analysis to yield findings that were interpreted in essentially the same way as those based upon the more time-consuming postsession coding. In this analysis, data points for baseline and modification were compared for faulting and positive talk for each partner in each of the three experiments. Using only agreeing coded events (i.e., consensus) of the two coders in postsession coding as criteria, it was found that, with only minor exceptions, the interpretations of the results using only the on-line data points of coder 1 or of coder 2 were entirely adequate to arrive at correct interpretations of whether or not the intervention was effective. The same comparisons were also made using statistical significance as the basis for determining whether there was a difference between baseline and modification. Here there were 24 tests, of which 23 yielded exactly the same conclusion based on on-line data as those based on results for postsession coding. It was concluded from the results of this study that experienced and trained coders could code verbal responses, such as faults and positive talk, as they occur with a sufficiently high degree of accuracy to produce findings that yielded essentially the same interpretations as those based upon data derived from postsession analyses. The great speed of on-line coding combined with rapid data feedback such as may be afforded by a computer printout holds great promise for carrying out quick and reasonably accurate coding in routine practice.[8]

HOME ASSESSMENT

Assessment of communication in the home is sometimes necessary to augment or supplant information based upon response displays in the office. The sources of information for home assessment are the interview, tape recordings, and client recording. The interview is especially useful for response specification, but it is not suitable for systematically monitoring anything other than an occasional, easily noticed outburst.

Tape-recording is a much better means of obtaining a response display of couple verbal behavior. Tape recorders can be turned on at given times and in given places to obtain a sample of partner interchange. The recording can then be replayed and analyzed by the practitioner.

Records of verbal behavior kept by marital partners can be used as widely and as productively as can client recording of other behavior. However, because of the possible intricacy of the verbal behavior involved, special care needs to be given to delineate the recording task. Verbatim records of who said what are appropriate only for purposes of specification because few details of any verbal interchange can be recalled accurately and recorded properly. Base-

---

[8] A transcript of marital communication is presented in Appendix A; coding for this transcript using frequency counts, time interval classifications, and durations is illustrated in Appendix D. For additional details concerning content coding, the reader is referred to texts on behavioral research as well as to special articles such as those of Bijou, Peterson, Harris, Allen, and Johnston (1969) and Johnson and Bolstad (1973).

lining and monitoring presuppose careful, prior response specification by the practitioner and full understanding of the recording task by the marital partners. Frequencies of well-defined verbal response classes may be readily counted. Time-interval coding is especially useful when one is trying to keep track of events that may be difficult to discriminate. This type of coding consists of determining whether or not at least one instance of a given response occurred for a particular time interval. For example, marital partners could record each half hour from 5:30 P.M. to 9:00 P.M. whether or not at least one positive comment was made. Although they may not be able to keep accurate count of the number of positive comments that were made, they can probably discriminate whether or not at least one occurred in each half-hour period. Measurement by time duration may be feasible for calibrating the gross aspects of verbal behavior, such as the length of talking, arguments, and silences.

ELECTROMECHANICAL DEVICES

Electrical and mechanical devices are not required for competent assessment and modification of marital communication, but such devices may assist the practitioner in carrying out these activities more precisely, rapidly, and accurately than would otherwise be possible.

Timers, such as watches with second hands, and stop watches, are particularly valuable for time-interval coding, in which the practitioner codes whether or not a given verbal event occurs in selected time intervals. Timers, especially stop watches, are of course useful for determining the duration of verbal events, such as speeches or silences. Kitchen timers, pocket alarms, and alarm watches may be used to signal the beginning or the end of given time intervals. Such timed signals can be employed to cue periods when clients should keep records or engage in conversations of certain types. Counters, such as golf and mechanical tally counters, are valuable for enumerating verbal events that occur fairly frequently and would be difficult to count by pencil and paper.

Perhaps the single most useful electromechanical device is the familiar tape recorder. The tape recorder makes it possible to record response displays in the office or at home, replay the tapes for purposes of assessment and modification, and provide a durable record of the verbal behavior. Inexpensive portable cassette models having good fidelity are widely available and may be applied most flexibly and productively by the practitioner.

There has been a lack of methods for evoking and objectifying behavior under controlled conditions that allow for precise intervention to promote desired changes in these behaviors. The author and some of his former colleagues therefore conducted research to develop a special signaling system referred to as "SAM" after its acronym, SSAMB (Signal System for the Assessment and Modification of Behavior) (Thomas, Carter, Gambrill, and Butterfield, 1970). Through the use of light signals, the apparatus provides for client-controlled signaling as a component of client-to-client interaction and for intervention in ongoing interaction by means of signals sent from practitioner to client. The components of the system consist of client button boxes to transmit signals, client light boxes to receive light signals, a practitioner control box to receive light signals, a practitioner control box to regulate circuits of the signal system, monitor signal activity, and intervene by signals in the interaction, a relay box, an event recorder to record client or practitioner signals, and a stereo tape recorder—one track of which is used to record the verbal responses of clients and the other to register tones, clicks, and other sounds produced by the activation of signals.

The system was designed so that each client button box can be used to activate lights on a subject light box as well as on the therapist monitoring and control box. In addition to client-to-client signaling, the circuits of the therapist control box make it possible for the therapist to have client signals illuminate only the monitoring lamps on the therapist box, with no lighting of the client reception lamps (private mode), or to activate client reception lamps with or without the client's being able to send signals (public mode). All of these operations activate relays in the relay box, and these, in turn, activate an event recorder to record all signal activity.

When used in assessment, the SAM affords the opportunity to collect verbal behavior, signal behavior, and examine a variety of relationships of signal and verbal data. Specification can be done rapidly, accurately, and unobtrusively by having either the therapist or the marital partners activate signals with designated meanings (such as "like" or "dislike") during ongoing interaction. In this way, the therapist may indicate what he notes as problems, on the one hand, and as strengths, on the other; also, instead, marital partners may likewise do the same type of signaling. On replay of the taped interaction along with the signal data, it is then possible to identify undesirable as well as desirable aspects of the verbal behavior. Client or practitioner coding can also be used for purposes of obtaining baselines and for monitoring particular elements of verbal behavior during interaction.

When used in modification, light signals may be activated by the practitioner or the client with precision and relatively little ambiguity. These signals may be used to indicate practitioner approval for designated verbal behavior as it occurs, to indicate disapproval of inappropriate verbal behavior during ongoing interchanges, or to cue desirable responding where this seems appropriate.[9]

A system such as SAM may be readily constructed with the assistance of someone familiar with electronics or by consulting a company that specializes in behavioral equipment. Simple light-signal systems, without the control and monitoring box and signal recording elements, have been used successfully along with tape recorders in assessment and modification. Reference to a report on the electromechanical details of SAM may suggest possible applications and adaptations (Thomas, Carter, Gambrill, and Butterfield, 1970).

A valuable adjunct to any signal system is a means by which verbal and signal data may be replayed immediately after recording. One such apparatus has been designed, constructed, and reported (Butterfield, Thomas, and Soberg, 1971), and a related apparatus has been constructed that combines the functions of SAM with those of the replay apparatus and also has the important advantages of being computer compatible and easily portable (called P-SAM, for short). The core of this system is an eight-channel encoder-decoder.[10]

It is also possible to computerize a signal system by having the light-signal system interconnected with the computer so that the computer takes over the functions of control, monitoring, and recording. Possibilities and illustrative data for computer-assisted assessment and modifications have been reported by the author and his colleagues (Thomas, Walter, and O'Flaherty, 1974b). These studies indicated that using the computer-assisted SAM (CASAM for short), it may be possible to employ on-line baselining and monitoring in routine interpersonal helping with marital verbal behavior and that signal effects in ongoing interaction may be precisely measured so that clinical decisions can be made on the basis of the results. Some of the relevant findings were summarized in the previous section on coding. Computer-assisted treatment of marital communication ulti-

[9] For additional details concerning the possibilities of using SAM in assessment and modification of verbal behavior, see Thomas, Carter, and Gambrill (1971).

[10] Details of this system are described more fully in Thomas, Walter, and Carter (1971) and Thomas, Walter, and O'Flaherty, (1972). The encoder-coder is a modification of the Lehigh Valley Electronics (now BKS/LVE) four-channel tape recorder, Model 112-10.

mately may be done rapidly with the additional benefit of yielding outcome data to be used for making clinical decisions that are as precise as information now available only through conducting careful, time-consuming single-couple experiments.

The increasing availability of relatively low-cost closed-circuit television equipment affords the opportunity for practitioners to employ video recording and replay in work on marital communication. Weiss, Hops, and Patterson (1973) have used video feedback to code aspects of marital interaction. Katz (1975) has described several uses of closed-circuit television that may have particular applicability in work with marital communication. These involve the use of video feedback for what Katz calls "self-confrontation"; video feedback combined with partner and practitioner interrogation and inquiry, dubbed "Interpersonal Process Recall" by Katz; and use of video feedback for purposes of training new patterns of marital communication.

Among other devices that may have special application to marital communication is the automated system developed by Katz (1974) for eliciting and recording self-observations during dyadic communication. With this system, self-report data are recorded on a moment-to-moment basis during dyadic interaction, using client-activated pushbuttons, while videotape recordings are simultaneously made of the interaction as well as the signal data; thus, upon replay using split screens, one for the interaction and one for the self-report data, self-report data can be placed in correct temporal relationship with the other aspects of the interaction. The Chapple Interaction Chronograph (1949) has been used successfully for recording such formal properties of speech as duration of talk and silence and latencies of reaction and initiation. Careful studies illustrating possible uses of such recording have been reported by Matarazzo and Wiens (1972) and, with a related computer-assisted device, by Jaffe and Feldstein (1970). A free-operant approach in which a leverlike device is operated by a subject at predetermined response rates to maintain clear visual and audio communication with someone else on a television monitor has been employed by Nathan (1965), Nathan, Smith, and Rossi (1968), and Lindsley (1969).

Synopsis

The purpose of carrying out assessment of couple communication is to establish the necessary conditions for remedial work in this area. These conditions consist of an explicit agreement to work on marital communication, identification of the behavioral components of couple communication that are to be the focus of modification, determination that there are no other problems that should take precedence over communication, isolation of possible controlling conditions for the target aspects of marital communication, determination of the behavioral and environmental resources available to be used in remediation, and specification of concrete behavioral objectives.

To obtain the relevant information, this chapter sets forth the details of eight basic steps:

Preliminary Steps
1. Inventory of problem areas
2. Selection of and contract for the target area
3. Commitment to cooperate

Steps Involved in the Assessment of Marital Communication
4&5. Response specification and identification of probable sources of difficulty
   a. Objectives and general approach
   b. Initial inquiry
   c. Response display procedure
      (1) Topic selection
      (2) Discussion of topic
      (3) Scanning
      (4) Postdiscussion inquiry
      (5) Other procedures of display
   d. Response specification procedures
   e. Data types for possible sources of difficulty
6. Assessment of behavioral and environmental resources
7. Specification of behavioral objectives
8. Respecification of contract for target area

Additional steps that may be useful under special conditions were also described. These are baselining, the probe for assessment, and assessment feedback.

Specialized procedures that make assessment activities more precise, accurate and systematic were presented in detail. These involve the Verbal Problem Checklist, coding, home assessment, and electromechanical devices.

CHAPTER FOUR

Modification of Marital Communication

MODIFICATION OF marital communication is undertaken after assessment has been completed to increase acceptable target behavior and to decrease unacceptable target responding. Modification may best be carried out by means of a series of ordered activities that directly followed assessment. The steps of modification are as follows:

9. Formulation of the modification plan
10. Implementation of the plan
11. Monitoring of outcomes
12. Maintenance of change

The activities associated with each of these steps are taken up in detail below.

Formulation of the Modification Plan (Step 9)

Planning for modification draws on the results of assessment and what is known about the methods of modification. The objective is to select and plan for the implementation of a program of modification appropriate for alteration of the target behaviors.

The target behaviors, selected as part of the specification of behavioral objectives, include (1) *Alpha* problems, for which general intervention procedures (not only the specialized methods discussed here) would most often be appropriate; (2) decision making, for which the methods presented in Chapter 7 would be suitable; and (3) marital communication proper, for which the methods presented in this chapter are directly relevant. The aspects of target behavior that are most pertinent here are the verbal behavior of the partners (as well as occasional nonverbal difficulties) along with such sources of communication difficulty as referent conditions, unfavorable setting events, restricted marital arrangements, and structural deficits. The methods of modification include corrective feedback and instructions, rules for marital interaction, interactional cueing, practice, feedback, response contingencies, and exchange systems. Each method is applicable to one or more of the target behaviors.

SOME PRINCIPLES

There are several principles that help the practitioner to weigh information obtained in assessment and chart directions for modification. Principles 1–8 follow.

1. *Tailor plans for modification procedures to each partner and the couple.*

The assessment yields individualized information about the partners and the couple which makes it possible to prepare an individualized modification plan for the partners. Intervention tailored to the particular needs and conditions of the couple stands a better chance of success than a general plan that is not responsive to these conditions.

2. *Formulate the modification plan for a few key target responses.*

Because of the time and effort required to initiate changes in any given area of behavior, one or a few responses should be the initial targets. This restriction avoids overloading and weakening the program with too many target responses, a common failing of inexperienced practitioners. If additional responses need attention, they can be phased in at a later point, after progress has been made with the original target behaviors.

3. *Include both partners as targets of modification even if one contributes much more than the other to the interactional difficulties.*

The impression that one partner is being singled out or picked on should be avoided as should the idea that the helper is not impartial. Where possible, the impression should be fostered that each partner has strengths and limitations to about the same degree and that both contribute more or less equally to any disordered communication they have.

4. *Choose a setting for modification (e.g., office, home, or both) that is consonant with the modification objectives and distinctive capabilities of the interventional methods.*

Modification of couple verbal behavior in the office setting, with the worker present, has many advantages. Among these are that the verbal responses are directly displayed and observed by the helper, modification can be undertaken by the practitioner with the partners, feedback to the couple can be given immediately or with little delay, and rehearsal and practice can be carried out repeatedly, if necessary. Direct modification in the office is also well suited to the development and training of the partners' verbal responding, which could not be done effectively in the couple's home. The main disadvantage of modification in the office, of course, is that the stimulus conditions there may not be sufficiently similar to those of the home so that transfer and generalization may readily occur. Ideally modification in the office should be combined with intervention in the home.

The alteration of verbal behavior in the home is ordinarily carried out through the practitioner's instructions to the couple, given in the office by interview, concerning conditions to be established and behaviors to be produced in the home. The practitioner's activities during the interview are designed to establish conditions in the natural environment that will mediate changes in the target behavior (Kanfer and Phillips, 1969; Thomas and Carter, 1971). As desirable as intervention in the home is, however, it cannot be carried out successfully unless certain conditions are present. (1) The partners must correctly discriminate the behavior to be carried out and the appropriate stimulus context for its emission; (2) the behavior to be carried out must be present in each individual's repertoire; (3) the stimulus conditions under which this behavior is to be emitted must be present in the environment and capable of cueing the desired behavior; and (4) the practitioner must have sufficient influence over the clients so that the requested behavior has a good chance of being carried out (Gambrill, Thomas, and Carter, 1971). In general, new forms of verbal responding can be developed and trained at home, although generally somewhat less efficiently and effectively than in the office. The home is particularly well suited to intervention that places emphasis on establishing appropriate stimulus conditions for evoking already established verbal responses.

5. *Direct intervention toward altering the sources of communication difficulty, when these are known.*

Instead of directing modification toward target verbal responses alone, irrespective of their maintaining conditions, attention should be given first to alteration of the sources of the disordered communication. For example, if marital arguments and disagreements are occasioned mainly by the referent condition of poor child management, modification should be directed first to the couple's child management rather than to the verbal behaviors relating to the arguing and disagreement. If the improvement in child management reduces the disordered communication, as it should if poor child management is in fact a source of the communication difficulty, then, of course, it is unnecessary to work directly on the communication itself. If the communication difficulties persist, they may be taken on directly unless some other plausible sources of the communication difficulty have been identified.

6. *Give priority in modification to alteration of the sources of communication difficulty deriving from such factors as referent conditions, unfavorable setting events, restricted marriage, and structural deficits before focusing on partner interaction itself.*

To the extent that a couple's communication difficulties in fact derive from such sources as referent conditions, unfavorable setting events, a restricted marriage, or structural deficit, successful alteration of these maintaining conditions may well eliminate the need for training one or both partners to interact differently. If such alteration does not improve communication sufficiently, however, then modification can be directed toward partner interaction itself.

7. *Where possible, combine modification to accelerate desirable verbal responding with intervention intended to decelerate responding for unacceptable behavior.*

As we have noted, an increase in desirable responding in verbal behavior will not necessarily relate to a decrease in undesirable responding, nor will a decrease in undesirable responding be related necessarily to any increase in desirable responding. There are so many acceptable and unacceptable categories of verbal response that change in the frequency of responding in one category, even if very large, need not affect the frequency of responding in the remaining response categories. In consequence, one cannot hope to "accelerate out" unacceptable response categories by accelerating selected positive response categories. Another reason, reviewed more fully before, is that the desirable and undesirable behaviors of marital partners appear to be independent in their effects on marital satisfaction. Negative behavior contributes more to marital dissatisfaction than the positive behavior contributes to marital satisfaction.

8. *When focusing on partner interaction, modify the complimentary target behaviors of both partners, where possible.*

Thus, the interfering verbal responses of one partner should be reduced while the target behaviors of the other partner are being accelerated. For example, if the primary target behavior is to increase the undertalk of partner A and partner B overtalks, there should be a complimentary effort to reduce the overtalk of partner B. Likewise, responses that are likely to be reciprocally facilitating should be increased. For instance, if the primary target is to increase the positive talk of partner A, a complimentary and reciprocally facilitating behavior might be the positive talk of partner B.

Interventions focused only on the verbal responding of one partner may not be successful, or if they are, may be short-lived. Two important studies have found that efforts to modify the behavior of subjects in interacting groups depend greatly upon whether the behavior of their partners is also modified. Simkins and West (1966) found that to increase the duration of talking in freely interacting triads, it was necessary not only to reinforce the talking of the critical subjects but also to reinforce the noncritical subjects for having the critical subjects talk to them and to penalize the noncritical subjects for talking to each other. Bavelas, Hastorf, Gross, and Kite (1965) tried to alter the group structure of four-person groups by increasing the amount of talking done by the person ranked third in the group. Using green lights from the experimenter to signify positive contributions to the discussion and red lights for hampering contributions, it was found that it was necessary not only to give green light signals to the target person for his talking but also to give red light signals to the others when they talked.

Modification Methods for Couple Communication

There are at least seven modification methods directly applicable to the modification of couple verbal behavior. These are corrective feedback and instruction, rules for marital interaction, interactional cueing, practice, feedback, response contingencies, and exchange systems. Each of these is called a method because it consists of a distinctive set of practitioner activities and conditions for altering partner behavior. Even so, within each method there are generally different practitioner procedures that can be employed along with a variety of possible applications.

The first three methods are particularly suitable to the alteration of conditions antecedent to couple verbal behavior. These are corrective feedback and instruction, rules for marital interaction, and interactional cueing. Method 4, practice, involves evocation and training of the target response through either rehearsal or "live" performance. The last three methods involve stimulus conditions that may affect couple verbal behavior following its emission. These are response feedback, response contingencies, and exchange systems. These seven methods, along with several others having possible application that will also be discussed, are those from among which selection is made to compose a program of modification.

CORRECTIVE FEEDBACK AND INSTRUCTION

Corrective feedback and instruction (CF-I) consists of verbal or written statements presented by the practitioner to marital partners. The statements have the following components: (1) brief reference to the positive aspects of couple behavior or verbal responding; (2) description and explication or, preferably, taped replay of not more than three (and generally one or two) of the most important problems discovered in the assessment; (3) brief explication of the major dysfunctions for the couple associated with engaging in these behaviors; and (4) instructions concerning what steps the couple might take to behave differently.

CF-I differs from ordinary advice in that it is based upon careful evaluation of data collected during assessment; begins with positives so as to set events favorably for forthcoming information; designates particular behaviors as problematic and dysfunctional; consists of specific, definite practitioner statements (although not presented officiously or necessarily formally); is followed by a period in which the partners have an opportunity to carry out the instructions, usually at home; and entails practitioner monitoring to check on the adequacy with which the clients follow through on the instructed behavior.

The function of CF-I is catalytic inasmuch as it serves to initiate responses that are essentially already available for evocation and that depend upon subsequent evocation and reinforcement to be sustained in the long run. Because it performs this initiating function, CF-I generally constitutes an early step in a modification program. Several conditions necessary for the use of CF-I are that the responses in question are in the partners' repertoire, that responses may be evoked by instructions, and that contravening conditions are absent. Futhermore, it has been found that instructions are more likely to be carried out if compliance is reinforced (Ayllon and Azrin, 1964; Cossairt, Hall, and Hopkins, 1973; Bennett and Maley, 1973; Leitenberg, Wincze, Butz, Callahan, and Agras, 1970) and noncompliance has aversive consequences (Ramp, Ulrich, and Dulaney, 1971).

When used in intervention in the office, CF-I may be given on one occasion or several, with new and different instructions as necessary, after each practice session. When used in the home, CF-I can likewise be employed on a one-time basis or in sequence after practice to catalyze a series of different behaviors. A useful variation of CF-I is as an instructional probe to determine whether or not given verbal responses can be initiated discriminatively by instructions. If the responses can be so initiated, the practitioner then moves directly to methods designed to provide more reliable stimulus control of the behavior. If the probe fails to produce the intended responses, other, usually more painstaking procedures may have to be undertaken.

CF-I can be presented in a written statement, which enhances emphasis, clarity, and precision of expression. When a written statement would be too formal, however, the practitioner may deliver his comments orally, having carefully prepared them in advance. This next example is a segment of CF-I given verbally to the partners.

> On the positive side, both of you are intelligent, alert, and verbal. At several points you displayed a fine sense of humor. You also came out fairly well in conversation control. Here, no one dominated the conversation and both of you seemed to have your say.
>
> However, there were several difficulties revealed by the assessment that I would like to call to your attention. The first involves a pattern of faulting. [*At this point, the practitioner replayed portions of the tape to illustrate the faulting pattern of the partners.*]
>
> A faulting pattern is evident in this segment of your communication. Much of the time, in general, each of you responded to a statement about a problem of the marriage with an objection, a denial, or a countercomplaint. This is what I mean by a pattern: fault-objection, fault-denial, or fault-fault. This appeared regularly and, when it occurred, it didn't go anywhere, you each became more angry and it was thus counterproductive. Furthermore, the faulting tended to be personalized, and, in some cases, it was downright abusive and nasty.
>
> Thinking now about some of the ways you could discuss things more favorably, may I suggest that you keep difficulties from being personalized and leave the blaming out of it. Rather than get locked into the pattern I mentioned, you should try to move out of it by avoiding the faulting and stressing the positives. With a reduction of faults, objections, and denials and an increase in appropriate positives, the pattern will likely be broken.
>
> Another suggestion is that . . .

As mentioned earlier, CF-I can be given sequentially, following practice sessions. This next excerpt was taken from a written "Statement to Partners" presented just after a practice session that, in turn, was preceded by an earlier CF-I.

> In analyzing your communication during your last discussion, I observed that you changed in two important ways. First, you were noticeably more specific in talking about complaints and problems than you have been; you provided examples and helped each other to be more concrete. This was very good and I hope you will become even more specific in talking about topics. Second, I observed that Mr. O did not make nearly so many derogatory statements to Mrs. O as he did earlier. This is also an important change that I hope will continue to be demonstrated in your communication. I hope these positive changes will encourage you to make further improvements in the way you talk to each other.
>
> However, some of the concerns of communication pointed out to you last time are still apparent. These involve Mr. O's defensiveness and rationalizations and Mrs. O's frequent repetition of her complaints. The pattern now seems to be that Mrs. O presents a complaint or problem, Mr. O responds in a defensive manner, Mrs. O repeats the complaint, and Mr. O is defensive again, and so on. Even though you are being more specific and less critical in your discussions, this pattern I just referred to still prevents you from being effective in your communication . . .

Although there have not been many studies conducted in this area, several have yielded relevant findings. Hursh, Schumaker, Fawcett, and Sherman (1973), for example, found that direct instructions were more effective than written instructions in altering the behavior of subjects (behavior modifiers) who were in training. Instructions alone have been shown to bring about desired behavior changes in selected areas (Ayllon and Azrin, 1964; Merbaum and Lukens, 1968) and combining instructions with reinforcement, as above, increases the likelihood of achieving compliance with the instructions. Cossairt, Hall, and Hopkins (1973) studied the effects of experimenter instructions, feedback, and praise on selected behaviors of teachers. They found that instructions and feedback produced inconclusive results but that the package consisting of instructions, feedback and social praise produced more of the target behaviors. Perhaps most directly relevant here is a study of the effects of CF-I in the modification of problematic marital communication. In this initial demonstration, Carter and Thomas (1973b) reported on two exemplary cases out of a larger sample in which CF-I was shown, in general, to bring about successful change of the problematic components of the partner verbal repertoires dealt with in these interventions.

RULES FOR MARITAL INTERACTION

Rules are oral or written statements that prescribe desired behavior or proscribe unacceptable behavior, provide information concerning what rule-compliant behavior is, and serve as discriminative stimuli for the desired behavior. Conditions relevant to their use are very similar to those that apply to CF-I. Specifically, the behavior should be capable of being evoked by rules, the responses in question should be in the partners' repertoires, and there should be no contravening conditions. Rules work best when they are clearly and simply stated, when behavior relating to them is carefully monitored, and when behavior consistent with the rule is reinforced and behavior inconsistent with it is not.

Although the initial objective in the use of communication rules is catalytic in that they serve to stimulate particular verbal responses, the ultimate goal is to have the cueing control transferred to stimuli that are more natural components of the environment. Ordinarily the target behavior of the rules must be brought under the control of rules before control can be transferred to stimuli of the natural environment. This means that emphasis at first should be placed upon ensuring that the rules work—that is, that behavior consistent with the rules is reliably produced by the rule.

General Rules

Although each couple has its own characteristic profile of strengths and limitations, there are many communication difficulties that are shared by large numbers of couples. The general communication rules given below embrace many of these difficulties.

The rules have been grouped into four categories, each relating to a characteristic source of difficulty for marital communication. The first group (Rules 1–3) has to do with reducing the ill effects of setting events, such as unpleasant emotions and outside pressures, that may intrude upon and interfere with marital interaction. The second group (Rules 4–6) has the objective of helping the couple separate decision making, which often involves disagreement, persuasion, and conflict, from noncontroversial verbal interchange. The third group (Rule 7) is directed toward structuring an explicit time for noncontroversial marital communication. The last group (Rules 8–23) pertains to partner interaction itself and is oriented toward some of the behaviors each partner can engage in to try to increase the likelihood of having mutually gratifying verbal interchange.

Rules to Set Events Favorably for Marital Communication

1. Greet your marital partner after a period of being separated, even if only for a few hours, with a smile and pleasant talk such as a happy salutation, a compliment, humor, or the recounting of interesting, different, or "success" experiences.

2. Set aside a period of transition between work, or any potentially stressful activity, and other parts of the day. This transition is designed to provide a "decompression period" each day so that any pressures, frustrations, fatigue, anger, or anxiety that may have been generated by work or other activity will be less likely to affect marital communication.

3. Never discuss serious subjects or important matters that involve potential disagreement when you or your partner is highly fatigued, emotionally upset, sick, injured, in pain, or under the influence of drugs or alcohol.

Rules to Separate Marital Decision Making from Noncontroversial Verbal Exchange

4. Set aside a special agreed-upon time every day (or as required) to take up matters involving decision making, family business, disagreements, and problems.[1] This "Decision Time" should allow for the relaxed and uninterrupted discussion of all decision-making and problem-solving activities. No other activities should be concurrent, such as eating, driving, or watching television.

5. Save all complaints about your partner, disagreements, and joint decisions, especially those that might be controversial, for the scheduled Decision Time when these matters are taken up. Partners should keep a pad of paper on which all matters to be taken up at the Decision Time are written down as they arise.

6. In the decision sessions, try to reach a specific solution. If there are decision-making difficulties, adopt the appropriate decision-making rules presented in Chapter 7.

Rule for Structuring Couple Conversation

7. Set aside a scheduled time for noncontroversial marital conversation. The "Talk Time" should be every day if possible. This serves to cue conversation, using time as the control stimulus, and, hopefully, also serves to "prime" couple interaction, thus making future interaction more probable. Among the topics that might be discussed are the experiences of the partners during the day or at other

---

[1] This is similar to "Administrative Time," as employed by Weiss, Hops, and Patterson (1973), a fixed time set aside for couple problem solving.

times, noncontroversial plans or decisions that involve individual partners, the couple or the family, and jokes and gossip.

Rules for Noncontroversial Discussion

8. Each partner should have a special "Topic Turning Signal" to cue his or her mate to change from a controversial subject during Talk Time or any other time of conversation. The signal should be an agreed-upon word or phrase, as neutral and noninflammatory as possible.

9. Do not fault your spouse, and save matters of complaint and proposed change for the Decision Time.

10. Stay on the topic being discussed until each of you has had a say.

11. Avoid talk about what happened in the past or what might happen in the hypothetical future, if potentially controversial. Dredging up complaints about the past and creating criticism about what might happen in the future are almost always inflammatory and very capable of converting a conversation into an argument. Again, complaints about any present difficulties should be reserved for the Decision Time.

12. Be specific in what you talk about and avoid overstatement and generalities, especially if these are intended to have persuasive effect.

13. Acknowledge the main points of what your partner says with such words as "I see," "I understand," "Yes," "Um-hm."

14. Try to keep the nonverbal aspects of your communication consistent with the neutral and positive aspects of the verbal message. For example, avoid expressing compliments with scowls or an indifferent tone of voice. Thus, say nice things with a pleasant tone of voice and a pleasing facial expression.

15. Be as accurate as you can in describing objects or events for your partner.

16. Praise your spouse for the things he or she says that you like, using words that you think are particularly likely to be appreciated.

17. Discuss topics with your partner that you know he or she will like to talk about. If your partner fails to discuss topics to your liking, do not hesitate to cue him or her to discuss the desired subjects. For example, use hints or direct requests when you want the partner to praise you, support you, say something endearing, or discuss one of your special subjects.

18. Never increase the aversiveness of what you say or exaggerate things in order to emphasize a point. If you seriously wish to persuade your mate and the topic stands a chance of being controversial, write it down and save it for the next Decision Time.

19. Don't mind-read or make presumptive statements about what your partner said when he or she has in fact not made such an assertion.

20. Never quibble about minor or trivial details.

21. Respond fully but not excessively when your turn comes.

22. Repeat to your partner what you think he or she said if you have had trouble in understanding what is meant or if your partner has not always said what he or she intended.

23. Help each other to follow the rules, first, by having a neutral method of noting significant departures from them, and, second, by regularly praising your spouse for rule-consistent talking.

Procedures for the Use of Rules

General rules for marital communication, such as those above, are useful to orient professionals who work with marital partners. A copy of these rules may be given to marital partners who are endeavoring to improve their communication and would like some guidelines. Their main use in practice, however, is as guidelines for the practitioner in selecting aspects for implementation with a given couple. Procedural steps to implement this use of rules are given below.

1. Formulate a set of communication rules tailored to each partner of the couple, using relevant rules from among those given above, supplemented, as necessary, on the basis of assessment information. An example of individualized rules is presented below.
2. Orient the partners to the need for the rules, the difficulties they are directed toward remediating, and the advantages of engaging in the behavior relating to the rules.
3. State the rules for the partners, providing verbal illustrations and elaboration, and give the partners a written copy.
4. Solicit the partners' agreement to use the rules to try to improve their marital communication.
5. Specify and operationalize as fully as possible the relevant behavior relating to each rule.
6. Have the couple practice responses relating to the rules.
7. Have the partners carry out the rule-related behavior frequently in the natural environment.
8. Have the rule-related behavior recorded by one or both partners.

9. Review the recording, provide feedback, and adjust the rules and their implementation as necessary.

Individualized Rules

In the following example of individualized communication rules, the partners were requested first to have Talk Time for at least thirty minutes at an agreed-upon hour each evening. These talk sessions served to take care of what was probably the major problem for both —namely, not talking to each other because no regular time had been established for doing so or underresponding very much when talking occurred. Even with the Talk Time, however, it was found, in response displays in the office as well as in records the partners kept of the Talk Time, that several difficulties persisted, for which some tailor-made rules were formulated. The behavior relating to the rules was to be practiced during the Talk Time, but the partners were also to carry it out as often as they could at other times.

Communication rules for the wife were:

1. State what you want to hear Harold talk about. (The wife had complained frequently that Harold did not talk about subjects she wanted to hear discussed. However, she never cued him concerning what she wanted to hear.)
2. Avoid nagging and complaining. (The wife faulted the husband frequently. An earlier part of the modification program included practice in decision making, and the couple were to save complaints relating to decision issues to be taken up then at Decision Time.)
3. Listen to what Harold says and be supportive of and acknowledge his points. (The wife was low in acknowledgment.)
4. Express yourself fully when you speak. (She characteristically underresponded.)
5. Do not presume anything about what Harold says. Clarify precisely. (The wife engaged in a lot of presumptive attribution.)
6. Compliment Harold on what he says that you like and do so generously. (Positive talk was very low for the wife.)

Rules for the husband were:

1. Reply fully to Shirley's questions. (The husband also tended to underrespond.)
2. Be specific and concrete rather than general and vague. (The husband tended to specify very poorly.)

3. Do not presume, and clarify precisely. (The husband also engaged in presumptive attribution.)
4. Compliment Shirley on those things you like and do so generously. (The husband also was low on positive talk.)

INTERACTIONAL CUEING

Interactional cueing consists of cues given by one or both partners in the interactional situation that are intended to occasion particular verbal or nonverbal responses of the partner. Cues may be employed to start or to stop given behavior. Examples of "start cues" would be "How did you like the movie?" or "How did you like the supper I prepared?" Stop cues, of course, are intended to reduce or eliminate particular ongoing behavior. "Let's not talk about that now," "Let's talk about that after supper," "I'm grumpy, don't discuss anything controversial tonight," and "Remember, that's a no-no subject," are all instances of stop cues. Bach and Wyden (1968) have suggested that partners call "foul" to try to stop arguments that entail the partner "hitting below the belt." Both types of interactional cue presuppose a response capability to start or to stop responding, as the case may be. Interactional cueing may be employed most productively when the partners possess easy capability to respond as requested, when the cue is given clearly and strongly and when the cued behavior is reinforced. Like CF-I and rules, interactional cues are essentially catalytic and depend for their long-term success upon reliable evocation and proper reinforcement.

The examples above were of verbal cues consisting of common words rather than special words. Ordinary words are desirable as cues because no special code words need to be learned. When employed as cues, however, ordinary language often produces unintended and undesirable effects because of particular conditioned meanings and characteristic responses of the partner. The wife may try to cue her husband for a compliment, for instance, by saying "How did I do?" and, instead of complimenting her, he might reply with "You're always asking for compliments" or "Why don't you tell me how well I do once in a while?"—thus risking escalation of the conflict. In some cases, the precise labeling of the offensive comment with a new word might work. Thus, the wife might say "That's a fault," "That's an overgeneralization," or "That's a presumptive attribution." Unusual code words might also be effective in some cases. For instance, as a special code to cue a compliment, partners might agree to "How's Aunt Matilda?" To avoid the conditioned meaning of some words that may produce inappropriate responses, previously neutral non-verbal cues may be employed. Special movements of the arms, fingers or legs can be used to convey many signals; armbands, special hats or clothing can be used to signify that certain topics are taboo, such as unpleasant talk; and colored pieces of paper, plastic chips, poker chips, or coins can be exchanged in cueing, as well as in token systems. Electromechanical light-signal systems, such as SAM (Thomas, Carter, Gambrill, and Butterfield, 1970; Thomas, Carter, and Gambrill, 1971), have been used effectively to cue selected aspects of partner responding without interfering with ongoing verbal interchange.

Interactional cueing is a valuable tool to place in the hands of marital partners because it may be used flexibly and easily. It enables partners to remedy difficulties immediately as they come up and to train the spouse in different ways of responding. Practice in partner cueing can be initiated in training sessions conducted in the practitioner's office. At first the practitioner may himself model how it is done and may even cue the partner who is to do the cueing. Then the partners can practice cueing each other in free interaction, using ordinary conversation or prescribed discussion topics to display verbal responses. The main objective of providing training in partner cueing is to have partners employ cues at home and elsewhere in the natural environment to improve the marital communication. After initial training in cueing, the partners can be given assignments in partner cueing. The practitioner can obtain records of the cueing behavior and thereby monitor progress.

PRACTICE

Practice consists of the repeated evocation of target responses carried out as rehearsal or in a real-life situation. The target responses here, of course, are generally verbal, but they also may be nonverbal. Practice has been widely used for many years in and out of therapy to train higher levels of responding. As a method of intervention it is related to a variety of training procedures, such as role playing (Corsini, 1966), behavioral rehearsal (Bandura, 1969; McFall and Lillesand, 1971; Lazarus, 1966; Wolpe, 1969), reinforced practice (Leitenberg, 1972), and coaching (Thomas, O'Flaherty, and Borkin, 1976). The purpose of practice is to evoke responses that are weak or absent from the repertoire until the appropriate level of performance is achieved. Practice is most effective when carried out under surveillance of the practitioner or others suitable as monitors and under conditions that permit early feedback to the partners.

Although emphasis here is on the response-evocation aspect of practice, it is important to recognize that all practice is preceded by some characterization or model of the desired responding. Thus, exemplars may be presented by practitioner demonstration, verbal description, verbal instruction, or by a rule. Furthermore, some feedback is almost always present and, if properly given, can greatly increase desirable responding and reduce undesirable responding. Although practice is described here as a separate method of intervention and can be so used, it is generally best employed along with other methods that alter antecedents, such as CF-I, rules, or interactional cueing, and methods that modify the consequences of practice, such as the use of contingencies and exchange systems.

Practice may be implemented with a variety of procedures. For instance, partners may rehearse verbal skills by discussing topics such as those used in the response displays for assessment. Thus, they might be requested to discuss the strengths in their marriage, and the target responses could be to engage in positive talk, where appropriate, and to omit faulting. Assignments may also be given to practice at home, and these sessions can be tape-recorded for subsequent replay and appraisal. Coaching, to be described more fully in the section on decision making, is a procedure of practice aimed more toward repertoire construction than toward accelerating one or a few responses. In general, coaching calls for response evocation in restricted behavioral areas for which there are clear-cut objectives that must be achieved before the next area of response can be entered. In coaching for decision making, these areas are stages of decision making. Couple verbal behavior is directly monitored throughout by the practitioner, verbal feedback and correction are given by the coach, as necessary, and light-signal feedback is given concurrently during the coaching to indicate whether or not the partners are making appropriate progress. Although coaching was developed as a method of providing training in component areas of decision making, it may be readily applied to marital communication, with or without the electromechanical assistance of light-signal feedback. Chapter 7 provides details.

Piaget (1972) has described a technique called R.I.D., which stands for "recognize, initiate, and drop." In this form of negative practice, the partner imitates precisely his own maladaptive behavior that he wishes to eliminate, and the undesirable behavior is repeated many times. Piaget has also described techniques he calls "receiver skills," pertaining to the listening behavior of a partner. One of these is called acknowledgment training in which the partner who has just heard the other speak acknowledges that he has received and understood the message by saying "thank you," "okay," or words to that effect. Intake verification, another technique, requires that after receiving a message, the partner must paraphrase that message and repeat it to the first speaker.

FEEDBACK

Feedback involves the delivery of stimuli following target responding concerning the desirable or undesirable aspects of the responding behavior or its consequences. Feedback thus has an informational function and can be valuable in itself.

Replay of audio tapes of couple verbal responding combined with verbal feedback by the practitioner are examples of what generally enters into therapist feedback. The focus may be on the verbal behavior of one or both partners or the patterned interaction between them. One useful procedure is to replay a brief segment of the tape, stop the tape recorder, and analyze that part. This type of explication can highlight (1) the stimulus antecedents of what the speaker says, (2) the relationship between his intentions and what he actually said, (3) the consequences of what the speaker said, as well as (4) what he might have said instead. Explication can also be directed toward what the listener thought the speaker said and why he said it as he did. The limitations, strengths, and patterns of verbal responding may thus be identified.

Videotape replay, using closed-circuit television, is a related procedure. In addition to the opportunities for explication referred to above in connection with audio tape replay, videotaped replay permits analysis of nonverbal behavior such as facial expression, and placement and movement of the limbs and body.[2] Feedback may also be given orally following a live response display, as is illustrated in Appendix F, which contains a transcription of therapist feedback given after the couple had completed discussion of a decision-making topic. Whatever the procedure—taped replay and explication or verbal feedback after live response display—the objectives of feedback are to provide discrimination training for the partners, to alter the speaking or "listening" behavior, and to break disordered communication patterns.

Feedback of information following verbal behavior alone may alter the behavior, as has been shown in a study by Favell (1973), in which feedback served to reduce staff tardiness. However, informa-

[2] In addition to the discussion of videotaped replay in Chapter 3, the reader is referred to Katz (1975) and to Weiss, Hops, and Patterson (1973) for additional details.

tional feedback alone is often insufficient to bring about the desired behavior changes. Thus, Wincze, Leitenberg, and Agras (1972) found that token reinforcement reduced the delusional talk of psychotics much more effectively than did therapist feedback alone. Several studies on the effects of light-signal feedback in altering verbal behavior have shown that light feedback alone was not so effective as light feedback combined with back-up reinforcement (Kazdin, 1973; Patterson, 1964; and Straughan, Potter, and Hamilton, 1965). Eisler, Hersen, and Agras (1973) found, in attempting to modify the nonverbal interactions of partner smiling and eye contact, that videotaped feedback combined with verbal instructions was no more effective than instructions alone in increasing couples' "looking" behavior. Alkire and Brunse (1974) found, in fact, that videotaped feedback could result in deleterious effects for the couples receiving it. The problem with feedback, then, is that while it generally informs the recipient and sometimes changes his behavior favorably, its behavioral function is uncertain. Because of this uncertainty, feedback should generally be augmented with other methods of modification to ensure a better chance of success.

RESPONSE CONTINGENCIES

The concept of response contingency is employed here to refer to response consequences that bring about a change in the target behavior. These response consequences generally consist of the presentation, removal, or withdrawal of stimuli following emission of the behavior to be altered; and the changes thus achieved consist of the acquisition, strengthening, continued maintenance, weakening, or elimination of the responses in question. As indicated in Chapter 1, many studies have indicated that such aspects of verbal behavior as content, fluency, frequency, and formal properties of speech are responsive to manipulation of consequences. This has also been shown for a number of population groups, such as autistic children, retarded children, and psychotic and nonpsychotic adults.

The particular functions of the response consequences may involve positive reinforcement, negative reinforcement, extinction, differential reinforcement, response shaping, and punishment. Alteration of response contingencies is critical to the modification of verbal behavior because any sustained, long-term change depends very much upon whether or not conditions have been arranged so as to provide effective consequences for the target verbal-responses. Without proper response consequences, even if the initiation of change is very successful in the short run, the changes achieved in verbal responses are very likely to be short-lived. The six main response consequences to change behavior are given below along with their conditions and principal uses.

1. *Positive reinforcement* presupposes an established verbal response that can be reinforced and is used mainly to strengthen or maintain that behavior. The change operation consists of presenting a stimulus following the emission of a given verbal response, with the consequence that there is an increase in the future rate of responding for that response. For example, when a wife says "thank you" to her mate after he had complimented her, the result is that he tends to compliment her more frequently in the future.

2. *Negative reinforcement* presupposes an established verbal response that one wishes to strengthen or maintain. The operation consists of removing an aversive stimulus following the emission of the verbal response, with a consequent increase in the future rate of such responding. An example would be an increase in the rate of the husband's saying "Yes, dear, I'll do what you say," when these words serve to reduce the persistent and aversive nagging by the wife that he perform certain unpleasant maintenance jobs around the house. (Whether or not he actively does the chores is, of course, another matter.) Positive reinforcement is generally much more suitable in intervention to increase particular verbal responding.

3. *Extinction* is used to weaken or eliminate a response that has been sustained by reinforcement or by punishment. In the case of responses previously sustained by reinforcement, the extinction operation consists of withholding the reinforcer when the verbal response is emitted, with consequent reduction in the rate of responding for that response. In the case of punishment, the operation consists of withholding the punisher whenever the response is emitted, with consequent increase in the rate of responding for the target response. Consider, as an example, persistent counterfaulting of partner B as a positive reinforcer for the faulting responses of partner A. Extinction of the faulting of partner A would consist of partner B's withholding all criticism and complaints whenever his mate faults.

4. *Differential reinforcement* is used to strengthen or maintain pro-social verbal responses and to eliminate or weaken unacceptable responses. The operation consists of presenting a stimulus following the emission of an acceptable verbal response and withholding reinforcement for the emission of an unacceptable verbal response. The functional consequence must then be an increase in the acceptable response combined with a decrease for the other response. An example would be a wife's saying "good" when her husband speaks concretely with a resulting increase in his referent specificity, combined with her inattention and lack of verbal reinforcement when the husband speaks generally and nonspecifically, with a consequent reduction in such verbal responding.

5. Given a low rate of verbal responding in a given area, *response shaping* may be employed to establish new classes of verbal response in that area. The technique of response shaping is thus especially applicable to response acquisition and development. The operations consist of (1) presenting reinforcing stimuli following the emission of verbal responses that successively approximate the desired verbal responses, combined with (2) withholding reinforcement for verbal responses that do not approximate the desired terminal verbalization. The functional consequence, for this to be called response shaping, should then be an increase in the rate of verbal responses that approximate desired terminal responses and, ultimately, an appropriate level of responding in the new response class. An example might be the shaping of a husband's positive talk from a base-rate level of essentially zero, beginning with the wife's reinforcement of his talking on *any* subject, then of positive talk on any subject followed by any talk about the wife, and, finally, reinforcement of positive talk about the wife. Each level of response must be successfully achieved before the response criterion is raised so that reinforcement is provided only for the higher level of response.

6. Given established verbal responses that are unacceptable, *punishment* may be used to weaken or eliminate such responses. One operation consists of presenting an aversive stimulus following the emission of the undesirable verbal response, with the functional consequence of reducing the rate of such responding. This reduction may be large or small, permanent or temporary. An example would be the wife's saying "That's wrong" when the husband overgeneralizes, with a consequent reduction in the rate of overgeneralized statements. Another operation is the removal of a positive condition following an undesirable verbal response, with a consequent reduction in the rate of responding for that behavior. An example would be the husband's refusal to join his wife at the dinner table whenever she nags needlessly, with a consequent reduction in the wife's nagging. Punishment should be used advisedly and sparingly, if at all, and only after reinforcement and other methods have been tried and found ineffective.

According to research in operant behavior (e.g., see Honig, 1966), the procedures described above are more likely to be effective when they are employed with scrupulous attention to the following aspects involving reinforcement or punishment:

1. The category of verbal behavior to be changed must be clearly and precisely defined.
2. The response to be reinforced or punished must first be emitted, otherwise the relevant stimulus consequence cannot be given after the response. Clearly, one cannot reinforce a response until after it has been emitted. Although this is axiomatic, since we are dealing with techniques of altering response consequences, it is unfortunately sometimes overlooked.
3. Response consequences must not be delayed; in general, the more immediate the consequences, the better. Positive reinforcement, for example, has been found to be most effective when given approximately one-half second after the response.
4. Providing response consequences after every target response (a continuous schedule of reinforcement or punishment) is most effective for establishing the intended response. For instance, in attempting to increase a particular verbal response with reinforcement, provision of reinforcement after every desirable response rather than less often is most effective for establishing that response.
5. After responses have been established, the schedule may be thinned to an intermittent schedule of reinforcement or punishment, thus increasing the chances of producing responses that will endure after the consequences become more uncertain or are terminated.
6. Stimuli that are effective for purposes of reinforcement or punishment for one individual may not be appropriate for another. Each individual has his own profile of effective response consequences and the practitioner should seek out those most likely to work before formulating the modification plan.

The ultimate objective in using response contingencies is to have each partner in the marital dyad introduce the appropriate consequences so as to regulate the verbal responding of the other. In effect, each partner is reprogrammed, as necessary, to effectively alter the verbal behavior of the other. By this means, the potential for initiating and maintaining changes is developed and lodged in a significant part of each spouse's behavior-guiding environment—namely, in his partner's behavior. To this end, each partner must be able (1) to identify the verbal responses of the partner that he wants accelerated and those that he wants diminished, (2) to use the alteration of response consequences to change the partner's verbal behavior, and (3) to support the partner's efforts to reprogram his behavior with positive consequences and not sabotage such efforts with countercontrol and negative consequences. At the outset of intervention, partner practice and training may be required and many of the other methods of modification discussed here may have to be employed to reprogram partner behavior.

EXCHANGE SYSTEMS

A system of exchange as applied to marital behavior is a means by which given response consequences, such as reinforcement for engaging in desirable behavior or punishment for engaging in undesirable behavior, may be exchanged for particular verbal responses. The exchange is simply a means of achieving behavior-guiding response consequences. It can be mediated by tokens (tangible media of exchange, such as poker chips) or points (intangible means of exchange, such as tally marks signifying points earned) or contingency contracts (agreements between parties to exchange given desired behaviors for given privileges). The proper use of such exchange systems presupposes what appears at first to be an unusual combination of circumstances. On the one hand, the verbal responses in question should be within the response capability of the partner; on the other, the responses are not capable of easy evocation by instructions, rules, or cues, and natural reinforcing conditions do not sustain the responses at the desired level. It turns out, however, that this combination of conditions is not at all unusual and that exchange systems have rather wide applicability.

There are advantages and disadvantages in each exchange system. Among the advantages of the token system is that the receipt of a token right after emitting desirable behavior is itself an immediate, discriminable consequence that often has reinforcing value and also serves to bridge the gap between the desired behavior and the back-up reinforcement. Point systems are more abstract inasmuch as there is no physical exchange following each desired behavior. The contingency contract is likewise abstract and sometimes has the advantage of seeming to appeal to the maturity and adult responsibility of the participants. In work with children, a rough rule of thumb is that one generally moves from tokens for very young children, to points for youngsters just before and at the beginning of adolescence, then on to the contingency contracts for older children and young adults. An analogous ordering may not apply at all with adult marital partners.

Suggested steps in implementing an exchange system are:

1. Select the appropriate form of exchange—tokens,[3] points, or contingency contract.
2. Specify exactly and fully the desirable and undesirable behaviors to be included in the system.
3. Determine that the target behaviors are within the response capability of the partner.
4. Specify exactly and fully all privileges.
5. Allocate values for potential earnings for behaviors and costs for privileges, for token or point systems, and full details of exchange, for contingency contracts.

As an example of a point system in which some verbal responses were included, consider the case of Bob and Mary Johnson, a couple in their early thirties, with three children. The husband was professionally employed and the wife was professionally educated, presently occupied full time as a houseperson and very active in an outside voluntary organization. The couple complained at the outset of vague communication difficulties and indicated that they had some resentment toward each other and that their sexual adjustment was not satisfactory. Focus here will be mainly on the verbal behavior of the partners. Specifically, the wife wanted her husband to give her more "free" (i.e., unsolicited) compliments, engage in "personal" talk every day (e.g., discuss his goals and concerns in intimate matters relating to the two of them), and refrain from criticizing her cooking and cleaning. The husband wanted his wife to cut down on her nagging as well as her analyses of his "downs."

Assessment indicated that sexual frustration, lack of fulfilling outside social interaction, and a paucity of outings were among the possible sources of the wife's concerns about communication. (The marriage had certain "restricted" features for her.) The husband, for his part, was resentful and reluctant to talk to his wife evidently because of her nagging, frequent analysis of his "downs," long annoying phone calls made by his wife concerning her organizational work, especially at supper time, and sexual frustration. For both partners, an important unfavorable setting event was their constant fatigue, deriving largely

---

[3] Further details about how to construct a token economy, which are also generally equally applicable to point systems, can be found in a variety of sources, such as Alvord (1973), Atthowe and Krasner (1968), Ayllon and Azrin (1968), Rimm and Masters (1974), and Staats, Minke, Finley, Wolf, and Brooks (1964). Details of how to construct a contingency contract are to be found in such sources as Cantrell, Cantrell, Huddleston, and Wooldridge (1969), DeRisi and Butz (1975), Homme et al. (1971), and Stuart (1971).

from a very demanding and exhausting schedule of work and activity, including night classes that both were taking.

Before initiating an exchange system in which communication behaviors were included, a plan was introduced that called for the partners to relax their schedules greatly, allowing for more free time before bed and more rest for both. The exchange system was a point system, chosen because it had special appeal for both partners. The system was constructed to include communication behaviors and all the other main concerns of the partners, some of which, it turned out, were precisely those that the assessment suggested were possible sources of communication difficulty. The point system is presented in Table 4-1, which shows that in addition to the communication behaviors, the system addressed the referent conditions for the wife (e.g., sexual frustration, need for outings, and the aversiveness for her of the husband not washing up before sex and his taking naps during busy hours) and the husband (e.g., sexual frustration, need for a period of free time in the evenings, reduction of the long phone calls when he was home in the evening). The late supper, requested as a privilege for the husband, consisted of a special supper to be served with candlelight after the children were in bed, to be followed by sex. The system was set up so that the points earned by one partner could be exchanged for desirable behaviors by the other partner. Thus, in this system, the acceleration of desirable behaviors for one partner earned, as payoff, an increase in desirable behaviors of the other partner—a reciprocally benefiting exchange.

The point system was in operation for eight weeks, with the results shown in Table 4-2. Prior to intervention, Mary had nagged Bob very frequently, engaged in long phone calls and frequently analyzed his "downs." She never cued him for compliments. Following intervention, nagging, long phone calls, and analysis of "downs" disappeared entirely and Mary cued Bob for compliments on an average of three times a week. For his part, Bob never gave compliments prior to intervention nor did he engage in personal talk. Following intervention, freely given compliments averaged about four per week and personal talks a little over two per week. Both partners were noticeably calmer and without resentment. Although they were not the primary focus of the present discussion, all the other desirable behaviors increased considerably for Bob and Mary, and none of the undesirable behaviors was engaged in. To the extent that these other noncommunication behaviors were in fact referent conditions for the communication difficulties, the improvement in these conditions may have had beneficial effects for the communication.

The use of a contingency contract to mediate the exchange of a

TABLE 4-1. A Reciprocally Beneficial Point System for Bob and Mary

DESIRABLE BEHAVIORS			
For the Husband	*Payoff**	*For the Wife*	*Payoff**
Free compliment	5	Late dinner, sex	7
Cued compliment	1	Supper at given time,	
Personal "talk" (five		cued	3
minutes)	7	Free time from 7–8	3
Outing for Mary	5	Initiate sex	5
Initiate sex	3	Cue Bob for compliment	5
Giving sex when asked	5	Giving sex when asked	3
"Surprise"	3–15	Making coffee and juice	
		the night before work	5
UNDESIRABLE BEHAVIORS			
For the Husband	*Fine*	*For the Wife*	*Fine*
Not washing up before sex	−10	Nagging	−10
Criticism of kitchen regimen	−10	Organization phone calls	
Taking naps during busy		over 5 minutes	−10
hours	−10	Analyzing Bob's "downs"	−10
PRIVILEGES			
For the Husband	*Cost**	*For the Wife*	*Cost**
Late dinner, sex	14	Free compliment	0
Supper at given time, when		Cued compliment	4
cued	6	"Personal" talk	10
Free time from 7–8	3	Outings for Mary	7
Sex before Mary's bedtime		Sex before Mary's bedtime	
when Bob asks	3	when Mary asks	5
Coffee and juice	2		

Earnings Quota for Week: 53 Points
Maximum Point Carryover for Week: 15

---

* Payoffs for initiating sex and costs for providing it were not equal for Bob and Mary because of different probabilities of engaging in the behaviors, different preferences, and the need to have internal balance and some consistency of cost and earnings totals for husband and wife.

husband's verbal behavior for desired nonverbal behavior of the wife is illustrated by procedures employed with another couple with whom I worked recently. In his instance, the problem contract was to work on communication as well as sex. The main problem with sex was its low frequency, especially for the wife, combined with insufficient "sweet talk" of the husband during intercourse. The wife wanted the husband to give her more compliments, one important form of which for her was "sweet talk" during sex. The husband, in turn, was dissatisfied with the way the wife took care of the house, feeling that she did not keep it clean and orderly. One part of the modification program

TABLE 4-2. Monitoring Data for a Point System for Marital Partners, Expressed in Rates of Desirable Behavior Per Day

DESIRABLE BEHAVIORS*	PRE-INTERVENTION RATE	DAILY RATE FOR EACH WEEK OF INTERVENTION								
		Week 1	Week 2	Week 3	Week 4	Week 5	Week 6	Week 7	Week 8	Week 9
Wife's Behaviors for Husband										
Late dinner, sex	.00(0/28)	.14(1/7)	.14(1/7)	.00(0/6)	.16(1/6)	.00(0/7)	.00(0/7)	.16(1/6)	.14(1/7)	.14(1/7)
Supper at given time (cued)	.14(4/28)	.14(1/7)	.71(5/7)	.83(5/6)	.71(5/7)	.57(4/7)	.50(3/6)	.66(4/6)	.66(4/6)	.50(2/4)
Free time for husband 7:00–8:00 p.m.	.00(0/28)	.14(1/7)	.85(6/7)	.83(5/6)	.85(6/7)	.42(3/7)	1.00(6/6)	.66(4/6)	.71(5/7)	.83(5/6)
Cue for compliment	.00(0/28)	.42(3/7)	.57(4/7)	.71(5/7)	.50(3/6)	.42(3/7)	.42(3/7)	.14(1/7)	.14(1/7)	.16(1/6)
Giving sex, when asked	.07(2/28)	.00(0/7)	.40(2/5)	.42(3/7)	.00(0/6)	.42(3/7)	.00(0/7)	.28(2/7)	.14(1/7)	.00(0/6)
Making coffee and juice	**	**	**	.66(4/6)	.83(5/6)	.16(1/6)	1.00(5/5)	1.00(5/5)	.40(2/5)	1.00(4/4)
Initiate sex	.00(0/28)	.14(1/7)	.14(1/7)	.28(2/7)	.16(1/6)	.14(1/7)	.14(1/7)	.14(1/7)	.14(1/7)	.16(1/6)
Husband's Behaviors for Wife										
Free compliment (non-cued)	.00(0/28)	.14(1/7)	1.00(7/7)	.28(2/7)	.33(2/6)	.71(5/7)	.42(3/7)	.85(6/7)	.71(5/7)	.83(5/6)
Giving cued compliment	.00(0/28)	.42(3/7)	.57(4/7)	.57(1/7)	.50(3/6)	.42(3/7)	.42(3/7)	.14(1/7)	.14(1/7)	.16(1/6)
"Personal" talk (5 minutes)	.00(0/28)	.28(2/7)	.42(3/7)	.28(2/7)	.50(3/6)	.28(2/7)	.28(2/7)	.28(2/7)	.28(2/7)	.28(2/7)
Outing with wife	.03(1/28)	.14(1/7)	.14(1/7)	.42(3/7)	.16(1/6)	.28(2/7)	.28(2/7)	.28(2/7)	.28(2/7)	.50(3/6)
Initiate sex	.10(2/28)	.00(0/7)	.40(2/5)	.42(3/7)	.00(0/6)	.42(3/7)	.00(0/7)	.28(2/7)	.14(1/7)	.00(0/6)
Giving sex, when asked	.00(0/28)	.14(1/7)	.14(1/7)	.28(2/7)	.16(1/6)	.14(1/7)	.14(1/7)	.14(1/7)	.14(1/7)	.16(1/6)

* Desirable behaviors for each spouse are privileges for the other.
** Not part of the program at this time.

involved an exchange agreement. In return for tidying up the house, the wife would earn generous "sweet talk" during sex. If she failed to clean the house that day, there would be no "sweet talk" during sex. But if the wife did the housework that day and the husband failed to engage in "sweet talk" during sex, she could omit tidying up the next day. To increase the likelihood of the couple's having sex, they were instructed to leave plenty of time each evening for relaxation before the time when they ordinarily might have sex and to have sex frequently (i.e., every day or two).[4] Prior to modification, the wife tidied up the house approximately once a week, the husband never engaged in "sweet talk" during sex, and the couple had sex about once a week or less. During the two weeks that this contingency contract was in operation, the house was tidied up nine times, the couple had sex six times, and on five of these occasions the husband engaged in "sweet talk." There were other aspects of this modification program not germane here. (Shortly after completing modification, maintenance was undertaken that served successfully to sustain the gains achieved in modification.)

Exchange systems may entail the exchange of particular marital verbal behavior for nonverbal behavior, as illustrated above, or the exchange of the verbal behavior of one partner for verbal behavior of the other. In either case, it is important to determine that all the behaviors included in the system are part of the partner's repertoire. This has been highlighted in a study by Wieman, Shoulders, and Farr (1974) in which training in communication skills was required before the partners were able to produce the communication behaviors required in the exchange agreement.

In addition, exchange systems require considerable mediation and negotiation skill to set up, careful recording by partners, and monitoring by the helper along with periodic readjustment. One must remember that it is only under exceptional circumstances that behaviors are changed greatly and dramatically; more commonly some of the target behaviors included in the system are accelerated to some extent. When behaviors are changed, moreover, research indicates that, at least for token systems, there will not necessarily be much generalization to other responses of the individuals involved or to other stimulus conditions in which the target behaviors may be displayed (Kazdin and Bootzin, 1972). Even so, however, exchange systems are an important

---

[4] Contracts or exchanges, such as those illustrated here, should be undertaken only when the practitioner is reasonably sure that many of the desirable behaviors will be readily evoked or can be easily prompted. If not, the quid pro quo arrangement can fail to yield mutual increases in desirable behaviors.

and generally effective method of change and they have a special place in modification of marital communication because there are few viable alternatives to such systems.

OTHER METHODS

In addition to the methods described above, almost any other intervention technique may be applicable, if not to verbal behavior itself, at least to possible related referent conditions, such as sexual problems or anxiety. Special mention should be made of model presentation in which exemplary verbal behavior, tailored to the partners' situation, is presented. The forms of presentation include a written transcript, audio- or videotape, or, not uncommonly, therapist-verbal description. Such model presentation should be made just prior to the opportunity for partners to display the desired behaviors. The presentation of models is essentially a catalytic procedure and works best for responses that are already in the repertoire or, if novel, are not difficult to evoke. Model presentation should be combined with practice afterwards, and this, in turn, should be followed up with response consequences intended to sustain the changes.[5]

MODIFICATION PROGRAMS

Modification methods such as those described above are not ordinarily used singly. Rather, it is generally the case that a modification program consists of more than one method of modification suited to the marital partners in question. Although such programs may include two, three, or four methods, it is prudent to use no more than are necessary—the minimally effective intervention package. Methods involving antecedents, such as CF-I, rules, and interactional cueing, may be used mainly by themselves when they readily reestablish responding and such responding is easily maintained. Otherwise, it is important to include practice and response consequence methods (e.g., feedback and response contingencies) with methods entailing alteration of antecedents. A possible exception is the exchange system, which can sometimes be used alone very successfully. Although emphasis has been placed, and properly so, upon exchange systems as means of mediating response consequences, all such systems also have instructional and cueing features and presuppose that the behaviors

---

[5] For additional details concerning modeling research and procedures, the reader is referred to Bandura (1969).

in question are already sufficiently well established in the repertoires of participants to be evoked in response to proper contingencies.

Implementation of the Modification Plan (Step 10)

The objective of implementation is to carry out the intervention according to the modification plan. Ordinarily, only the agreed-upon target behaviors are worked with. If the plan cannot be carried out as formulated, the practitioner seeks the reason for this and acts accordingly, returning to appropriate earlier steps of the procedure (e.g., to Step 2, Problem Contract) and progressing again through the steps of assessment and modification.

The first task of implementation is to see that the program takes effect. Every effort, including very tight monitoring and checking, should be employed to be sure that the program is carried out as projected and that it works properly. During intervention, after changes have begun to take effect, it is important to be vigilant about possible shifts or drifts in program. For example, the problem contract may not be adhered to as initially agreed; the class of verbal responses that serves as the target behavior may shift; or the partners may neglect modification procedures or undertake ad hoc modification that departs from the plan.

Monitoring of Outcomes (Step 11)

The purpose of monitoring is to obtain information regarding the effectiveness of the intervention as well as the adequacy with which the modification program is carried out. This information provides feedback to guide the behavior of the practitioner. If the modification program is not being implemented according to plan, adjustments must be made immediately. If the modification program is being carried out as intended but behavioral objectives are not being attained, the program is inadequate and alternatives must be considered.

Monitoring is actually a process that begins with the recording of data and progresses through its storage, processing, and display and the taking of appropriate action by the practitioner. Verbal behavior may be recorded by the marital partners or by the practitioner in the form of coding or ratings, such as those provided by the Verbal Problem Checklists, or by electromechanical devices. The adequacy of the modification program may be determined by practitioner observation, interviews with the partners, and review of tapes and records made by the partner.

The monitoring process is illustrated here with an example from a point system designed to modify selected verbal and nonverbal behaviors for Bob and Mary. The particular behaviors and point allocations were described earlier (Table 4-1). To obtain data on program adequacy and outcome, the partners recorded the frequency and points earned for engaging in desirable and undesirable behaviors, points spent as well as the total points earned. Recording forms prepared for this purpose were reviewed prior to the couple's weekly appointment. Data review consisted of examining the information for completeness (e.g., to be sure that all entries were made as they were supposed to be), internal consistency (e.g., to see that each desirable behavior of a partner, when engaged in, was also recorded as a privilege with given cost to the other partner), and accuracy (e.g., to check that all point entries and totals were correct). In the ensuing interview with the partners, the adequacy of the data was further checked by determining whether the recording was carried out as requested and whether it was complete. Then, the adequacy of the categories for the behavior in the exchange system was checked and any necessary adjustments in the points for the exchange were taken up.

For purposes of data display, an ongoing chart of daily rates of the desirable behavior was maintained for each week, so that it could be determined readily whether proper progress had been maintained (Table 4-2). For example, consider the data for Week 9 as if they had just come in and had been added to the data for the other weeks. It may be seen that the wife's cued compliments were down, as was the daily rate of giving sex when asked. The latter, of course, is dependent upon the husband's initiations, and these, as may be seen, had dropped. Making coffee and juice the night before had increased. Altogether, however, the total amount of desirable behavior produced by the wife during the last week had neither dropped off nor increased appreciably over the prior weeks. On the husband's part, free compliments had increased, which perhaps accounted for the drop in the wife's cued compliments, and the husband's initiation of sex had dropped off as well. However, outings had increased. Again, however, the total amount of desirable behavior produced for the husband was about the same as in preceding weeks. No unacceptable behavior was reported for either partner, and none had been reported since the intervention program began. The practitioner must stay on top of the data in order to make adjustments for and trouble-shoot possible program problems and to provide appropriate, early feedback to the partners.

Maintenance of Change (Step 12)

The conditions that maintain desirable behavior during modification are not always the same as those that would or should sustain the desirable behavior after the modification program has been termi-nated, and the successful maintenance of behavior after intervention cannot be taken for granted. True, experienced practitioners can cite cases in which successful modification persisted without any special interventional efforts to insure maintenance. And there have also been studies that indicated a floodgate effect, in which desirable verbal behavior, once initiated, persists even under adverse conditions, such as those involving extinction (e.g., Thomson, Fraser, and McDougall, 1974). In general, however, it is probably safe to assume that success-ful change of verbal behavior is likely to be specific to the stimulus conditions that prevailed in the modification program (Tracey, Briddell, and Wilson, 1974; Garcia, 1974; Johnston and Johnston, 1972). Studies of the generalization of change with token systems have also indicated that the effects are largely specific to the stimulus conditions in which the tokens were used and, also, that the changes of behavior were restricted mainly to the target behaviors to which the token exchange was applied (O'Leary and Drabman, 1971; Kazdin and Bootzin, 1972). And, as has been indicated, changes in the verbal behavior of one partner may be fragile if the complementary behavior of the spouse is not altered as well (Simkins and West, 1966; Bavelas, Hastorf, Gross, and Kite, 1965). Rather than ignore or assume gener-alization, it is thus increasingly clear that generalization must be programmed (O'Leary and Drabman, 1971; Kazdin and Bootzin, 1972).

Maintenance involves the reduction of dependence upon the prac-titioner combined with efforts to increase the influence of more natural external conditions. An ideal maintenance program involves transfer-ring control for the desirable behavior entirely to the natural environ-ment. For example, Talk Times originally set up and monitored by the helper would eventually be controlled in maintenance by time and date without any practitioner participation. Another program of main-tenance is to have behavioral guidance transferred to the partners so that they carry out such activities as charting, monitoring, evaluating, and analyzing data, programming contingencies, and making necessary program adjustments. Still another maintenance program consists of continued practitioner management wherein efforts to maintain the gains of modification are carried out by the practitioner through continued contact with the partners. Thus, the partners could return periodically to review their performances on their own and to receive booster training sessions as necessary. This last type is the least desirable program, but when the other types of maintenance cannot be undertaken, continued contact with the practitioner for purposes of maintenance is preferable to losing the gains achieved in modification.

Procedures to institute maintenance are considerably less well developed than those for modification, especially in regard to verbal behavior. In the absence of procedures specifically applicable to verbal behavior, the practitioner must necessarily turn to what has been found to be useful in other behavioral areas. These maintenance procedures serve mainly to reduce reliance upon the practitioner or to increase the efficacy of external, behavior-influencing conditions. Among the procedures that relate largely to reducing dependence upon the practitioner are reducing practitioner surveillance, such as having fewer and briefer appointments, thinning reinforcement schedules, and gradually phasing out external cueing conditions. Among the procedures that have application to increasing the capability of partners to maintain changes are training spouses in such activities as self-monitoring, reinforcement, behavioral problem solving, and program management. Transfer of control to more natural environmental conditions can also be accomplished by shifting the dispensation of reinforcers from the practitioner to the individuals in the normal environment, priming natural reinforcers, training partners to emit behaviors most likely to produce reinforcement from the environment, practicing desired behaviors in the natural environment, training in self-reinforcement and self-cueing, using stimulus and reinforcer variance and diversity, and fading stimulus conditions originally associated with practitioner management.

In carrying out maintenance, procedures such as those described above are introduced, outcomes are then monitored, and, later on, the practitioner does a follow-up check. If everything is doing well at follow-up, the intervention is finished for that area of behavior.

Several features common to most maintenance programs are illustrated by the case of the Millers, who recently completed a successful program of modification of their marital communication. Briefly, the partners were taught to chart and analyze their own verbal behavior. They also understood and carried out the procedures of change, in this case Talk Times, interactional cueing, communication rules, and use of each partner to reinforce the desirable behavior of the partner. Appointments were reduced in frequency and telephone checks with the practitioner, held as frequently as every other day during modification, were gradually phased down to every other week, every three weeks, every month, etc. In the later period, when it was clear that the partners could accurately recall all the desired behaviors for which recording had initially been implemented, the recording was gradually phased out. Finally, follow-up sessions were scheduled at two-month intervals. At this point, program monitoring, management, and adjustment were carried out essentially autonomously by the partners themselves.

CHAPTER FIVE

Verbal Behavior and Marital Decision Making

DECISION MAKING IS an important method of handling problem situations for which marital partners have no immediate or agreed-upon response alternatives. If carried out well, the decision making increases the likelihood that appropriate solutions to such situations will be adopted. Good marital decision making makes adjustment to problematic life situations more rewarding inasmuch as the couple thereby alters their environment more effectively in behalf of their objectives. Without competent decision making, the couple would generally be much less effective in coping with problem situations, experience more negative consequences in the face of such situations, have more interpersonal conflict, experience more personal stress, and end up more often being dependent on others.

Opportunities for marital partners to make decisions, and to agree or disagree, are numerous. Decisions need to be made concerning the allocation of funds, such as how much to save and to spend and who is to receive what amount of money; the purchase and mainten-ance of material objects, such as clothing, furniture, a home, an automobile; the allocation of consumables, such as food, drink, and drugs; the labor of family members, such as how much a wife or husband should work; the care of dependent family members, such as the sick, the young, and the elderly; family size, such as whether to have more children, whether to adopt, and if so what type of child to adopt; power and authority, such as who has control over what (or whom), under what conditions and in what ways; contact with relatives, such as the frequency and kind of relationships to have; time, such as how much time family members should spend together and how much should be devoted to private activities; vacation and recreation, including what activities to engage in at what times; religion, including belief in God and the observance of religious practices; and political matters, such as political and economic ideology and the amount and type of political participation. Issues such as these may require literally thousands of deliberations and may generate considerable disagreement and controversy.

Components of Marital Decision Making

Marital decision making is verbal behavior that serves to mediate the transition from a problem situation confronted by the couple to a response that constitutes a solution. If successful, the verbal behavior makes an appropriate solution more probable.

There are at least five components of marital decision making: (1) a problem situation for which there is no immediate agreed-upon response alternative; (2) selected predecision verbal responses of the partners; (3) a decision response agreed to by the partners intended to lead to an appropriate alteration of the problem situation; (4) solution behavior that consists of verbal or nonverbal responses to remedy the problem situation; and (5) evaluation responses in which the adequacy of the solution situation is appraised. Each component is discussed more fully below.

The first component, a problem situation, is conceived here as one for which there is no immediate agreed-upon response alternative, a view consistent with that of D'Zurilla and Goldfried (1971) and Skinner (1953) on this subject. The problem may be generated outside the family (e.g., issues concerning the allocation of money arising from a partner's being laid off at work), out of the interaction of the partners (e.g., the desire to limit family size), or out of individual conditions (e.g., overeating by a partner, leading to obesity). To be relevant here, the problem situation or the solution behaviors must affect both mates to some extent, and partner preference rather than factual information or expert knowledge must be critical.

The second component of marital decision making, the predecision verbal responses, have often been identified with the decision-making or problem-solving process itself. For example, D'Zurilla and Goldfried (1971) define problem solving (which embraces decision making for them as well) as a behavioral process that "(a) makes available a variety of potentially effective response alternatives for dealing with the problematic situation, and (b) increases the probability of selecting the most effective response from among these various alternatives" (p. 108). Some of the verbal responses that precede a final decision response and make it more likely are (1) defining a problem situation as one requiring a decision; (2) partializing and making specific the component issues of the problem situation; (3) noting the interrelationships of the relevant problem components; (4) establishing priorities concerning which of the components should be addressed first; (5) arraying information relevant to the problem, weighing the importance of facts, and noting possible gaps in information; (6) generating alternatives that may be pursued; and (7) evaluating the alternatives for their solution potentialities, action feasibility, and possible payoffs.

Each of these verbal responses can set conditions for and control the verbal responses that come next. It is in this way that the responses of each "step" make their contribution to the selection of the final decision response. In the ideal case of a rational progression, there is thematic continuity of the responses for each step, logical justification for progressing from one step to the next, and, altogether, an ordered, logically consistent sequence. The predecision responses may even be implicit and still exercise some guidance over the decision response. Although the presence of these predecision responses does not guarantee a good final decision, without them the final response may never get produced at all, or the decision response may be poor.

The decision response itself is the third component of marital decision making. This is a verbal response selected implicitly or expressly from among several alternative responses. The choice reflects the preferences of the partners. The decision response should serve as a discriminative stimulus for particular solution behavior and is selected in preference to other possible behavior.

The fourth component is behavior directed toward remedying the problem situation. Such solution behavior may be verbal or nonverbal; in the extreme case, it may consist of doing "nothing," if that is the behavior consistent with the decision response. The solution behavior is the most important component of decision making inasmuch as it is this behavior that does or does not alter the problem situation. The solution behavior generally consists either of acting directly on the stimulus conditions of the problem situation so that these are changed or behaving in other ways while leaving intact the stimulus conditions of the situation.

The final component consists of evaluation responses that indicate the adequacy of the solution behavior. To carry out this evaluation, called "verification" by D'Zurilla and Goldfried (1971), the decision makers must obtain information on the adequacy of the solution in relation to the decision response, the problem situation, and the time and effort involved in carrying out the solution behavior itself. The evaluation responses obviously provide a basis for determining whether the solution behavior should be continued.

Improving Decision Making

In their review of research on decision making and problem solving, D'Zurilla and Goldfried (1971) summarize a number of factors likely to improve decision making. Among these are the following: (1) a definition of all aspects of the problem in specific, operational terms; (2) a full and comprehensive description of all the problem elements; (3) consideration of all relevant facts; (4) generation of alternatives in a brainstorming, freewheeling fashion in which criticism and judgment are deferred until the point of evaluation; (5) statement of the solution in very specific terms, at the point of decision; (6) selection of the decision response likely to be reasonably successful and satisfactory (i.e., that "satisfices") rather than one that necessarily maximizes given outcomes; (7) inhibition of action until the point of decision has been reached; and (8) verification of the adequacy of the solution after the solution response has been carried out.

Decision Making versus Communication

Although the difference between verbal behaviors in communication and in decision making is a matter of arbitrary classification, it is of practical importance because the procedures used by the practitioner are quite different.

Decision making and communication both involve verbal behavior, message sending, and behavioral guidance. However, verbal behavior in marital decision making arises from a problem situation with respect to which the marital partners are interdependent and involves verbal responses directed toward achieving a decision that will mediate a solution to the problem situation. Further, verbal behavior in decision making ordinarily entails one of the components of decision making, including the problem situation or its elements, possible solution alternatives, evaluation of solution alternatives, the solution response itself, the action to be taken in regard to the solution response, or postdecision evaluation. Communication, by contrast, implicates verbal behavior that ranges much more widely. The content is not restricted to component aspects of decision making, the verbal behavior generally does not arise from a problem situation with respect to which the partners are interdependent, and the purpose of talking is not to formulate a decision response that, in turn, would guide action. In this connection, the reader might compare the transcript of marital decision making in Appendix F with the transcript of marital communication in Appendix E. Here the differences referred to above are clear.

There are additional possible relationships, two of which are mentioned to clarify the distinction further. One is *contested decision making,* consisting of communication difficulties associated with an unresolved decision issue. Examples might be arguments, disagreements, or other problematic verbal behavior relating to such aspects of decision making as opposing solution alternatives that each advocates to resolve a problem situation affecting both partners, action relating to the decision in regard to who should do what under what conditions, whether or not something is a problem, what components the problem embraces, and opinions and evaluation in regard to solution alternatives. These are often very obvious communication difficulties, and the practitioner may not readily note the decision-making components because of the salience of the disordered communication or because only one rather than several of the component aspects of decision making is evident. Such contested decision making, segmented as it is and rife with communication problems as it can be, should be regarded as disordered decision making and treated accordingly. An example of marked communication difficulties coincident with a decision issue is illustrated in Appendix A.

Still another type of verbal behavior involving communication and decision making consists of isolated elements of content involving potential decision issues. This type involves *decision fragments in marital communication.* For example, the husband may return from work and report to his wife that his job is getting so bad that he can't stand it, without any further discussion. This element of information has been shared, and it may affect a later decision concerning whether or not the husband will stay on at that job. Other examples are incidental reporting on problem components (e.g., "The car also has a bad battery," in the context of the implicit question of when to get a new car) and providing additional information concerning decision alternatives ("I notice that rain is predicted for the Green Lake area next week, our vacation week," thus increasing the attractiveness of other places to spend the vacation). Other fragments might be the sharing of information about the preferences of partners for decision alternatives, with no further discussion, or reporting on the feasibility of actions relating to decision alternatives, again without lengthy discussion. To the extent that fragments such as these are a minor aspect of the decision-making process, are nonproblematic, and occur in a larger context of verbal behavior that mainly would be called marital communication, it is best to place primary emphasis on the larger context of marital communication rather than on the incidental decision-making features. Several examples of decision fragments are to be found in Appendix E.

Decision Processes

Decision making has been viewed by most writers as consisting of activities that unfold in ordered sequence.[1] The steps emphasized here are:

1. Agreeing to work together on a problem.
2. Selecting one specific part to work on.
3. Generating possible solutions without judgment or evaluation.
4. Selecting a solution (or solutions) for implementation.
5. Deciding on action (i.e., who will do what, when, and how).
6. Taking the specified action.
7. Evaluating the action.

There are at least three relevant patterns of decision making, considering the decision behavior preceding action itself. The first is a *stepwise pattern* in which the decision activities (e.g., Steps 1–5 above) are carried out more or less in order. This process can unfold at one time without interruption or on several occasions, with the partners resuming the process roughly where they left off after interruptions.

The second is the *nonstepwise pattern,* in which the activities coming before action are not carried out in order and stages may be

---

[1] Although writers do not agree precisely on what the stages should be, D'Zurilla and Goldfried (1971) identify five general stages that, in their view, come close to representing a consensus: (1) general orientation, such as "set" and attitude, (2) problem definition and formulation, (3) generation of alternatives, (4) evaluation and selection of an alternative, and (5) verification.

repeated or omitted altogether. The process may occupy on
sion session or may extend over many sessions because of interrup
tions or because the partners reach a dead end in decision making
beyond which they cannot go without obtaining more information.
In contrast to decision fragments mentioned before, the behaviors
here are larger, more extensive exchanges involving decision-making
responses. The transcript in Appendix F illustrates essentially a nonstepwise pattern of marital decision making.

The third type is the *defaulted pattern,* in which the decision activities are delayed or avoided, with the result that, in effect, the
decision is made for the partners. In this pattern, outside events or the
behavior of others affects such conditions as the problem situation for
which a decision was originally required, the alternatives available
to the partners, or their evaluation of alternatives. In consequence,
all or significant aspects of the decision response are thus determined.
For instance, the decision about when to replace the family car can
be made by default simply by waiting long enough. Eventually, there
will be a deterioration of the car's condition or a change in partner
resources that will determine when another car is purchased.

O'Flaherty (1974) found in a detailed experimental study of the
behavior of eleven couples who had decision-making difficulties that,
when asked to try to reach a decision on a real issue they currently
faced, prior to being coached to improve their decision making,
most of the couples failed to get beyond discussion of the nature of
the problem. In those few instances where it went beyond this into
generation of alternatives and evaluation of options, the partners
quickly reverted to discussion of the problem. Even worse, Briscoe,
Hoffman, and Bailey (1975) found that their study participants, who
were low-income members of a community board, failed to identify
and isolate the problem under discussion, to state and evaluate alternative solutions, and to select a solution and make explicit decisions
for implementation. If incomplete decision making persists, decision issues will eventually be determined by factors other than
decision processes of the participants.

Although the stepwise pattern may be the most rational and
effective, the nonstepwise pattern and, in some special cases, the default pattern may be appropriate and adequate. As Aldous (1971)
has observed more generally, families don't use a sequential, rational
approach to problem solving, and they endeavor to satisfice rather than
optimize in regard to their solutions.

The decision-making process may be carried out in either the
analytic or the persuasive mode. Responses in the *analytic mode*

are essentially descriptive and not persuasive, accurate and not exaggerated, whereas those in the *persuasive mode* involve prescription, direct influence, and, in some cases, demands. The analytic mode fosters the selection of a good decision response inasmuch as it allows the participants to explore, examine, and weigh information without undue pressure to change and without interfering emotion, such as anxiety and anger. The persuasive mode is generally dysfunctional in decision making inasmuch as participants thereby fail to explore other alternatives or consider relevant information, become emotionally upset, or adhere steadfastly to less than desirable solution alternatives. As Walton and McKersie (1966) have emphasized, persuasion and influence are most appropriate for bargaining in essentially competitive situations whereas the analytic mode (which these authors identify as problem solving) is most appropriate for the cooperative aspects of decision making. The persuasive mode does have a place in decision making, but this is restricted mainly to the stage of selecting a decision response when alternatives are not equally advantageous to both partners.

Types of Decision Issues

Decision issues are not all the same and the differences are often critical in assessment and modification. Three important types of issues are distinguished here.

Recurring decision issues are those that occur regularly or periodically. They usually involve many different decision areas. For example, a decision difficulty for recurring decision issues might be evidenced by inadequate couple decision making in regard to where to take a vacation, how much money to spend on clothing and food, how often to have the car fixed, use of time for recreation on weekends, and what to serve for holiday dinners. *Nonrecurring decision issues,* by contrast, occur episodically, occasionally, or essentially once in a lifetime. Examples include whether to have a dying parent live out his remaining days in the partners' home, where to live, whether to send a child to college, whether to change jobs, and whether the wife should work. Partners who have recurrent difficulties in making decisions are the best candidates for methods of modification in which the objective is to change the decision process, such as in a training procedure, whereas couples having difficulties with nonrecurring issues can generally be assisted by methods that focus more on the outcome than the process.

Whether the issues are recurring or nonrecurring, there are two subtypes of each, if the outcome payoffs are considered for each partner. When both partners obtain approximately equal benefits from a solution alternative, which is one subtype, the situation is more conducive to cooperation than if the solution alternatives yield unequal partner benefits, the other subtype. Again, this distinction is germane to modification, in this instance because procedures involving disagreement and conflict resolution may be needed for decision issues that produce unequal benefits for partners.

Another type is the *nonconjoint issue,* which is so labeled because shared couple decision making is not needed to produce a decision. Here, there are three important subtypes. One is the decision that involves an outcome mainly affecting one person alone (e.g., what food to eat, what clothes to wear, or whether to get contact lenses, where cost is not a factor). A second nonconjoint type is the issue for which there is a factual solution. "Factual" solutions, for present purposes, are those that involve mathematical computation, logical manipulation, or documentary evidence. Examples would be whether the family could afford to send a child to college, given present savings and income, whether cigarette smoking is harmful to health, or what the divorce laws are in the state. A third nonconjoint type is the issue for which expert opinion, such as technical, medical, religious, legal, or psychological knowledge, would be most suitable. Most relevant here are issues that entail the practitioner's expertise as a professional helping person. Ordinarily, clients cannot be expected to solve technical problems in regard to such matters as their own sexual adjustment in the marriage, child management, or severe adjustment difficulties of the individual partners. It is wrong to expect them to solve any serious problem for which they do not have the requisite knowledge and skill. Instead, partners should be directed to an appropriate expert. If that happens to be the practitioner himself, then intervention of a different type from that described here would be called for (e.g., sexual therapy for sexual maladjustment, a child-management program for child-management difficulties).

In summary, the following types of decision issues have been identified:

1. Recurring
   a. Equal outcomes for partners
   b. Unequal outcomes for partners
2. Nonrecurring
   a. Equal outcomes for partners
   b. Unequal outcomes for partners

  3. Nonconjoint
    a. Individual issues
    b. Factual questions
    c. Questions involving expert judgment

Decision Outcomes

Decision making may result in a variety of outcomes. From the point of view of remediation, perhaps the least eventful is the decision finally arrived at out of the initial uncertainty of the partners concerning possible decision alternatives. Ordinarily here, the decision process involved in remediation serves to generate and facilitate the selection of an alternative. Decision outcomes are more intricate and important when partners disagree about solution alternatives. Among the alternatives for resolution of disagreement are:

1. Compliance with a partner, consisting of a decision response consistent with the partner's initial position.
2. Compromise, a final decision response that falls somewhere between the initial positions of the two partners.
3. Trade, comprised of an exchange of benefits in which the final decision response consists of (a) a proposed solution that is closer to the initial preference of one of the partners than the other and (b) some compensating condition for the partner whose initial position is less favored.
4. Default, in which necessary decision-making activities are delayed or avoided with the result that, in effect, the decision is made for the partners by outside events or the behavior of others.
5. Delegation of the decision, in which resolution is achieved by delegating the decision-making prerogative for this issue to one partner or the other, thus also changing partner role responsibilities.
6. Mediation, in which the partners agree to allow a third party, such as the practitioner, to assist them in reaching agreement.
7. Arbitration, wherein the partners agree to let a third party, such as a trusted relative or the helping person, make the decision for them.
8. Forced resolution, in which the partners are constrained through the use of force by others to resolve the disagreement. This, of course, is not a viable alternative with voluntary participants, nor is it desirable in any case.

In the absence of resolution, there are additional alternatives of non-resolution:

9. Continued negotiation, in which the partners actively interact in an endeavor to achieve some resolution.
10. Negotiation moratorium, in which the partners agree to stop negotiation for the time being, with the possibility that it may be resumed.
11. Continued disagreement, wherein the original disagreement continues and there is no negotiation to resolve it.
12. Uncertain status.

The alternatives indicated above are generally many more than most marital partners entertain when they disagree. It is not un-common to find that disagreeing marital partners are locked into their respective positions as if the only alternatives for each were to have his or her position prevail or give in to the partner. Compromise is ruled out inasmuch as the partners also see this as an intolerable loss. And the partners rarely entertain two of the other most viable alternatives, namely, trade or mediation. Nor do most partners see the possible advantages, in extreme cases, of some of the nonresolution alternatives, such as a negotiation moratorium, which can greatly reduce the conflict and contention until negotiation can be resumed.

In general, partners in disagreement tend to exaggerate the importance of that particular decision issue and the value of the outcome for them personally without realizing that the issue is but one of many, that the outcomes for decision issues will not and need not always favor both partners equally, and that any decision has to be evaluated on its own terms as well as for its possible effects on other aspects of the partner relationship.

Decision-making Difficulties

Some of the diverse difficulties that marital partners may display in their joint decision making are enumerated here.

Difficulties of Predecision Verbal Response

1. Failure to recognize a problem situation as one for which marital decision making would be appropriate.
2. Misconception of the problem situation.
3. Failure to break down the problem situation into workable components.

4. Failure to operationalize and make problem components sufficiently concrete and specific.
5. Tackling too many things at once.
6. Not identifying other problem components that may be critically related to the parts the couple had intended to work on.
7. Not placing proper priorities on the problem elements that may be worked on.
8. Discussing problem elements excessively and not moving on through other relevant predecision stages.
9. Focus on trivial or imaginary problem elements.
10. Failure to array relevant information and to consider available facts.
11. Misinterpreting facts.
12. Not recognizing gaps in available information.
13. Not recognizing what other specific information is needed.
14. Not generating good, relevant, or ample alternatives for action.
15. Evaluating alternatives prematurely.
16. Not evaluating alternatives.
17. Evaluating alternatives improperly.
18. Advocating one alternative when there are others that might be more suitable.
19. Not agreeing on an alternative where some agreement is required to address the problem.
20. Not making a decision response.

Difficulties Involving the Decision Response
21. Making a needless decision.
22. Selecting a poor decision alternative, considering its consequences.
23. Selecting a poor decision alternative, considering the nature of the problem situation.
24. Not making operationally specific the agreed-upon action alternative.

Difficulties Involving the Solution Response
25. Not carrying out the solution response.
26. Carrying out the wrong solution response.

Difficulties of Postaction Evaluation
27. Failure to evaluate outcomes.
28. Failure to evaluate the action response properly in view of the problem situation it was to address and in light of other consequences.

General Difficulties

29. Use of the persuasive rather than the analytic mode where the analytic mode would be more appropriate.
30. Failure at any stage to have responses controlled by relevant responses that occurred in prior decision stages.
31. Failure to engage in relevant predecision verbal responses in an order that would allow the decision response to be properly guided by relevant prior considerations (e.g., evaluating solution alternatives before generating solution options or specifying a component of the problem to work on).
32. Failure to inhibit action prior to decision, with consequent premature action by one or both partners.

COMMUNICATION DIFFICULTIES AND DECISION MAKING

Certain shortcomings of marital communication may adversely affect partner decision making. Any of the following, if serious enough, could interfere with successful marital decision making: undertalk, underresponsiveness, overtalk, overresponsiveness, quibbling, overgeneralization, presumptive attribution, misrepresentation of fact or evaluation, content avoidance, content shifting, content persistence, poor referent specification, temporal remoteness, opinion surfeit, opinion deficit, excessive agreement, excessive disagreement, too little information, too much information, illogical talk, and negative talk surfeit. There are some others that are potentially less serious, but, if extreme, may interfere to some extent also. These are affective talk, obtrusions, excessive question asking, excessive cueing, and acknowledgment deficit.

Social Structure of Family Decision Making

To highlight some of the structural limitations of family decision making, consider the following description of making decisions in an imaginary and somewhat ideal organization. In this organization, the problem situations requiring decisions would be readily identifiable but, if not, there would be standards defining what is and what is not a problem for which decision making would be required. Once a problem is identified as such, there would be a means to connect the problematic issue with a decision-making process so that decision issues would ultimately be dispensed with. There would always be a time for participants to meet to make decisions, and during this time there would be no outside distractions. A recognized decision-making procedure would then be followed that would provide for systematic input, cueing, and priority ordering of decision issues, the collection and display of information, generation of possible solutions, their evaluation, and a means by which a decision would be reached, including resolution of conflict. Then there would be a mechanism for converting the decision to action and ultimately evaluating the outcome. Participants in the decision making would have the experience, training, and competence to handle the issues, and, if needed, a variety of persons would be made use of for decisions and activities requiring diverse competencies. Conditions for decision making in most families, of course, differ markedly from those described above, thus laying the groundwork for possible decision difficulties.

The following are some of the social-structural shortcomings that lead to decision-making difficulties in families.

1. The family faces a very large number and variety of decision issues, which include many nonroutine, nonrepetitive decisions as well as recurring decisions for specific situations that frequently shift as family members grow older, the needs of members change, and family resources vary. The decision-making task would be much more manageable if the family faced fewer decision issues and, especially, if the issues were more routine and repetitive so that standard practices could be developed and applied repeatedly. As it is, with so many decision issues, there tends to be what Weick (1971) has referred to as a predominance of unfinished business—i.e., more unsolved than solved problems.

2. Standards defining what is and what is not a problem situation in the family are often vague, ambiguous, shifting, or nonexistent. To the extent that this is the case, there can be confusion of members concerning what is normal, natural trouble and what is not, uncertainty concerning what is developmental or exceptional in the life span, what will go away in contrast to what deserves special attention (Weick, 1971). Criteria defining a decision problem, if available, would embrace aspects of physical and mental health, child and adult development, changeability of behavior, home economics, and many others—a truly immense domain. In most families there is no systematic way by which the problem situation may be connected up with decision making. That is, recognition that a problem situation exists does not necessarily result in some particular mechanism by which the problem situation is addressed.

3. Decision making rarely happens at designated times set aside exclusively for this activity without the intrusion of extraneous influences that so often go along with the more or less disorderly, distracting, and disruptive nature of life in families. There is thus a relative absence of conventional stimulus control in family decision making, thereby allowing decision behavior to occur informally and to be confounded with other activities where partners may be together, such as eating, reading the newspaper, watching television, grooming, intimate relations, and getting dressed or undressed.

4. There is generally no established procedure in families for systematic, regular, and orderly carrying out of the decision process. In consequence, one or more of the following simply don't exist: a method for determining decision issues; priority establishing mechanisms; ways to collect and display data, generate alternatives, and evaluate options; methods to resolve disagreement and conflict; and reliable mechanisms to carry out decisions.

5. The family group is small, and each member tends to have a fixed role with power centralized in the mother and father (Aldous, 1971). Without real training and sometimes with little experience, the members, furthermore, are often incapable of or incompetent to handle the myriad decisions they encounter. The range and quality of solutions are restricted to and dependent on the abilities and skills of just a few persons. The limitations of any incompetent, deviant adult members therefore have special force. Whereas in larger groups a single defective decision maker can often be neutralized and corrected for, a maladept adult decision maker whose only counterpoise in the family is a mate and perhaps a few children may bias decision making most unfavorably.

6. Much of what the family does has to do with group maintenance, and, according to Weick (1971), it is a structure better suited to providing sustenance and comfort for the members than to problem solving. As a result, Weick contends, the family may often suppress conflict and the generation of problem-solving alternatives when these are inconsistent with group maintenance.

7. Being nuclear and isolated, the family is very much an encapsulated problem-solving unit, sealed off from the external environment so that it receives little new input and develops processes that tend to be resistant to revision (Weick, 1971). If members are poor decision makers and use defective procedures, there is little input to provide for correction and positive change.

Altogether, the above limitations may result in such difficulties as family members not making decisions when they need to do so, not carrying out a decision-making process after a problem situation has been recognized, endeavoring to make decisions at unfavorable times, encountering distractions and disruptions during decision making, making decisions in haste, making poor decisions, and failing to carry out decisions.

These social-structural factors clearly set up conditions that dispose many families to have disordered decision making. To this sociological context of family decision making it is necessary to add sources of difficulty specifically applicable to assessment and intervention with particular couples. It is to this topic that we now turn.

Sources of Decision-making Difficulty

In considering clinically applicable sources of decision-making difficulty, emphasis is placed on contemporary precipitating or maintaining conditions that may operate singly or in combination to account for the significant aspects of a given couple's decision making. The sources of decision-making difficulty are the same as those that affect marital communication—repertoire deficit, referent conditions, setting events, structural deficit, and partner interaction. For relevant background on these sources, the reader is referred to Chapter 1.

REPERTOIRE DEFICIT

The individual response repertoires of the partners may involve deficits in the communication skills necessary for decision making or in any of the decision-making skills themselves. In regard to the latter, there may be deficits in discriminating a problem situation as one calling for decision, withholding action until a joint decision has been reached, particularizing problem components, generating possible alternatives for solution, evaluating these alternatives, deciding on action, and specifying what is required for implementation. Repertoire deficits of decision-making skills are particularly common. They are remedied most readily, of course, by providing training in these skill areas.

REFERENT CONDITIONS

As applied to decision making, referent conditions consist of particular conditions in the life situation of partners not embracing communication or decision making proper that require behavior change of one or both partners and that coexist with and give rise to decision-making difficulties. For instance, sexual difficulties of the partners, such as psychological impotence for the male combined with inorgasmic responding of the female, may occasion aborted, ineffective, and needless decision making. Such decision making is inappropriate because the solution lies beyond partner preference and requires, instead, outside intervention to change the sexual responding and adjustment of the partners. Referent conditions that may occasion disordered decision making are the same as those that may give rise to problematic couple communication (see Chapter 1 and Table 3-2). Decision-making difficulties deriving from a referent condition generally require that the referent condition be addressed before intervening with couple decision making proper.

SETTING EVENTS

Setting events affect the verbal behavior in decision making in very much the same way as they do the verbal responding in marital communication. For instance, the unfavorable setting events of sex deprivation, anxiety, anger, fatigue, sickness, or the effects of alcohol and drugs may adversely influence any or all of the verbal responses relating to such decision-making activities as definition of the problem situation, predecision verbal responses, selection of a decision response, and action carried out, as well as postdecision evaluation. Thus, an important decision made by a couple when both members are on the down limb of the blood-alcohol curve but long before sobriety can be pessimistically colored by the irritability and depression induced at this point by the alcohol. Because of the generally adverse effects that unfavorable setting events may have upon marital decision making, conjoint decision making should not be undertaken unless the setting events are favorable. Decision-making difficulties that may be traced to unfavorable setting events direct the practitioner first to an alteration of these events and only later, if difficulties persist, to the decision-making process itself.

STRUCTURAL DEFICIT

When stimulus conditions that otherwise successfully occasion marital decision making are absent, there is a structural deficit. Such a deficit may be remedied by providing a specific time and place for decision making, a Decision Time. The deficit should generally be remedied before or instead of working with decision-making skills themselves.

PARTNER INTERACTION

Partner verbal behavior in decision making is an especially important contemporary controlling condition inasmuch as each mate has the capability of exercising enormous positive as well as negative guidance over the content and direction of the decision making. The partner functions in interaction here very much as she or he does in connection with marital communication. In particular, partners may reinforce bad decision making, may fail to cue appropriate decision-making responses, may speak so as to elicit interfering emotional states of the partner, or may punish or fail to reinforce the appropriate decision-making behaviors of the partner, among others. Decision-making difficulties arising from partner interaction are very common. When they are discerned as the main source of difficulty, the practitioner generally works directly on the verbal behavior of one or both partners in the decision-making process.

CHAPTER SIX

Assessment of Marital Decision Making

ASSESSMENT OF couple decision making yields essential information for the formulation of a modification plan. Information gathered in assessment bears on three major questions:

1. What is the nature of the decision-making difficulty?
2. What are the probable sources?
3. What are the behavioral objectives of intervention?

Procedures applicable to the assessment of marital decision making are presented below. It is assumed that the reader is familiar with the material presented in Chapter 3 on the assessment of marital communication, details of which will not be repeated here.

Overview of Basic Steps

The activities involved in assessment are as follows:

Preliminary Steps
1. Inventory of problem areas
2. Selection of and contract for the target area
3. Commitment to cooperate

Steps Related to Decision Making
4&5. Response specification and identification of probable sources of difficulty
   a. Objectives
   b. Interview inquiry
   c. Response display procedure
   d. Postdiscussion inquiry

6. Assessment of environmental and behavioral resources
7. Specification of behavioral objectives
8. Respecification of contract for target area

If decision making is the presenting concern of the couple or it is discovered to be of concern early in work with the partners, the practitioner can begin with Step 1 and progress through the series more or less in sequence. However, if the practitioner has already completed an assessment of marital communication, as outlined in Chapter 3, the preliminary steps will already have been completed, and some details of couple decision making and communication will have been obtained. Continued assessment focusing on decision making itself can then resume at the appropriate point, usually with Steps 4 and 5.

Preliminary Steps

Three preliminary steps precede the assessment of couple decision making itself. The rationale and procedures given in Chapter 3 are applicable to decision making and will not be repeated here.

INVENTORY OF PROBLEM AREAS (STEP 1)

In obtaining the spectrum of presenting concerns, partners may indicate directly that they have difficulties in making decisions or may mention concerns in this area indirectly. For instance, they may refer to a high frequency of arguing, inability to resolve disagreements, or unresolved problems affecting the family for which couple decision making would be appropriate.

SELECTION OF AND CONTRACT FOR
THE TARGET AREA (STEP 2)

It is necessary that both parties agree that marital decision making is an area deserving attention and, at that point, that there are no other concerns of greater importance.

In work on decision making, in contrast to marital communication, it is not necessary to ascertain at the outset that separation or divorce are not imminent. Couples can often be effectively assisted in carrying out the process of decision making in this area or in making particular critical decisions. However, if the partners have already decided that the marriage is to be dissolved, with the likelihood that each will thereafter be making most of his or her decisions individually, a contract should be deferred until more information has been obtained concerning possible areas of mutual decision that the couples could be assisted with conjointly.

COMMITMENT TO COOPERATE (STEP 3)

The procedure followed here is the same as that outlined in Chapter 3 (p. 47).

Steps Relating to Decision Making

RESPONSE SPECIFICATION AND IDENTIFICATION OF PROBABLE SOURCES OF DIFFICULTY (STEPS 4 AND 5)

Steps 4 and 5 are discussed together here because the procedures generally yield information relating to both steps.

Objectives

It is especially important to be clear on assessment goals for these steps because the procedures for the assessment of marital decision making are just emerging and the practitioner may wish to try out new procedural alternatives or expand on those to be described below.

Whereas specification of communication difficulties generally consists largely of an early, detailed topographical denotation, response specification for marital decision making involves first obtaining selected critical details, without which intervention objectives and methods could not be chosen properly. Then, more focused and detailed specification is generally undertaken. Among the critical areas of information are the following:

1. The nature of the decision issue, whether recurring or non-recurring, and whether decision alternatives favor partners equally or unequally. Difficulties involving recurring issues lead the helper more toward methods to alter the decision process than do issues that are predominantly nonrecurring. Likewise, there are different modification

methods and procedures for issues involving unequal and equal outcomes.

2. The pattern of marital decision making—whether it is mainly
a stepwise, nonstepwise, or defaulted pattern—and the particulars
of the characteristic pattern. There is little information on characteristic patterns, but available studies (O'Flaherty, 1974; Briscoe,
Hoffman, and Bailey, 1975) and my own observation suggest that
the defaulted pattern is the most common for couples having difficulties in decision making. In any case, knowledge of the nature of the
pattern and the particulars of its unfolding are behavior-controlling
for the practitioner inasmuch as critical strengths and limitations are
thereby highlighted. For both areas of information considered here, the
list of decision-making difficulties in Chapter 5 (pp. 121–123) may
be helpful to keep in mind.

3. The role of communication difficulties in marital decision making. If communication difficulties significantly interfere with the decision making, then these also need to be specified and considered in
the modification plan. Knowledge about the sources of decision-
making difficulty directs the practitioner to undertake intervention
oriented toward their removal. Again, earlier discussions on this topic
in Chapters 3 and 5 are relevant but are not repeated here.

Throughout assessment and modification of marital decision making, one must also be alert to the possibility that there may be a
more important concern, such as an *Alpha* problem, that needs attention first or instead of marital decision making.

Interview Inquiry

Illustrative areas of content to be explored and for which specific
examples should be sought by means of interviews with the partners
are as follows:

1. The areas in which the couple has difficulty in making joint
   decisions.
2. The areas of continuing dispute or disagreement.
3. The areas in which the couple successfully makes joint decisions.
4. How the marital decision making is characteristically carried
   out.
5. When and under what conditions joint decisions are made.
6. Whether time is made available regularly for purposes of
   marital decision making.

7. Decisions made that are not carried out.
8. Current unresolved decision issues.
9. Particular aspects of marital decision making that the partners would like to see improved.

It cannot be emphasized too strongly that examples and specific response description are required for these areas rather than vague description or unspecified generalization.

Response Display Procedure

The sample of verbal behavior obtained in the Response Display Procedure provides information about the decision-making skills of the partners, the possible role of partner interaction as a source of difficulty, and the extent to which there are communication difficulties that interfere with couple decision making. Partners should be asked to discuss decision making in their marriage or the three most important unresolved decision issues in their marriage. One of the best ways to discover decision-making behavior is to have the partners endeavor to reach an actual decision on a current unresolved decision issue. The topic is chosen from a list of unresolved, recurring, joint decision issues obtained from the partners beforehand. Almost any topic on the list will generally serve the purpose. In selecting, however, some priority may be given to decision issues that the partners want to consider first, issues that should be decided sooner rather than later, and those that are easier rather than more difficult.

The marital partners are then requested to discuss the issue between themselves to try to reach an actual decision on the matter as they normally would. The partners are not told in advance how much time they have, but they should be given at least twenty minutes, unless a decision is reached before that time. The practitioner sits inconspicuously to one side or withdraws from the room if the discussion is audible or is to be taped for later analysis. One or two such response displays are ordinarily enough if responses are found to be reasonably typical of the partners' decision making.

The practitioner should know what to look for during the discussion and in any later replay of taped sessions. The scanning and tracking provide a basis for detecting or excluding major factors relating to significant decision-making strengths or difficulties (see Chapter 5, pp. 121–123), the role of partner behavior in interaction as a source of decision-making difficulty (see Chapter 1, pp. 21–23), and significant communication strengths and limitations (see Table

3-1 and Chapter 2 for examples). The observer should also be alert to detect other sources of difficulty, including structural deficits for decision making, referent conditions (see Table 3-2 and the relevant section of Chapter 5), and unfavorable setting events (see Table 3-3 and the relevant section of Chapter 5).

Postdiscussion Inquiry

Following the response display, postdiscussion inquiry should be undertaken to determine the adequacy of the decision-making sample. If the partners' decision making is found to be atypical because it is carried out in the presence of the practitioner or for any other reason, additional response displays on unresolved recurring decision issues should be obtained. What is typical or atypical, of course, may be especially illuminating. For example, the decision-making display of couple G transcribed in Appendix F was atypically good, and later inquiry indicated that the partners rarely sat down at a given time to have a discussion aimed at making a joint decision. This suggested structural deficit for decision making was remedied in part by having the couple set aside regular Decision Times to take up unresolved, joint decision issues.

The principal objective of the postdiscussion inquiry is to follow up any leads that may reveal the part played by sources of decision-making difficulty, especially referent conditions and setting events.

Postdiscussion inquiry can run from five to thirty minutes, or even longer in exceptional cases. Additional response displays with post-discussion inquiries should be conducted as necessary, until the practitioner ceases to learn anything relevant that is new and until one or more of the sources of decision-making difficulty has been identified with some certainty.

In those cases when an adequate response display cannot be obtained in the office, partners can be requested to carry out actual decision making on unresolved issues in their home, recording the sessions on tape for subsequent analysis by the practitioner. Although a poor substitute for on-the-spot or postsession analysis of response displays, written records kept by marital partners at home can yield valuable information, especially if they turn up specific instances that were not obtainable otherwise. Written records are particularly useful in obtaining information about problem situations for which decisions are not made and the failure of partners to follow through on decisions.

ASSESSMENT OF BEHAVIORAL AND ENVIRONMENTAL RESOURCES (STEP 6)

The objective and procedure here are the same as those described for marital communication in Chapter 3 (p. 61).

SPECIFICATION OF BEHAVIORAL OBJECTIVES (STEP 7)

Once assessment has been completed and the information appraised, it is possible to specify final behavioral objectives. The information on the couple's behavior will often point to more than one possible objective. Given the variety of profiles of problem, it is helpful to have general priorities as a basis for selecting appropriate objectives.

Attention should be given first to any relevant behaviors not involving conjoint decision making proper. These include (1) *Alpha* problems, such as serious drug abuse by one or both partners; (2) communication difficulties if they turn out after all to be much more serious than any difficulties of marital decision making; and (3) decision issues involving decision prerogatives of only one partner, expert judgment, or factual information. If there are major difficulties in these areas, they should be addressed instead of or before any difficulties of conjoint decision making.

Turning now to conjoint decision making proper, the target behaviors may be grouped into one or more of the following five important classes of behavior:

1. Reacting properly to a problem situation for which there is no immediate, agreed-upon response alternative.
2. Engaging in appropriate predecision verbal responses.
3. Producing decision responses appropriate to the problem situation to which they relate as well as to other factors.
4. Evoking appropriate solution responses, given the decision responses.
5. Carrying out adequate postsolution evaluation.

Any or all of these may be specified as the behavioral objectives for intervention.

In addition to specifying behavioral objectives, it is useful at this point to distinguish recurring from nonrecurring decision-making difficulties. If the sources of decision-making difficulty have been identified, and they usually can be, these sources themselves should be the operational targets of intervention. If there is more than one source of difficulty, the practitioner must try to select the source or sources that should be considered first. The following are suggested priorities from first to last, given information that these particular sources of difficulty are operative: referent condition; conditions disadvantageous for making joint decisions, such as structural deficits or unfavorable event setters, provided that the partners have the capability of engaging in reasonably adequate decision making given the impetus and opportunity; repertoire deficits; and partner interaction.

If the difficulty mainly involves nonrecurring decision issues, the operational targets of intervention generally consist of the target behaviors themselves rather than their sources. For example, if a couple has difficulty deciding whether or not to get divorced, it would generally be most appropriate to assist them with making this decision rather than get into a probably fruitless, academic, and misguided search for the sources of this single instance of difficulty. Such a couple, of course, would probably want help only with this one important life decision, not with their decision-making processes. In dealing with nonrecurring decision difficulties, it is sometimes appropriate to give assistance with particular predecision responses, solution responses, or postdecision evaluation.

RESPECIFICATION OF THE PROBLEM CONTRACT (STEP 8)

To go beyond the general agreement formulated earlier to work in the area of marital decision making, the practitioner respecifies the contract in the light of the behavioral targets now to be operational in the intervention.

Other Steps

It may be desirable to obtain a baseline of decision making before intervention, especially when doing research or evaluating practice outcomes systematically. In routine practice, however, it is generally not necessary to obtain a baseline. Difficulties of decision making often times consist of a variety of deficits, for which baselining is ordinarily needless. This is especially obvious, of course, for responses that have never occurred. When dealing with behavioral deficits, it is ordinarily enough in demonstrating improvement to observe new responses developed that were not in the repertoire or were infrequently produced before.

Assessment probes can often be fruitfully carried out to obtain assessment information not available otherwise. This is especially the case in determining the extent to which marital partners are capable of carrying out effective decision making, if only the right circumstances are present. Couples can be requested to establish a regular Decision Time during which they would not be disturbed. The results of such a probe should be informative no matter what happens. Thus, if the partners displayed characteristic decision-making difficulties even under these favorable conditions, then intervention oriented toward improving their decision skills would be desirable. However, if the couple completed their decision making satisfactorily under these conditions, the use of Decision Times could be built directly into the modification program.

Assessment feedback may also be appropriate just prior to starting intervention. The reader is referred to Chapter 3, where this and other procedural steps are discussed more fully in the context of marital communication.

CHAPTER SEVEN

Modification of Marital Decision Making

CONSISTENT WITH the approach to modification presented in Chapter 4 on marital communication, modification of marital decision making is preceded by assessment and formulation of a modification plan, which are followed by implementation of the plan, monitoring of outcomes, and maintenance of change. This chapter focuses on aspects of modification bearing directly on marital decision making—specifically, on some principles for planning modification of marital decision making, orientation for marital partners before such modification, rules for marital decision making, and the new modification methods of operating agreements, coaching, information display through interview guidance, and assisted decision making.

Some Principles for Planning Modification

Principles 1–8 given on pages 79–82 in Chapter 4 are as applicable to planning modification for marital decision making as for marital communication. It is assumed that the reader is familiar with these principles, which will not be repeated here. The following five principles should be considered in addition.

9. *Difficulties involving nonrecurring decision issues (i.e., one-time life decisions) should generally be addressed before any decision-making difficulties for recurring issues.*

Current nonrecurring issues (e.g., whether to get divorced) are generally pressing. Also, they can usually be taken up in less time than recurring issues. The latter ordinarily require alteration of decision processes for the couple whereas the former are restricted more to particular decision outcomes.

10. *The operational targets of intervention for difficulties in handling recurring decision issues should generally be the sources of such difficulties, if these sources have been identified.*

If a condition giving rise to a difficulty can be removed, doing so is preferable to engaging in modification that does not take such maintaining conditions into consideration. If the maintaining conditions for decision difficulties are not altered, any change achieved in decision behavior might be short-lived.

11. *Before endeavoring to modify sources of decision-making difficulty rooted in partner interaction, attention should generally be given to alteration of other sources of decision-making difficulty.*

Partner interaction oriented toward improved decision making will not be successful to the extent that decision difficulties are also sustained or occasioned by referent conditions, setting events, structural deficits, or repertoire deficits. Thus, there is little point in starting a training program to improve the partners' decision-making interaction if their failure to make decisions at home stems mainly from the structural deficit of not having an appointed time and place for making decisions.

12. *The operational targets of intervention for difficulties in handling nonrecurring decision issues should generally be particular responses relating directly to these issues.*

Assistance in resolving an infrequent, difficult life decision for partners can be given effectively without also addressing their decision processes in general or the sources of that exceptional decision difficulty.

13. *A problem-solving approach to marital decision making should be emphasized rather than a bargaining approach.*

The problem-solving model of marital decision making emphasizes cooperation, sharing of information, honesty and forthrightness, exploration of alternatives, and the satisfactory solution of the problem rather than only meeting the self-interests of the individual partners. The analytic mode, discussed before, is appropriate to a problem-solving approach. In the bargaining approach, by contrast, there is more stress on competition, manipulation, deception, payoff for oneself alone, restricted use of information, commitment to positions, and less interest in solving problems than in personal gain (Walton and McKersie, 1966). The persuasive mode of decision making, described earlier, is more characteristic of bargaining. In extreme cases, as

Walton and McKersie (1966) have indicated, bargaining can lead to distortions of judgment and perception, loss of efficiency and of mental functioning, and substitution of objectives, such as that of defeating the partner rather than solving the problem.

The problem-solving approach to marital decision making is generally most suitable for marital partners because they must live together in interdependence; their well-being involves numerous solutions and exchanges, not just one or a few; and their conflicts of interest are usually minor compared to the broader interests and common objectives of the partner relationship. A problem-solving approach should pervade all aspects of intervention, even when there are, in fact, clear conflicts of partner interest on given issues. This bias toward problem solving will help to solve problems of mutual interest, foster important concessions and changes, and avoid the disadvantages of the bargaining approach. Although conflicts of interest can generally be resolved satisfactorily in the context of the problem solving, it must also be noted that there are occasions, to be specified later, when disagreements may best be resolved by disagreement-resolution procedures that call for limited bargaining, explicit conceding, and resolution by trade and exchange.

Before starting intervention, a plan for modification should be formulated, following the approach presented earlier in Chapter 4.

Orientation for Marital Partners

Couples seeking assistance for disordered decision making generally have distorted and incorrect conceptions of the process, have been exposed to poor models of decision making, and have typically experienced conflict, frustration, and struggle rather than success in their efforts to make decisions jointly. Orientation of the partners serves to instruct them, provides a rationale for subsequent procedures of intervention, and indicates some of the desirable decision-making behaviors that partners may produce.

Many couples will benefit from being informed in regard to all of the points outlined below. However, for some couples selected points should be emphasized strongly, and others muted or eliminated. In any case, the orientation should be tailored to the individual couple to enhance its relevance and effectiveness.

Among the points that may be made in the orientation are the following:

Need for Improved Decision Making

1. Most marital partners would benefit from improvement of their joint decision making.

2. If partners cooperate and follow the regimen carefully, their decision making can almost certainly be enhanced, and this should produce a general improvement in their life situation relating to the decision issues.

The Nature of Marital Decision Making

3. Marital decision making is a common, everyday occurrence. Couples are routinely confronted with many decision issues as well as with frequent, new and unexpected issues. The business of making decisions is continuous and ongoing. Not only does the typical couple make scores of joint decisions in any given week, but there is always a certain amount of unfinished business, with many deliberations in different stages of solution.

How Marital Decision Making Should Be Viewed

4. Marital decision making is an expected, normal activity, not an activity to be feared, avoided, or exaggerated in significance.

5. Decision making is a rational way to improve the quality of life together by endeavoring to reach solutions that remove aversive problem situations and enhance desired outcomes.

6. Decision making in marriage is a valuable tool of living that deserves to be continually developed and improved.

7. The objective of marital decision making is to solve problems together, not to allocate blame, inflict punishment, resurrect the past, or rectify old injustices.

8. Partners should understand that if disagreements are to be resolved, each must undertake some adjustment and change.

9. Partners should treat each other as equals.

10. Spouses should adopt an analytic as opposed to a persuasive stance. The analytic stance emphasizes description in the present, not the past; exploration and problem solving rather than persuading with the goal of winning; treating the mate's opinion as no less valid than one's own, whether or not one agrees with it; and cooperation rather than competition.

The Recommended Process

11. Problem situations affecting both partners should be addressed through joint decision making.

12. There should be no undue delay in getting together with the spouse to address problem situations together.

13. Partners should inhibit action on an issue until a decision is reached. Premature action by one partner alone, or both together, should be avoided.

14. Partners should endeavor to achieve a workable and reasonably satisfactory solution, not an ideal outcome.

15. Critical activities in decision making are as follows:

    a. Recognition that a problem situation exists requiring joint decision.

    b. Agreement of the partners to try to work together toward a solution.

    c. Isolation of a specific and workable component to work on.

    d. Generation of solution alternatives, without evaluation or judgment during this time ("brainstorming").

    e. Selection of a solution (or solutions) for implementation.

    f. Deciding on action (i.e., determining what is to be done, who will do it, when it will be done, and how).

    g. Taking action.

    h. Reviewing action.

When undertaken in sequence, this procedure is a useful one to follow to improve disordered decision making. It should be acknowledged that although successful marital decision making can be carried out by couples who do not explicitly and self-consciously go through each of these steps in sequence, each step does contribute important information toward achieving a good decision response and solution.

Rules for Marital Decision Making

Rules may facilitate marital decision making to the extent that the desirable behavior is capable of being cued by the rules, the behavior in question is reinforced at some point following its emission, and there are no contravening conditions. The function of rules for decision making as for marital communication is catalytic inasmuch as the rules serve largely to initiate behaviors that ultimately should be evoked and reinforced by other conditions.

The general rules presented below have been grouped into three categories: establishing facilitative conditions (Rules 1–3), decision-making procedures (Rules 4–13), and behaviors relating to partner interaction (Rules 14–16). The language used is the same as if we were speaking to the partners themselves.

Rules to Establish Facilitative Conditions

1. Set aside a special agreed-upon Decision Time during which issues relating to your joint decision making may be taken up in a relaxed, uninterrupted session. Whether it is scheduled daily or several times a week, the Decision Time should be set aside regularly even though there may be occasions when you have nothing to discuss, in which case you can agree to stop the meeting.

2. Marital decision making should be undertaken when you are reasonably calm, rested, and clear-headed. Under no circumstances should you try to make joint decisions when either one of you is highly fatigued, sick, injured, in pain, extremely hungry, emotionally upset, or under the influence of drugs or alcohol.

3. Marital decision making should be carried out as a pure activity so that your full attention can be given to it. There should be no other activities concurrent with the decision making, such as eating, driving, watching television, sex, reading the newspaper, or paying bills.

Rules Relating to Decision-making Procedure

4. Write down all complaints, disagreements, and problem situations affecting you jointly as they come up, and save them for Decision Time. Make it a practice to record decision issues on a special pad kept in an accessible place.

5. Matters involving young children and older, impaired relatives should be taken up mainly by you and your partner. Children and others directly affected by the decision who can participate productively and responsibly should of course be included.

6. Address only "workable" decision issues. These are problem situations that (a) largely entail matters of your preference as partners; (b) involve interdependent outcomes for both of you; and (c) do not depend essentially upon outside expertise (e.g., medical, legal, religious, psychological, educational, or business), factual information, or individual prerogative alone.

7. There should be an agreed-upon agenda of decision issues prepared at the beginning of each session.

8. Carry the decision issues to the point of some conclusion, if at all possible.

9. If necessary, break down the decision-making process into manageable components and discuss each in order. The following procedure is suggested for this purpose:

   a. Agree to work together on a given problem situation.

    b. Choose a particular part of the problem to work on, being sure that this is workable.

    c. List possible solutions, generating these without criticism or evaluation. As in "brainstorming," judgment should be deferred and both of you should endeavor to freewheel and be original.

    d. Select a solution (or solutions) for implementation, being sure it is feasible.

    e. Decide action concretely (i.e., determine what is to be done, who will do it, when it will be done, and how).

    10. In pursuing the above procedure, both of you should agree to follow the steps in order, indicate your understanding of which step is in fact being worked on, summarize the results for each step before moving on to be sure that you agree on what has been accomplished, and, if necessary, agree that each step has been completed before moving to the next.

    11. All decisions made should be followed through and monitored so that the current state of progress can be reported at the next Decision Time.

    12. In carrying out the solution, try to adhere to the solution jointly agreed to. There should be no changes in plans or backing out on agreements without discussion beforehand at a Decision Time.

    13. At any point in the decision process, decision making may have to be delayed to allow you or your partner to obtain additional information, clarify opinions and evaluation, or, in some cases, seek outside expertise where this applies to a limited aspect of the decision issue.

Rules Relating to Partner Interaction

    14. Each partner should be allowed to have his or her say, keeping the contribution relevant to the decision issue being discussed.

    15. Communication rules should be followed so that disordered communication does not interfere with the decision making. (The reader is referred here especially to Rules 8–23, given in Chapter 4.)

    16. Praise your partner whenever he or she engages in good decision-making procedure, even if you disagree with the substance of what is said. If action alternatives are being evaluated, for example, the full expression of disagreement by your partner, if held back before, should be commended by you because preferences of partners can be dealt with appropriately only if they are expressed and aboveboard.

The above rules are a general set from among which a particular subset should be individually tailored for a given couple. Procedures to implement and individualize rules with particular couples are the same as those outlined in the section on this topic for marital communication (Chapter 4, pp. 89–91).

Operating Agreements

An operating agreement is an agreement formulated by marital partners concerning how a decision issue between them is to be resolved in the immediate future. Such an agreement is unique to the partners' situation and is something of a "ground rule" inasmuch as it is an expedient solution that may or may not be long-lasting. The objective is to give marital partners experience in formulating workable agreements when they have unresolved decision issues and to bring the couple's behavior in regard to the decision issue under the control of the jointly worked-out agreement.

The main behaviors entering into the formulation of an operating agreement are (1) identification of the areas of disagreement; (2) discussion by the partners to resolve the decision issue with an agreement; and (3) action and follow-through consistent with the agreement.

Formulation of operating agreements is most suitable when there is a clear disagreement regarding how a decision issue should be resolved and the partners possess sufficient interaction and decision skills to come to an agreement reasonably well on their own, given occasion and impetus to do so. Operating agreements may be worked out for disagreements involving recurring as well as nonrecurring decision issues. Decision issues relating to transitional life situations and temporary, short-term arrangements are often well suited to fashioning operating agreements. In any case, operating agreements are particularly applicable to decision issues in which there appears, at least at first, to be unequal rather than equal solution outcomes for the partners. Resolutions reached in operating agreements are generally a compromise between the original positions of the partners prior to agreement, a compliance with the position of one or the other partner, or a novel alternative.

PROCEDURE

In assisting marital partners to formulate operating agreements, the following steps are suggested.

1. In an interview, the decision issues needing resolution are identified and specified, the process of making operating agreements is described and illustrated, and the partners are requested to formulate operating agreements for each decision issue at home, at a Decision Time set aside for that purpose.

2. At home, partners discuss the issues and formulate mutually acceptable operating agreements, which are then written down and brought to the next session held with the worker.

3. In the next interview, the agreements are reviewed by the practitioner to be sure that they properly handle the decision issues, are operationally specific, and are reasonably satisfactory to both partners. Partners are requested to have some sessions again to rework inadequately stated agreements and formulate new ones as necessary. Satisfactory agreements are then made operational; that is, the partners are asked to begin implementing the agreements, and monitoring procedures are initiated.

Table 7-1 presents a useful monitoring format along with illustrative monitoring data which were recorded, in this case, by the wife. In this example, the decision issue involved disagreement of the partners about the husband's doing odd jobs around the house. The husband procrastinated in doing the jobs or didn't do them at all. The jobs were mainly minor repairs that, in this couple's division of labor, were best done by the husband. The operating agreement was that the wife was to request that the husband do the job and indicate a time by which it was to be done. The husband, in turn, was to say whether or not he could do the job by the time indicated and, if he couldn't, they were to agree on a different deadline. Then he was to complete the specified job by the specified time.

4. In subsequent interviews, the monitoring data are reviewed and the program is adjusted as needed.

If the partners cannot formulate operating agreements because they do not possess adequate interactional and decision skills, training in these skills should be given using methods such as coaching, to be described later.

CASE EXAMPLE

The use of operating agreements to resolve several important decision issues is illustrated by Mr. and Mrs. T. The partners were professionals in their early thirties, recently separated, who were considering the possibility of reuniting. Many of the decision issues related

TABLE 7-1.　Format for Monitoring Operating Agreements

Time and Date	Operating Agreement	Opportunity to Apply the Agreement	Agreement Related Behavior (Who Did What)
11:30 A.M. May 9	Odd-job agreement (as given in text)	I asked Bob to fix the light switch by May 12.	Bob said he couldn't do it until May 14; we agreed that he'd do it on the 14th.
2:00 P.M. May 14	Odd-job agreement	Date Bob agreed to fix light switch.	Light switch fixed.
4:00 P.M. May 15	Odd-job agreement	I asked Bob to fix the screen door by May 22.	Bob said he would.
11.00 A.M. May 17	Odd-job agreement	I asked Bob to take out the trash by 5.00 P.M.	Bob agreed and did it right away.
4:00 P.M. May 26	Odd-job agreement	Request of May 15.	Bob repaired the screen door—four days late.
1:00 P.M. May 27	Odd-job agreement	I asked Bob to repair a doorknob.	Bob agreed.
5:00 P.M. May 28	Odd-job agreement	Request of May 27.	Bob didn't repair doorknob; we argued and Bob said I didn't give him a deadline—and I should have. We then agreed that Bob would repair the doorknob by May 30.
9:30 A.M. May 30	Odd-job agreement	Agreement of May 28.	Doorknob repaired.

to the ambiguities of their transitional life situation. The husband was suffering from a fatal disease, but the amount of time he had to live could not be accurately anticipated. Although his physical condition was weakened by his illness, the husband was working and carrying out most other activities.

Some of the decision issues, operating agreements, and related behavior are given here.

1. Decision issue: how open should the marriage be? The husband wanted it "open" sexually whereas the wife wanted it "closed." Operating agreement: each partner could have friendships with members of either sex, which were not to be sexual relationships unless explicitly agreed to by the partners; further, each was to inform the other before going out on a date. Implementation: each partner had social relationships with others of the opposite sex, but neither partner had any sexual liaisons.

2. Decision issue: the husband's need for privacy. Operating agreement: it was decided that when either partner needed to be alone, he or she would say so. Implementation: this was carried out as indicated, and, in addition, a guest room in the house was converted to a den to which either partner could retreat to be alone.

3. Decision issue: how often to go out. The wife wanted to go out more often than the husband did. Operating agreement: the partners were to make sure that a "fun" activity was included in their lives at least once a week and try to have new experiences; also, because of the availability of money, they decided to spend more of it now rather than continue to pinch pennies. Implementation: the couple went on many more outings than before, including visits to restaurants, museums, and nearby cities.

4. Decision issue: how much money to spend. The wife wanted to spend more money than the husband. Operating agreement: to spend some of the money they had now rather than continue to be frugal. Implementation: in addition to the activities mentioned above, the couple bought new items for their house and rented special equipment to prepare their garden for spring planting.

5. Decision issue: the role of the wife in regard to the medical regimen required by her husband's illness. The wife, who was trained to carry out the regimen, wished to be relieved of most of these complicated and burdensome responsibilities; the husband was willing to hire persons to do the job, but they were unacceptable to the wife because of insufficient training. Operating agreement: the wife was to carry out the medical-care regimen for one month, with the arrangement being open for review at any time; the schedule required in caring for the husband was to be stipulated and negotiated weekly. Implementation: carried out as indicated.

6. Decision issue: clarification of who was to care for the two cars in the family. Operating agreement: each partner was to be entirely responsible for his or her own car. Implementation: carried out as indicated.

7. Decision issue: who was to do the menial jobs that neither liked. Operating agreement: the partners were to flip a coin to decide who did the job, if neither agreed otherwise to do it; and, this failing, someone would be hired to do the job. Implementation: the partners themselves did all the jobs by the means indicated.

8. Decision issue: how neatly each partner should keep his or her own belongings. Operating agreement: each partner agreed not to get "uptight" if the other's belongings were not kept neatly. Implementation: carried out as indicated.

9. Decision issue: how to handle the husband's teasing of the wife. Operating agreement: there would be no more such teasing. Implementation: carried out as indicated.

Coaching

Coaching is a recent modification method developed to train marital partners in family decision making. It is used during discussions between the marital partners of real-life decision issues they currently face. The three main components of the method are (1) decision making in ordered steps, with successful completion of each step required before progressing to the next; (2) concurrent feedback by the coach to the marital partners for on-topic and off-topic decision making, using either verbal or light signals; and (3) interventions in the decision making by the coach, as necessary to provide instruction, clarification, and guidance.

The method is called coaching because it resembles the training methods used in athletic and dance coaching and the instructional procedures used by tutors, music teachers, craftsmen, and by many practicum instructors in medicine and education. Here, complex response repertoires are developed, and training is accomplished by having the behaviors in question practiced in lifelike manner under the observation of the person functioning as coach. Guidance and correction are provided directly, quickly, and by a variety of influence techniques with focus on individualized, tailor-made change. If done skillfully, these elements of coaching combine to produce a powerful method of constructing response repertoires that may readily be generalized to the life situations in which they are to be used.

In a study done with the author and Joyce Borkin, O'Flaherty (1974) examined the efficacy of coaching for changing disordered marital decision making. In a series of single-couple experiments carried out with eleven couples who had difficulties in making decisions, it was found that 88 percent of the verbal units in each step of the decision making (i.e., sentences or parts of sentences that were "on topic" for each step) were appropriate for all couples during the coaching periods.[1] This compared with 22 percent for the precoaching sessions and 36 percent for the postcoaching assessment. It was concluded that for all couples in the series, coaching clearly served to produce the behaviors intended for each step in the decision making during the coaching sessions and to produce a modest but significant carryover of the decision-making skills when applied to a new decision area. A description of the coaching procedure along with a case study and evaluative data were reported subsequently (Thomas, O'Flaherty, and Borkin, 1976).

Coaching is most appropriate when employed with marital partners who have recurring difficulties with decision-making issues deriving from such sources as repertoire deficits and disordered partner interaction. The decision issues, as before, should be conjoint and should consist largely of matters of partner preference. Outcomes of the decision for partners may appear to be equal or unequal. If disagreements of partners are not handled by the coaching procedure, they can be taken up with special training modules, such as the Disagreement Resolution Procedure (Appendix H).

Main Procedures of Coaching

Following assessment, the practitioner completes the following principal activities in coaching. These are typically carried out in an office setting.

PARTNER ORIENTATION

In an interview prior to starting the coaching process, partners can be trained to make decisions and solve problems together in an orderly, stepwise fashion that will have application to a large number of decision areas in life. The practitioner points out the success of

---

[1] Specifically, appropriate verbal units were parts of the topic for Step 2, possible solutions for Step 3, evaluation and selection of possible solutions for Step 4, and specification of the decision response for Step 5. Percentage agreement of coders ranged from 80 to 90 percent for all cases in this study.

stepwise coaching in training other marital partners along with the value of their learning how to carry out each step together even if they later find that they can successfully make joint decisions without going through each and every step.

It is made clear that the solutions themselves will come from the partners, not the practitioner, and that the helper's role is only to assist the partners in moving through the procedure in an orderly way. The steps are described briefly, and the couple is told that the coach will henceforth introduce each step briefly and then allow the partners to discuss the topic together, with the coach staying out of the picture as much as possible. It is indicated that feedback will be given by the coach as the couple talks and that this will not keep them from continuing with the decision making. Light signaling is described, if it is to be used. If verbal feedback is to be employed instead, it is explained that the coach will comment occasionally on their progress in staying with what each step calls for. They are also told that the coach may interrupt briefly if they depart significantly from what is requested for the assigned step. It is emphasized that the partners' basic task is to follow instructions at each point so that the necessary responses for an appropriate, final decision response will be forthcoming.

LIST OF WORKABLE DECISION ISSUES

Partners are asked to indicate what decisions they currently need to make so that a list of possible topics to be used in training can be prepared. Examples might be decisions regarding where to take a vacation, how much to spend on a vacation, whether or not to buy a relative or friend a present, how much to spend on a gift for a family member, whether or not to buy a new car, whether a child should be allowed to work part time while going to school, whether to redecorate a room in the house, how much time the partners should spend together, whether a partner should take on part-time work in addition to present responsibilities, and so on. The topics should be screened for workability (i.e., they must be issues involving joint decision and be mainly questions of partner preference).

SELECTION OF TOPIC FOR DECISION MAKING

In selecting a topic from the list for coaching, preference should generally be given to the easier issues. Other factors being equal, "easier" issues involve narrow as opposed to large decision areas, single versus multiple solutions, issues for which partner objectives are not in conflict and in which negotiation and disagreement resolution would ordinarily not be heavily implicated, and issues that can readily be handled in one session. To the extent that the topics may be ordered, the more difficult ones should be saved for later work as training progresses and skills develop. In the absence of variations of evident difficulty, however, the practitioner should simply select for initial training the topic that seems to be most important for the partners at that time.

COACHING PROCESS

Sessions are conducted in an office setting in which partners are seated at a table facing each other, with the coach seated close by out of sight in the same room, or in an adjoining room where he can monitor the decision making and provide the feedback and intervening instructions as required. Before each partner is a Step Indicator Sign, visible to both partners during the session, which consists of a list of the steps and a large arrow that may be pointed to the step being worked on.

The three components of coaching—stepwise decision making, concurrent feedback, and intervening instructions—are elaborated below:

Stepwise Decision Making

Responses required to reach an operational decision have been broken down into five ordered groups, called steps, as follows.

Step 1. *Agreeing to work on the problem.* The partners' verbal agreement to work on the problem together is solicited by the practitioner immediately before beginning discussion of the decision topic.

Step 2. *Choosing one part of the problem to work on.* This step starts the couple decision making in their interaction together. The requisite here is that the part be narrow, specific, isolated from related changes, and manageable.

Step 3. *Listing possible solutions.* Possible solutions are generated at this point without evaluation or commitment. Emphasis must be placed on not evaluating or judging alternatives at this point. In "brainstorming" alternatives, it is important that the partners come up with as many ideas as they can without regard to practicality, reasonableness, or even merit. This free-wheeling approach ordinarily produces more and often better alternatives than have been thought of before. If there is initial conflict of interest and disagreement on the decision issue, it is essential that a range of possible alternatives to resolve the disagreement is included.

Step 4. *Selection of a solution for implementation.* By evaluating the feasibility of and consequences associated with the solution alternatives, the partners select a solution for implementation. The coach allows the partners to move on to the next step when they affirm that they have reached agreement on the solution alternative to be impelemented.

Step 5. *Deciding on action (i.e., what is to be done, who will do it, when it will be done, and how).* By specifying these details, partners make the action alternative operational and capable of being unequivocally carried out. When this step is completed, nothing should remain to be done except implementation itself.

A central feature of the stepwise decision making of coaching is that the behaviors requisite for each step are produced at that point and the step is successfully completed before the coach allows the partners to progress to the next. Each step has its target responses, acceptable related responses, unacceptable responses, and criteria that should be met before progressing to the next step. These are shown for Steps 2–5 in Table 7-2.

Concurrent Feedback

As partners engage in verbal interchange at each step, feedback is provided with light signals or verbally by the practitioner. If light-signal feedback is used, each partner has a light box placed before him in which the illuminated green light signifies "on topic" and the lighted red "off topic." "On topic" and "off topic" signs are placed conspicuously above their respective lights. The light signals may be provided with a system that makes it possible for the practitioner to illuminate either the green or red light for each partner at any point during the discussion.[2]

[2] An appropriate system having this and many additional capabilities is the Signal System for the Assessment and Modification of Behavior (SAM, for short) (Thomas, Carter, Gambrill, and Butterfield, 1970; Thomas, Carter, and Gambrill, 1971). The signaling apparatus may also be connected to a multiple channel encoder-decoder and a four-channel tape deck to assist in storing and retrieving the light signals along with the content of what is said (Thomas, Walter, and O'Flaherty, 1972). These apparatuses and computerized applications were described in the section on electromechanical devices in Chapter 3.

TABLE 7-2. Steps of Coaching and Related Responses

RESPONSE RELATING TO STEP OF COACHING	STEPS OF COACHING*			
	2	3	4	5
Target Response(s)	Selection of a particular part to work on	Generating possible solutions	Selection of solution (or solutions) for implementation	Deciding action (what will be done, by whom, when, and how)
Some Acceptable Related Responses	Persuading, evaluating, and providing information relating to possible parts to work on		Providing information and evaluation about alternative solutions; persuading, bargaining, and compromising. In exceptional cases, generating a new, suitable solution	Providing information and evaluation in regard to details of implementation
Some Unacceptable Responses	Target and acceptable responses for Steps 3–5	Target and acceptable responses for Steps 2, 4, and 5	Target and acceptable related responses for Steps 2, 3, and 5	Target and acceptable related responses for earlier steps
Criteria for Progressing to the Next Step	Selection of an isolated, specific, manageable component	Generation of enough possible solutions so that partners have enough suitable options for a solution response. This especially includes disagreement resolution responses for issues involving disagreement	Agreement of partners on a solution alternative they are willing to try to implement.	Specification of details required to carry out the solution

* Step 1 is handled before coaching is undertaken.

A simple, effective substitute for light-signal feedback is verbal feedback. Here, the coach provides praise or other words of approval when the partners stay on the topic for the step and verbal indications of disapproval for off-topic talk. For example, when the partners are on topic, the coach may periodically say "good," "you're doing fine," or "nice work." When off topic, he may say "you're getting off topic now," or, in more extreme cases, "remember, in this step you are to work only on the generation of alternatives, and not to evaluate them." Positive feedback should not be given in such a way as to interrupt the flow of decision making. It can be given less frequently as coaching progresses satisfactorily, but the partners should understand that the absence of comments generally means that the discussion is progressing well. Negative verbal feedback should be given every time there is more than a very brief departure from the target behaviors of the step the partners are working on. Such negative feedback ordinarily interrupts the flow of discussion, but it should do so only long enough for the partners to get back on topic. If partners are allowed to discuss topics irrelevant to the step and to follow practices that were dysfunctional before, they will not break old patterns and establish new, more adequate ones.

Intervening Instructions

In addition to concurrent feedback, the coach verbally intervenes as necessary at critical points during the coaching session. Some occasions for providing intervening instruction for purposes of redirecting the procedure follow:

1. To make step transitions, such as the introduction of a new step or requests to have the partners summarize at the end of a step.
2. To introduce a special training module, required when partners are unable to progress in a given step (e.g., use of the Disagreement Resolution Procedure for partners who can't agree at Step 4).
3. To cue more discussion on a given topic or to alter a persisting impediment in decision making when the light signals or verbal feedback has failed repeatedly. Here the coach specifies how the partners are not discussing step-related content, repeats the desired behaviors for that step and gives examples preferably drawn from prior correct responding of the partners at that step.

There are also occasions for the coach to intervene with substantive commentary:

4. To offer expert advice when this is directly relevant and essential to what the partners are trying to work through (e.g., regarding the capability of a five-year-old child to solve certain types of problems, where this capability is overestimated by the partners).

5. To give needed information (e.g., whether a certain day is a holiday).

6. To comment on the feasibility of alternatives in instances where given alternatives being seriously considered in Step 4 are clearly unrealistic (e.g., expecting a fifteen-year-old boy with little motivation and mechanical experience to repair a malfunctioning engine).

Finally, the coach must sometimes intervene simply to clarify what partners are saying so that he or she can continue to track the discussion properly.

FOLLOW-THROUGH INSTRUCTIONS

After coaching has been finished and a decision has been reached, the partners are informed that there are two additional steps to be completed: Step 6, taking action, and Step 7, reviewing action. In regard to taking action, spouses are requested to carry out the action agreed to and are informed that the practitioner will be checking with them again concerning their progress. The partners are also informed that after action has been completed the extent to which the problem situation giving rise to the decision issue was in fact remedied by the solution will be appraised with them.

MONITORING

Monitoring of the action taken is accomplished by checking with the partners periodically. If the intended action is being carried out successfully, the partners are commended, and the action is reviewed directly. However, if the solution has not been carried out as agreed to, the practitioner must find out the reason. If action has been delayed merely because partners have failed to proceed as agreed, then agreement to carry out the action as intended can be reaffirmed and times can be reestablished for carrying out the action. In exceptional instances, special modification procedures may be used to see that decisions are carried out as intended.

It is frequently helpful to have the practitioner check with the partners immediately after the action has presumably taken place to increase the probability of proper follow through. If the action has not been carried out because the action plan is defective, the practitioner starts coaching again at Step 5 to work out more satisfactory action details. Coaching is also reinstituted, in this case at Step 3 or 4, if the decision has not been carried out because a partner has found the previously agreed-on decision to be unacceptable.

REVIEWING ACTION

The objective of reviewing action is to provide some training for partners in the skills of evaluating the adequacy of their own decision making and to teach partners to take necessary additional action. Partners are requested to restate the original problem situation, to review the action taken, and to evaluate how well the problem situation was remedied. The practitioner should strongly support all aspects of the partners' analysis that indicate accurate and realistic appraisal. Inadequate aspects should be commented on and more appropriate evaluation provided as necessary. A critical part of appraisal is to identify with the partners what may still require attention, given the initial problem situation and what has been done, so that additional decision making can be undertaken. The coach should have the partners try to identify any additional decisions that may be required and then use coaching or other suitable methods to provide further training.

SPECIAL SITUATIONS

Occasions to Recycle to Earlier Steps

In the normal course of events, partners progress through the five steps in sequence. There are occasions, however, when even an expert coach will have to guide the couple back to an earlier step. Such recycling is required whenever it is discovered that a prior step has not been completed satisfactorily so that work on subsequent steps can go forward. If it is found in later steps, for example, that one partner has changed his or her mind concerning the agreement reached in Step 1 to work together on the solution of the problem, the coach should guide the couple back to Step 1 and try to reestablish agreement to work in a decision area. In special instances, a less formal, temporary recycling can be allowed to occur. For instance, if the partners are working at Step 4 to select an alternative and they think of another alternative at that point, the coach can simply allow the new alternative to be added to existing ones for evaluation in Step 4, even though, ideally, the solution alternative should have been generated in Step 3. Thus, very brief and relevant returning to earlier steps can be allowed occasionally, if the couple founders in going forward. Careful completion of each step will help reduce the need to recycle.

Forward Cycles

Jumping ahead one or more steps ordinarily results in getting off topic and is not allowed. However, there is at least one exception. If the partners happily hit on an alternative in Step 3, when alternatives are being generated, that both regard unequivocally as the best alternative and that the coach sees as workable, they should be allowed to go forward immediately to Step 4, if more evaluation is needed, or to Step 5, to specify details of action.

Occasions to Stop

If assessment and preparatory work have been properly carried out, there will be few occasions to stop a coaching session before its completion. There are occasions, however, when it is most prudent to terminate the session early. Some of these occasions are:

1. If partners have become too fatigued, emotionally upset, or ill to go on. For example, if coaching sessions exceed ninety minutes and the steps have not been completed, participants may have become too tired to continue productively, in which case the sessions should be stopped temporarily and resumed at another time. Partners who are just beginning coaching should refrain from discussing the decision issue in the interim between sessions and save any new ideas for the time when training resumes. However, partners who have already had considerable coaching and whose session has been interrupted might be encouraged to try to reach a decision on their own, using the stepwise procedure.
2. If the issue is discovered to be unworkable for joint decision making.
3. If requisite verbal skills are discovered to be lacking.
4. To allow partners to obtain information on necessary details or allow time during which partners' preferences may crystallize.

Failure to Produce Target Behaviors

Partners generally produce the desired behavior reasonably well for each step but occasionally they may simply not be able to do so despite the coach's best efforts. Some of the possible problems here are summarized in Table 7-3, along with the coaching step where the problem will be encountered, if it occurs, and the procedural alternatives for each problem. Appendix H, Training Modules for Special Coaching Problems, contains descriptions of the Alternative Generation Procedure, Information Display Procedure, Preference Display Procedure, and Disagreement Resolution Procedure.

TABLE 7-3.　Trouble-shooting Guide for Special Coaching Problems

PROBLEM	STEP OF COACHING WHERE EN-COUNTERED	PROCEDURAL ALTERNATIVE
Repeated failure of partners to agree to work on decision issue	1	Select a different decision issue
Repeated failure of partners to select a specific and manageable decision-issue component to work on	2	Select a different decision issue
Repeated failure of partners to generate an adequate number of solution alternatives	3	Use Alternative Generation Procedure (Appendix H)
Repeated failure of partners to evaluate and select an alternative for implementation	4	Use Information Display Procedure or Preference Display Procedure (Appendix H)
Repeated failure of partners to agree on a solution alternative	4	Use Disagreement Resolution Procedure (Appendix H)

Coaching Variations

Coaching is ordinarily "tight" inasmuch as it moves through each step in order and essentially disallows departures from step-relevant behavior. Tight coaching is most appropriate for narrow, specific, and structured decision issues for which feasible alternatives can readily be generated and, in general, for which occasions to recycle would be relatively improbable. To the extent that a situation departs from these conditions, it may be appropriate to consider "loose" coaching. Here, the coach allows more latitude about what is discussed in a given step, risking some off-topic discussion in return for what might be valuable clarification and exploration. Loose coaching sometimes produces partner responses that restructure the decision issue so that tight coaching is then justified. Loose coaching should be the exception rather than the rule. Whenever the coach finds himself inclined to adopt a loose style, he should seriously consider whether the part the partners have agreed to work on is sufficiently specific and workable. It is clear that if loose coaching is practiced on decision issues for which tight coaching would really be appropriate, irrelevant and off-topic responding is being strengthened, thus fostering continued difficulty in decision making for the partners.

In order to provide training in decision-making procedure, the coach ordinarily takes a completely neutral stance, focusing on procedure to assist the partners rather than on any substantive contribution he or she might make to the decision process or outcome. There are rare occasions, however, when departures from neutrality may also serve a training objective. For example, if partners need training in decision-making procedure and also want and need the coach's opinions as they may apply to the different steps, coaching can be carried out by having the coach add his contributions to those of the partners. Such "assisted" coaching may serve a modeling function for partners and may make it much easier in the early stages of training for the partners to progress successfully through each of the steps. A word of caution is in order, however. Neutral, value-free coaching is immensely more difficult to carry out than the assisted version, and coaches can all too easily be lured into participating substantively in the decision making by contributing *ad hoc* opinions and by biasing the feedback and intervening instructions in the direction of their own preferences. Assisted coaching should be used according to plan and only in the early stages of training before going forward with coaching that is neutral.

Case Examples: Coaching Process and Decision Structures

The case examples presented here illustrate important characteristics of the coaching process and decision behavior of participants along with different decision structures.

COUPLE A

Mr. and Mrs. A, in their early thirties, had recurring decision difficulties for which coaching, along with other procedures, was employed. The coaching session reviewed briefly below was taken from a later training session with the couple, and the summary indicates a relatively direct solution of the problem, with almost no intervening instruction on the part of the coach except to introduce and terminate each step. The time required to complete the session was short—approximately fifteen minutes. The decision issue in this training session was what to do about the family's three cars.

Step 1. The partners agreed to work together to try to reach a decision concerning the cars.

Step 2. The component aspect of the decision issue chosen to work on was whether or not to sell the sports car, an aging European import in less than excellent running condition. The wife wanted to sell the car whereas the husband was reluctant to do so and had been indecisive in prior discussions of the matter.

Step 3. Alternatives generated by the partners were as follows:
    a. Keep the car.
    b. Trade it in along with another one for a new car.
    c. Repair the car and have a mechanic sell it.
    d. Repair the car and sell it themselves.
    e. Repair the car and leave it at a gas station to be sold.
    f. Sell the car without repairing it.

Step 4. The husband wanted to sell the car as it was because he was reluctant to spend the money and the time to have the car repaired whereas the wife felt strongly that the car should be repaired before selling it to make it easier to sell and to bring a higher price. The couple finally agreed to sell the car and to have the wife handle all the details, including repair of the car.

Step 5. Details of implementation consisted of the wife's agreeing to take the car to the garage where it would be repaired, advertise to sell the car, and preside over the sale. It was agreed that she would take the car in to be repaired the next day and that additional steps to sell the car would be taken as soon as possible thereafter.

Commentary

The above case is typical of successful decision making in coaching with minimal guidance and correction from the coach. The responses constrained by the procedural steps are also very typical. First, Step 2 consisted of essentially one "component," the question of whether or not to sell one of the cars. Second, the component and the alternatives generated in relationship to it involved at least some conflict of interest. In this instance, the sports car had been purchased by the husband as his pleasure car. Although its sale would bring in money for the couple, the husband would thereby lose his plaything. The wife found the car unsightly and wanted to get what money could be obtained for it without having it depreciate further. The alternative chosen is also characteristic inasmuch as it reflected a change of position by one or both partners. In this case, the husband had not agreed to sell the car until he underwent the coaching. Rather than being a simple victory for the wife, however, there was also an element of trade inasmuch as the wife agreed to handle all details of the sale, thus relieving the husband of what for him were chores and unpleasant choices. Whether or not the conflict of interests is large, initially, the coaching procedure generally produces considerable behavioral change from the position partners held on the decision issue prior to coaching. This is one reason it is unnecessary to undertake Disagreement Resolution Procedures unless coaching fails to produce agreement.

COUPLE B

The following case is taken from an example reported by Thomas, O'Flaherty, and Borkin (1976).[3]

> The marital partners in this case were in their mid-forties. Among the current decision issues for them were the following: (1) what to do about their nine-year-old son's habit of eating in the TV room; (2) coping with the often unexpected weekend visits by their twenty-year-old son; (3) giving money to their fifteen-year-old son and his twenty-year-old brother; (4) letting the nine-year-old make more decisions; (5) working out leisure-time activities for the partners, both individually and together; and (6) handling disagreements of the parents in regard to the fifteen- and twenty-year-old boys. Decision-making difficulties of the parents involved not discussing subjects to completion, heated arguments, getting upset after discussion, and, on occasion, the wife's walking out of the room in the middle of a discussion and the husband's talking apologetically and hopelessly about his own behavior.

[3] In *Counseling Methods,* edited by John D. Krumboltz and Carl E. Thoresen. Copyright © 1976 by Holt, Rinehart and Winston. Reprinted by permission of Holt, Rinehart and Winston.

The excerpt below was drawn from a tape-recorded transcript. Verbatim coaching instructions are shown in italics. A summary of what transpired at each step is provided.

Step 1: Agreeing to work on the problem: *"You have listed this topic* (how to help Carl, the nine-year-old, make more of his own decisions) *as a possible topic to discuss during decision-making training. Do you agree to discuss this topic now and to try to reach a decision about it?"*

The couple agreed to discuss this topic.

"Because you both agree to work on this topic now, we will move on to Step 2, choosing one part of the problem to work on" (The pointer on the Step Indicator Sign is now moved to Step 2.)

Step 2: Choosing one part of the problem to work on: *"There may be several different parts of this topic which you would like to work on. Select one now for discussion and decision making. You may deal with any other parts later. Select a part that you think is important enough to work on and small enough to actually make a decision on now. Go ahead with Step 2."*

The couple began with a general discussion of the need for Carl to make his own decisions and with several illustrations of how the father didn't let him make them. In response to the generality of the discussion, the coach intervened to inquire what was meant specifically by Carl's decisions. The couple then gave an example of the father's selecting a book for Carl to read rather than having the boy make the selection himself. The couple then launched a discussion of possible solutions to this problem, at which point the coach intervened to ask what types of things the couple wanted the boy to make decisions about. In the ensuing discussion it was clear that the couple did not expect Carl to make adult decisions involving the family or the marriage; rather, they expected him to be able to make decisions within his capacity that pertained to his own personal situation. The coach then asked for examples of these types of decisions. Following further discussion, the couple indicated that they wanted Carl to be able to decide what to eat, what books to read, what to wear to school, and what TV programs to watch.

Then the coach asked: *"Have you agreed on the part of the topic you want to work on?"* The couple indicated that they had and, in response, the coach asked, *"What is the part that you agreed on?"* In reply, the husband repeated the particulars above concerning the areas in which they wanted Carl to be able to make decisions by himself.

Step 3: Listing possible solutions: *"List as many possible solutions, suggested actions, or plans as you can that you think could solve the problem or help in solving the part you have chosen to work on. In this step, each of you simply tries to suggest as many actions or solutions as you can without commenting on them or evaluating them. The objective of this step is to state all of the possible solutions or actions you can. Evaluating them or judging them will come later. Go ahead now to list all actions or solutions that you can think of that might help in handling the part* (or parts) *of the problem you have chosen to work on."* (The pointer on the Step Indicator Sign is moved to Step 3.

The following were among the possible solutions suggested: to offer Carl choices, e.g., 'Would you like egg or cereal this morning?' 'Which book would you like to read—A, B, or C?' (suggested by W, the wife); to give Carl a choice and then have the father leave the room to decrease the likelihood of the father's making the choice for the boy (suggested by H, the husband); to send Carl to the library and let him decide which books to get (by H); to have Carl get out the food he wants when food is prepared (by H); to have Carl select his own clothes (by H); to let Carl decide what TV programs he wants to watch (by W); when Carl asks a question involving a decision that he can make himself, to turn the question back and to ask him to decide by himself (by H); and when Carl asks the father a question, the father is to stop and think before answering to avoid making the decision for the child (by H). Several times during the discussion the couple got off topic but they were promptly brought back by the red light or, this failing, by the coach's instruction.

Then the coach asked: *"Would you review your list of possible solutions so that each of you knows what has been suggested?"*

Following a summary by the wife, who had written down the solutions on a pad provided for this purpose, the coach then said the following: *"These suggestions are sufficient for you to move on to Step 4, where you will consider them and select one* (or more) *suitable for helping with the part of the problem you have chosen to work on."* (The Step Indicator is now moved to Step 4).

Step 4: Selecting the appropriate solution: *"Select those actions you think are best for addressing the part or parts of the problem chosen to work on in Step 2."*

In regard to reading, it was agreed that Carl should be given choices and allowed to make his own decisions concerning which books would be read to him. He was also to make his own selection of books while visiting the library. It was concluded that Carl could watch anything he wanted on TV until 9 P.M., after which time, on Fridays and Saturdays, when he stayed up later, the parents would give him a choice of programs from among those not involving violence. When Carl asked questions of his father, it was agreed that the father would stop and think before answering, again, to try to avoid making decisions for the child. In regard to the suggestion that the child be allowed to choose his own food, the wife objected because it would be difficult to do at breakfast; however, it was agreed that this could be done at lunch. In regard to going to the library, it was again affirmed that it was possible for the child to walk to the library since it was really not far and involved few streets to be crossed.

Following the discussion, the coach said: *"Have you agreed on your selection? Would you summarize briefly what you have selected?"*

The couple then summarized.

Step 5: Deciding action: what is to be done, who will do it, when will it be done, and how: *"Plan the detailed action you will need to carry out the alternatives just selected. Decide what is to be done, who will do it, when it will be done, and how. You will have discussed some of these details already, but make sure you state them all clearly now, so that each of you knows exactly what you have decided to do. The aim of this step is to clearly specify all of the actions needed to carry out the alternatives agreed to so that, if necessary, you could each carry out your decisions satisfactorily without requiring further discussion in the future."* (The pointer is moved to Step 5.)

Most of the details discussed in connection with Step 4 were affirmed, but there were some additional specifications. For example, in regard to the selection of TV programs it was agreed that the husband and the wife would decide what is violent, preferably in advance, by discussing the matter beforehand. However, if it turned out that a program was unexpectedly found to be violent when they were watching it, they agreed that they would simply turn off the TV or change channels.

There was also discussion of what would happen if Carl made a decision with which one or both of the parents disagreed. At first, the husband wished to provide some means of reversing the decision but the wife argued that Carl must be allowed to make his own decisions even if they are occasionally incorrect, by parental standards. Finally, with some reluctance, the husband agreed that Carl should be allowed to make decisions in the areas specified without veto. The husband suggested that he should somehow be reminded if he begins to question Carl concerning the wisdom of any decision. It was then agreed, at the wife's suggestion, that if the husband began to disagree with a decision Carl had made, the wife would remind the husband that they had 'made an agreement,' and this was to be a signal for the husband to back off.

At the conclusion of the discussion the coach asked: *"Are you clear regarding the details of each action you have agreed to? Are there any other details that you need to consider? Would you briefly summarize what you have decided to do regarding helping Carl make his own decisions?"*

The parents then gave a summary.

Commentary

The coaching procedure illustrated with couple B is typical inasmuch as the style was "tight," a neutral stance was taken throughout, a fair amount of corrective feedback was given in the form of red-light signals, indicating off-topic talk, and there was occasional intervening instruction.

However, the decision issue faced by couple B was not so typical as that faced by couple A. With couple A, the decision issue was capable of resolution with a single solution alternative whereas more than one solution alternative was appropriate for couple B. One reason for this difference is that the coach allowed more than one part to be specified for couple B in Step 2. Thus, instead of working only on ways to help Carl make his own decisions in regard to what to eat, what books to read, or what clothes to wear, etc., all were allowed as component parts to be worked on. Had the coach been less experienced in coaching and more uncertain concerning the nature of the decision problem or the partners' capability, he should have taken just one part rather than several. Ordinarily, coaching that allows for multiple components in the problem definition can easily become unmanageable for training purposes. In this instance, however, we have illustrated a decision issue for which all parts and solutions relate directly to the central decision theme—how to have the son make more of his own decisions—and, consequently, the inclusion of more than one decision component was not excessive.

Cases A and B illustrate two different decision structures, as depicted in Figure 7-1. Structure 1 characterizes the decision structure for case A and Structure 2 for case B. Structure 1 is a simple, ideal prototype and is probably the most common one, if a single decision part is selected to work on. Structure 2 is no doubt an important type that is characteristic of many decision issues. Because it consists essentially of multiple versions of Structure 1, Structure 2 can be simplified and made more manageable for coaching purposes simply by reducing the number of component parts. There are, of course, other decision structures.

The coaching instructions for the steps can affect how the decision structure is captured, as can the discretion of the coach in determining the specificity and number of components chosen to work on, in Step

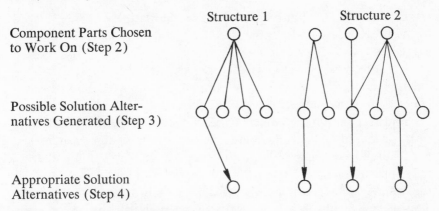

Component Parts Chosen
to Work On (Step 2)

Possible Solution Alter-
natives Generated (Step 3)

Appropriate Solution
Alternatives (Step 4)

FIGURE 7-1. **Two Decision Structures (——— stands for relevant and ———→ stands for selected)**

2, and the number and variety of solutions, in Steps 3 and 4. Ideally, the coach should grasp the decision structure he is working with early in the coaching process, select an appropriate part to work on, and guide the marital partners through it accordingly. This does happen and, of course, it can be exceedingly helpful in training. In some cases, however, it is not possible to anticipate all aspects of the decision structure. Even so, it is important for the coach to be aware that he is working within a decision structure and that his coaching behavior can influence the way the structure is worked through and the outcomes.

Information Display through Interview Guidance

Couples occasionally face what for them are very difficult life decisions relating to essentially nonrecurring, one-time issues (e.g., whether or not to separate, get divorced, have a child, adopt a child, take a job in a different community, or have a critical discretionary operation, such as sterilization). It is not at all uncommon for couples to have real problems with such life decisions but to have no special difficulty in making the smaller, every day decisions. The unusual complexity and important life consequences generally make these decisions unmanageable for some couples. If the partners are uncertain concerning how to resolve such a nonrecurring decision issue, have discussed it previously, and have not been able to reach agreement, the Information Display through Interview Guidance (IDIG) is an appropriate method to use. In IDIG, the interviewer takes a neutral position on the decision issue and assists the partners only in regard to the procedure by which they are to reach a mutually satisfactory agreement.

The objective of IDIG is to bring the decision response of the partners under the control of relevant information through the display of this information in a guided interview with the practitioner. Decisions are ordinarily much easier to reach if pertinent information is available. Such information here consists of the positive and negative consequences of following given possible solution alternatives, the preferences of partners for the solution options, as well as the willingness of each partner to adopt each alternative. Partners who have difficulty reaching decisions on nonrecurring issues often fail to display such information in their discussions because of such factors as inability to tolerate hearing unpleasant information, unwillingness to accept the other's point of view, dominance of the conversation by one so that the partner's point of view does not get expressed, or distorted presentation of information. The IDIG procedure allows for the systematic, step-by-step display of information relevant to the possible solution alternatives so that each partner can have his or her say and can attend to and understand the other's point of view without the simultaneous persuasion, disagreement, and misrepresentation that so often characterize discussions of such life decisions.

PROCEDURE

1. The interviewer explains that the purpose of the procedure is to help the partners reach a mutually satisfactory decision on the basis of careful consideration of relevant information. It is emphasized that the decision is theirs alone and that the interviewer will remain neutral throughout, assisting the partners only in regard to the method followed in reaching the decision. The procedure is described as consisting of interview guidance to draw out the pertinent information bearing on the decision issue.

2. The practitioner requests further specification of the decision issue, as necessary. The purpose, of course, is to make the decision issue as specific and manageable as possible. As in coaching, if there is more than one component, only one is selected, saving the others for subsequent decision making.

3. The interviewer requests possible solution alternatives for the decision component to be worked on, being sure that an adequate range is obtained, including disagreement resolution alternatives, if there has been prior disagreement on the issue. Again, alternatives are to be generated without evaluation, criticism, or judgment. Solution alternatives are written down for use in the next step.

4. In explaining the forthcoming information displays, the practitioner indicates that by directing questions at partners one at a time, he will solicit information on the consequences of following the alternatives, each partner's preferences for the alternatives, as well as his or her willingness to adopt each alternative. It is indicated that each partner will be allowed to speak in turn without comments or interruption by the other. Each spouse is then directly asked not to register complaints, persuade, or dispute points when the partner talks and, when his or her own turn comes, to present only the requested information, again without complaints or persuasion. However, the spouses are told that when one finishes, the other may ask questions for clarification. If at any point along the way a partner changes his position, he is encouraged to state this the next time he has a chance to speak.

5. In the information display, the practitioner proceeds systematically by asking the same question first of one partner and then of the other. He proceeds in this way throughout the topics, as suggested in Table 7-4. Thus, the coach begins by asking one partner what he or she regards as the positive consequences of following alternative A. Then the same question is directed to the other. Taking notes on the central points made for each topic by each spouse, the interviewer continues until each partner has had an opportunity to give the requested information on all topics.

TABLE 7-4. Topics and Order of Coverage for the Possible Solution Alternatives for the IDIG Procedure

| | POSSIBLE SOLUTION ALTERNATIVES | | | | | |
| | A | | B | | C | |
TOPICS	W	H	W	H	W	H
Consequences of Following the Alternative						
Positive	1*	2	5	6	9	10
Negative	3	4	7	8	11	12
Preference for the Alternative	13	14	15	16	17	18
Willingness to Adopt the Alternative	19	20	21	22	23	24

* Numbers refer to the order of taking up the topics for each spouse.

6. When the information display has been completed, the partners are asked if they have reached a decision and, if so, what it is. If the partners have not reached a decision at this point, the coach reviews his notes and summarizes the main points. If one alternative appears to be the best, given all the information, as is often the case, the practitioner points this out. The agreement of the partners concerning a solution response should, hopefully, be consistent with the information disclosed by the response display. In those unusual cases where it is not, the inconsistency can be explored to determine its basis, which often turns out to be relevant information.

If no decision has been reached, the practitioner asks the couple if they would agree to have him act as a mediator to help them try to resolve the disagreement. If so, the interviewer then pursues such options as compliant resolution, compromise, trade, delegation of the decision, or resolution by default. In his role as mediator, the interviewer is considerably more active than before in that he is endeavoring to bring the partners together on the basis of the information he has and what he considers to be feasible.[4] The practitioner still serves as procedural guide, however, and remains as neutral as possible. If resolution is reached, the interviewer goes to the next step. If there is still no resolution, however, the interviewer tries to formulate a non-resolution understanding, such as that described in the Disagreement Resolution Procedure (Appendix H).

CASE EXAMPLE

Mr. G, a professional, and his wife, a waitress, were far apart in education, social background, and interests. The husband was oriented toward intellectual and cultural matters whereas his wife found these boring and uninteresting. Mrs. G felt inferior to her husband, had a history of being anxious and upset, and was lonely and unhappy in the marriage. Mr. G acted superior to his wife, spoke to her condescendingly, hardly let her speak at all, and, when she did, paid little attention to what she said. He was dissatisfied because of his wife's complaints and was optimistic that, with professional help, their relationship could be improved.

In the first interview, the couple indicated that they were having

---

[4] Pruitt and Johnson (1970) found in a laboratory experiment that the suggestion by a mediator of a point of settlement halfway between the positions of two negotiators produced substantial concessions and that intervention by a mediator relieved any sense of personal weakness that otherwise may arise in making concessions.

difficulty deciding where to live. Mrs. G wanted to move to Stockton-ville, a city of approximately 250,000, which was the locale of her childhood home, whereas Mr. G wished to continue living in York-burg, a university town of approximately 50,000 located in an area having educational, intellectual, and cultural advantages.

Although the decision issue was specific to start with—whether to live in Stocktonville or Yorkburg—it was not as innocent as it seemed. It turned out that there was great conflict in the marriage, and it became increasingly clear that physical separation of the couple at this point might be the beginning of marital dissolution. With the couple's consent, the IDIG Procedure was employed to disclose rele-vant information bearing on the decision issue of where to live, the results of which are summarized briefly.

The positive consequences for the wife of Stocktonville were that she could be reunited with her friends, relatives, and parents, could again frequent familiar haunts (e.g., bars and dancing places), and again could get a job in the bar where she had worked prior to mar-riage. The husband saw no advantages for him in living in Stockton-ville and preferred to stay in Yorkburg because he could remain on his job, which he liked, could begin to develop friends with interests similar to his own, and could continue to take advantage of the ed-ucational and cultural opportunities in the area. The wife saw es-sentially no advantages for her in remaining in Yorkburg. She disliked the town, was lonely, had no friends, and felt alienated. The husband objected to moving because he would lose his job and might have difficulty in getting another one as good. He did not want to move away from the advantages of the educational community. Further-more, he disliked his wife's family and friends, and, it turned out, resented the idea that she would probably be associating again with some of her former male friends, of whom he seemed jealous. In regard to preferences, the wife clearly preferred Stocktonville whereas the husband unequivocally desired to remain in Yorkburg. As for willingness to adopt the alternatives, the results were equally clear; the wife finally admitted that she refused to continue living in York-burg, and the husband finally acknowledged that, all things con-sidered, it would be impossible for him to leave Yorkburg for Stock-tonville.

When the information display was completed and the partners were asked if they had made a decision, it was quietly but dramatically evident from the information shared that they had; the wife would move to Stocktonville and the husband would remain in Yorkburg. The consequence of the decision was equally evident—the physical

separation would coincide with marital separation and would probably
lead ultimately to divorce. She seemed relieved and he resigned as
they stood up, said good by, and left.

In this case, the IDIG Procedure structured the husband's responding so that the wife had an opportunity to express her opinions
fully and to have them heard completely by her husband, probably
for the first time. The procedure also highlighted for the wife the
husband's unwillingness to change, given the knowledge he had just
gained of his wife's strong preferences.

Assisted Decision Making

By joining the marital partners as an active participant, the
practitioner can freely contribute his own opinions to those offered
by the partners. Such "assisted" decision making by the practitioner
is an obvious departure from the practitioner neutrality emphasized
previously. This method of couple decision making requires the prior
consent of the partners and should be adopted only when both the
partners and the practitioner believe that the helping person's participation would be valuable. Assisted decision making provides an opportunity for the helping person to model use of the stepwise procedure and the selected responses he himself makes to each step in the
decision making. Among the possible uses of the method is in work
on nonrecurring decision issues for which the couple desires the
helper's substantive contribution to the decision or when IDIG is
found to be too demanding for the partners and they still cannot make
a decision.

The practitioner participates in all steps of the decision making,
but only after the partners have made their contribution to each step.
Special attention is given to carrying out decision making using the
stepwise approach, thus making sure that relevant topics are taken
up one at a time and that the information deriving from them influences subsequent deliberations. If the partners disagree on options, the
practitioner then obtains information such as that sought in IDIG
(and outlined in Table 7-4). The function of the helper entails openly
sharing information, giving his opinions, and, when appropriate, at
the evaluation and solution-selection steps, giving advice and gently
persuading partners to adopt a solution that, in his judgment, is indicated as the best one available by the information at hand. The practitioner must recognize that his influence with many individuals may
be exaggerated. In consequence, he should avoid pressing partners

to adopt a decision response that is clearly not preferred by them and that they might adhere to afterwards only half-heartedly at best. In the final analysis, the decision response selected must be the one preferred by the marital partners. If the partners do adopt a solution at variance with the one advocated by the practitioner, he should defer graciously and without hesitation, refrain from reopening discussion on the matter except at the request of the partners, and close the session positively and with no ill feeling.

Other Procedures

Although the main procedures for work on marital decision making have now been presented, there are others that may have value in special cases. These include audiotape and videotape replay and explication, corrective feedback and instructions, response contingencies, and exchange systems. These were discussed earlier in Chapter 4 in relationship to the modification of marital communication, but they may be applied equally well to special problems of marital decision making. When decision making may be traced to decision shortcomings of one partner, it may be appropriate in exceptional cases to employ the methods of D'Zurilla and Goldfried (1971) or of Briscoe, Hoffman, and Bailey (1975), in which people are trained individually in problem solving. The IDIG and assisted decision-making procedures may also be adapted to work with individuals who have decision difficulties involving recurring or nonrecurring decision issues. Finally, there will be occasions when virtually any modification procedure may have special application to an unusual feature of marital decision making. It should not be forgotten that the methods described earlier as especially applicable to marital decision making are part of a larger interventional technology with which the practitioner must be familiar and that marital decision making is but one aspect of the lives of marital partners.

Couple E: "I've Told You This for Twenty Years"

THE FOLLOWING transcript is one of several response display discussions obtained in assessment for Mr. and Mrs. E, a middle-class couple in their mid-forties with three children in late adolescence and one four-year-old. In this display, the couple discussed "The Concerns You Have in Handling Your Children," a topic selected for discussion because early information caused the practitioner to suspect that the couple's communication difficulties might relate to their child management.

The transcript illustrates that the partners communication difficulties did indeed involve disagreements about how the children should be handled. The transcription also illustrates clear-cut shortcomings in decision making in regard to these disagreements. Most importantly in terms of marital communication, however, the transcript illustrates a variety of communication difficulties, many of which may be seen as arising from or being maintained by the verbal behavior of the partner. This couple displayed similar difficulties of verbal behavior when discussing other topics. (For further commentary on the use of this response display in assessment for this couple, see Appendix C.)

The segments in brackets are instances of partner verbal behavior that ilustrate categories of verbal behavior presented in Chapter 2. Note that the bracketed segments have been selected for illustration purposes. Not all possible examples have been identified. Any category rating with a schedule such as the Verbal Problem Checklist would be based on all the information for a given response display. The categories associated with the numbers for brackets are given in Appendix B, "Code for Instances of Verbal Categories, Couple E."

(The asterisks and the short dashes beneath them extending to the right are for purposes of the coding described in Appendix D.[1])

H: I think personally, Mary, we've done a pretty good job with our children because I do feel that we've gotten genuine compliments from other people on * their behavior.

W: [₁Well, then, that must be important to you.]

H: Not as important as I feel that it is a sign * that we are achieving something. We have managed to get one of them into college. I don't know how the hell he got there, but, anyway, we have managed to get one of them there. (*Laughs.*)

I think that * we have four completely different entities and we realize this, but [₂where we really differ is on whether the whole household should stop and pay attention to a four-and-a-half-year-old * who yells, "Mom, Mom, Mom," at the slightest inclination of his mind, and I don't think that the whole household should cease . . .]

W: [₃(*Interrupting.*)] [₄I don't either.]

H: [₅ . . . to carry on while this kid stands there and * has a "hairy" in the middle of the floor.]

W: [₆(*Interrupting.*)] [₇I don't either.] [₈He didn't really have a "hairy" in the middle of the floor. He was coming in the door.]

H: [₉Well, and then the next situation is that, of late, you've thrown it up * to me that I have seemed to be siding with the oldest child . . . ah . . . constantly. . . .]

W: [₁₀(*Interrupting.*)] What do you mean by "siding"?

H: Well, that I seem to be talking to him and getting along * with him and doing this, that, and the other thing whereas a year ago you told me that I should do this and I should do that and the other thing with him and that I should try to get along with him better and so, okay, I took your * advice, and I did what you said should be done and I did my best to get closer to him. I let him have more leeway and didn't bite his head off as much, and * [₁₁now, I'm accused of playing favorites.]

W: [₁₂No, I never said you were playing favorites.]

H: Well, that's the impression I got from what you said.

W: No, I didn't mean you were playing favorites.

H: All right, now we're having a specific * problem with child number 2. Apparently child number 2 gave you a lot of problems this afternoon.

W: [₁₃No, he didn't give me a lot, I just said that I had a discussion with him.]

H: Ummmmmmmmm. * (*Silence.*) Presumably you got your point across, but at the same time he probably went away mad . . . not * any the wiser.

[1] The asterisks mark twelve-second intervals; the short dashes beneath asterisks mark faults of one or both partners for such intervals.

W: Why?

H: [14 Because you probably didn't tell him why I didn't * want him to drive the car.]

W: (*Exasperated.*) I didn't know why.

H: Well, the reason I didn't tell you why was . . .

W: [15(*Interrupting.*)] [16 You did tell me why.]

H: . . . because it would have caused an argument.

W: [17 You did tell me why.]

H: [18 He's gonna kill himself with it, for one thing, and, the other thing is the car can't stand his type of driving.] *

W: [19(*Interrupting.*)] Okay.

H: [20 I don't feel like doing a clutch job on it right now and the main bearing is about to go out of it, so [21 I don't want him to drive it, okay?] I've had enough report from the other kids * in the area that he goes to school just as Douglas did with the other one and this is a machine which is an absolute lethal machine. This is why I sold * the other one.]²

W: Richard, why are we having a discussion about the car?

H: Because the problem was that I had said that I didn't want him to drive that car.

W: That's right. That's right, and you don't. * And you told me because that some bearing number 006543 was going or something.

H: [22(*Interrupting.*)] Central bearing.

W: Now that's all you have to tell him.

H: Well, the other thing was a disciplinary prob*lem which you don't like the word of but the fact of the matter is that he's been going down and showing off the car to people and showing . . .

W: [23(*Interrupting.*) Where?]

H: . . . them just how fast it will do.

W: Where?

H: [24 Wherever there happened to be an audience.]

W: How do you know? *

H: [25 Because I've been told.]

W: [26 Oh, my. They could be telling you anything.]

H: [27 They could.] They could. (*Silence.*) But, ah . . .

W: You always tell the children not to repeat things unless * they see it themselves or you know not to . . . and yet now you . . .

H: [28(*Interrupting.*)] [29 Well, I've had two adults tell me too, okay?]

W: [30 Well, I don't care whether they are children or adults. *]

H: [31 I've had two adults tell me that they'd seen him driving that car like a maniac.] (*Silence.*) [32 So I think that settles that argument there.]

W: . . . and I suppose . . .

H: [33(*Interrupting.*)] [34 The next question . . .]

W: [35(*Interrupting.*)]. . . you agree with them? *

² End of bracket 20, which embraces the beginning and end of bracket 21.

H: [36 No, not necessarily.] [37 If he wants to kill himself ah . . .]

W: Did you agree with them?

H: No, I did not. I wasn't in a position to agree or disagree because I hadn't observed him driving the * car. Okay? [38 The next thing is . . .]

W: [39 (*Interrupting.*)] Well, even if you had I wouldn't have agreed with them.

H: [40 No, you fly into the defensive.]

W: [41 No,] I would have just said, "Thank you very much, I'm glad to know."

H: Oh, I * said that, yeah, like "Thanks for telling me, I'll look into it. That's fine." That's all I said. [42 The next thing is that] the fourteen-year-old you say has had a complete personality change * in . . .

W: [43 (*Interrupting.*)] He has.

H: . . . the last six or eight months and [44 I keep telling you that the best way to fix it is to give him a belt with the back of your hand sometime and he'll pay attention to you for a good long time] because * it will so surprise him; but, at the same time, not by belting him on the face necessarily to hurt him but to show him that when you say something you mean bus*iness and you want his respect. [45 You don't want his fear, you want his respect.] [46 You, at the moment, are getting absolutely no respect from him whatsoever.] [47 You deserve a lot * more respect than he's giving you.] [48 In my opinion, the only way you're going to get this respect is with a short, fast piece of corporal punishment] * . . . and you disagree with it. I will say this. Don't do it with the hand with the rings on because you'll lay his face open. * But give him the back of your hand right across the mouth and then [49 you won't get any more vituperance] from him and [50 you will have gained his respect because, right now * he thinks he has the upper hand.]

W: I don't think . . .

H: [51 (*Interrupting.*)] He doesn't.

W: [52 . . . I don't think he thinks he has the upper hand.]

H: [53 Mary, he does not expect you to come back with anything like that at all. Now, my father spanked me a number of times, * as fathers will do, and I gained some experience from it. I think my mother belted me three times * in my early teens and believe you me I learned a lot more from that.]

W: Um-hm.

H: [54 A lot more respect from that than all the thrashings that any of my teachers or my father could have * given me. I learned a respect . . . of her that I couldn't have learned otherwise. I've heard of it being done for girls— * this is something out of my realm and I'm not in a position to talk about that, but [55 I suggest to you that the reason why you don't want to do it is because it was never done to you.] * Have you noticed me jump on the kids the last little while when [56 they've given you vituperance] in front of me?

W: [57 What do you mean by "jump on" them?] *

H: Bring them up to a halt. Bring your attention to it. Including Fred.

W: Um-hm. [58 But "bring their attention to * it" is different from what you just said, though.]

H: I didn't belt Fred, no. I just told him that he should go over and tell you he was sorry. He didn't mean to speak to you that way.

W: [59(*Interrupting.*)] [60 No, "Bring their * attention to it" is different from the first of the two phrases you used before that, in my opinion . . .]

H: (*Sighing.*) [61 Well, not wishing to use the muscle on them at the * time, not feeling in the position, not feeling well enough to use the muscle on them, I haven't done so . . . It's a physical and mental strain, I think, * on the parent to use the muscle on a child.]

W: I don't even like the expression.

H: Well, uh . . . all right. Laurence * called me up on the telephone and said [62 ah . . . that you were going to do this and that; you wouldn't let him do that and so on and so forth] and [63 expected me to rescind your decisions] * . . . and [64 I not only didn't rescind your decisions] I added a little bit more on top of it.

W: (*Sarcastically.*) Good for you.

H: Right? Wasn't that the thing to do?

W: I don't know * whether it was the thing to do or not.

H: [65 Wasn't he trying to play you against me or me against you? . . .]

W: [66(*Interrupting.*)] I have no idea. I have no idea what he was trying to do.

H: Don't you recall the situation?

W: Um-hm. [67 Very well,] but I don't know what he was trying to do.

H: [68 He was trying to get * me to get on the phone with you and tell you that you were being too harsh on him and that he should be able to go to the movie with his girl friend and do what he wanted to do, if you re*call it. And I said, no, I didn't want him to go and I didn't want him to take the car and, furthermore, if I heard any more about it he was going to want for quite a while.] [69 Do you recall that?]

W: (*Exasperated.*) I told you that I * did.

H: But [70 you don't appreciate the fact that I dealt with him in that way.]

W: No, because afterwards I had some second thoughts about it, but, yet, I don't think that you could have done it any other way. *

H: Do you give me credit for the fact that I backed you up?

W: [71 Well, you'd back me up in that instance no matter what it was.]

H: Sorry. Would you * run that one by me again?

W: You would back me up in that type of thing no matter what it was or who it was.

H: I feel that parents should stand together when it comes to a decision to be made about the children.

W: That's because it was * something that I was doing that you would do . . . but you see, when it comes to something that I do that you don't agree with, then you don't, you know.

H: All right. [72 Do you feel that we've been harmful to the children in the past in saying that * ... ah ... just to make up, a case, "Okay you've been bad, you can't go out to have fun, to enjoy yourself * for the next three days," and then a couple of days later we say that "Well, you've been particularly good, we'll let you . . .]

W: [73 (*Interrupting.*)] [74 No, I don't think that's good, no.]

H: . . . off for good behavior."

W: [75 But I think it would be better if you said they weren't going out * one night rather than three and then backing down.]

H: (*Correcting wife.*) [76 *Than* backing down.]

W: [77 *Than* backing down.]

H: [78 You think we should back down.]

W: [79 No,] I'm saying that it * would be better to say that, you know, they're not going out for *one* night and sticking to it than picking *three* nights out of the blue for no reason and then . . . you know.

H: [80 (*Interrupting.*)] . . . and then letting them off on good behavior.

W: Right . . . okay? *

H: [81 So, you agree then, that child management is a situation where we both should be . . . ah . . . consis*tent?]

W: Well, I think it for a . . . [82 yes, I do.] [83 And I also think that you have it blown up into something that is ridiculous.]

H: You think it's a lot bigger item with me than it is to you. * And, yet, you complain to me that the children have no respect for you whatsoever.

W: [84 Well, if I can't complain to you who am I going to complain to?]

H: [85 The children.]

W: [86 Oh, well, then you don't want to be complained to.]

H: [87 No, I'm not saying * that at all.] I'm saying to you that if you feel that you don't have the respect of child A, that you should tell child A that you don't feel that you're getting the respect that you as a mother deserve. *

W: You're saying, too. [88 You're saying, too, that a discussion is a complaint.]

H: No, not necessarily at all because a discussion can * be a compliment, too.

W: [89 Well, let's say that if I can't discuss them with you, who am I going to discuss them with?]

H: Let me put it to you this way. * I consider that you have dealt with the situation by the time I come home . . .

W: [90 (*Interrupting.*)] . . . [91 so that you don't want it discussed.]

H: [92 No, no,] let me finish. [93 Let me define it properly.] * [94 I come home at five o'clock . . .]

W: [95 Don't go into *detail*.] (*Exasperated.*) I know when you come home.

H: . . . [96 and you've had a problem with a child at three o'clock and you tell me what the child did at three o'clock, * this is a form of a complaint to me.]

W: [97(*Interrupting.*)] [98 No, it isn't.]

H: . . . [99 and to me, I resent it in this regard that, okay, you're telling me what took * place at three o'clock] and [100 I get the opinion that you are disappointed that I don't do something about it . . .]

W: [101(*Interrupting.*)] [102 No!]

H: . . . [103 and yet I don't feel that I should punish a child for something they did two hours before.]

W: I'm not asking *_ y_ou to, I'm merely telling you what's gone on, and we're back the same old place where we started and that is that we can't discuss . . .

H: [104(*Interrupting.*)] What would you like to do about it?

W: [105 Just a minute!] [106 You can't discuss anything with you because you don't know how. *]

H: [107(*Interrupting.*)] What would you like me to do?

W: . (*Exasperated and raising voice.*) [108 Nothing! Not a thing.] I'm just telling you. (*With evident emotion.*) [109 If I win a million dollars, I won't tell you.]

H: [110 That's not the point.]

W: (*Raising voice further.*) [111 Well, it is, * because it will be complete.] (*Voice shaking and crying.*) It's the same thing.

H: (*Softly.*) No, I . . .

W: [112(*Interrupting.*)] [113 Yes, it is!] (*Crying.*)

H: (*Softly.*) I don't think you need to be emotional about it. * [114 Then why tell me?]

W: Why shouldn't I? [115 If I can't tell you who am I going to tell?]

H: [116 Tell the child at the time.]

W: (*Shrieking.*) [117 Well, I do!] [118 Well, then it's never supposed *_ to_ be discussed. Is that it?]

H: [119 No, I didn't say that.]

W: Well, then okay. (*Voice quavering.*) [120 Maybe one of them will have their appendix out and I won't bother telling you.]

H: [121 That's being ridiculous.]

W: (*Shrilly.*) [122 No, it isn't.]

H: [123 Let's get back on the track.] *

W: [124 It's the same thing.]

H: [125 The issue is that complaints are raised . . . quite some time after the fact . . .*]

W: (*Shrilly, exasperated, and loudly.*) [126 It's not a complaint!] I just finished telling you that!

H: How am I supposed to know?

W: Oh. (*Exasperated.*)

H: [127 How am I supposed to know?]

W: I don't know how you're supposed to know. * I suppose I have to tell you ahead of time this isn't a complaint. [128 In other words, you really don't want to discuss the children.]

H: [129 That's not the fact at all.]

W: [130Well, it must be!] Because apparently, if it's discussing, it's complaining. *

H: [131If you told me that child A did so and so and said so and so and that you objected to it and that you had done such and such about it ah . . .]

W: [132(*Interrupting.*)] [133Okay, * if they won a scholarship then I don't like that so when I tell you that I'm complaining.] (*Raising voice.*) It's the same thing.

H: (*Angrily.*) [134Let me finish.]

W: You're just going on and on about telling the same old thing over and over. * ___

H: [135Would you let me finish, please?]

W: [136You finished ten months ago.] [137You're telling me the same thing.] (*Sniffing.*)

H: [138I would like to know if you're bringing it up as a topic of conversation, * just what you did about it.]

W: [139No, I'm not, I'm . . .]

H: [140(*Interrupting.*)] [141I think I'm entitled to know what you did about it.]

W: (*Loudly.*) [142No!] I don't think it's necessary. (*Voice quavering.*) [143I think you're entitled to know.]

H: [144Well, then I think that's very poor child management.]

W: [145I think you * are entitled to know but I don't think it's necessary.] Well, then we just don't discuss it, that's what that ends up as. [146You don't want to hear about them.]

H: [147It's not that I don't want to hear about them.] I have to hear about * them. They're my children.

W: [148Well, no, you don't.] [149I won't tell you any more, because I'll be complaining.]

H: [150Then you will be . . . ah . . . then abrogating your responsibility as a parent.]

W: [151(*Interrupting.*)] [152No, I won't.] [153You just told me you don't * want to hear about it, so how can I . . .]

H: [154(*Interrupting.*)] [155I did not say that.] [156I did not . . .]

W: (*Shrilly.*) [157You did!]

H: [158I did not say that.]

W: (*Emphatically.*) [159Yes, you did.]

H: [160If you are * going to bring it up as a topic of conversation you mention the . . . you mention the problem and you mention how you dealt with it and then the whole thing will be taken care of.]

W: [161No, I'm not mentioning it] and [162I'm * not . . . I'm not even going to discuss it . . .] (*Silence.*) If you have to take everything . . .

H: [163(*Interrupting.*)] Once again . . .

W: [164 . . . that's discussed as a complaint * well, go and take it.]

H: [165Once again I feel like you've thrown a bomb . . . and run like hell.]

W: [166 (*With emotion.*) No, I haven't . . .] * ___

H: [167Well, you're running behind a veil of tears as far as I'm concerned.]

W: [168 I'm just plain not going to tell ya.]

H: [169 I think you've run behind a veil of tears] and [170 I don't think you are prepared to discuss the subject at all] and [171 I don't think you want any help on the topic at *_all_] and [172 I think that you're particularly annoyed by the fact that you don't have the children's respect] and [173 you understand that you don't have the children's respect] and [174 above all you're not prepared to do anything about it. *] I think as their mother you are entitled to their respect, [175 but you have to earn that respect. You don't earn that respect by being * _inconsistent_ with punishment or ignoring the fact that they've done something wrong. You do not . . . you do _not_ earn their respect . . . And I'm telling you this * and I've told you this for twenty years.] [176 I think it's very, very important, vitally important, to the child and to its upbringing] and I think *_that_ [177 you're abrogating your . . . your whole responsibility as a parent if you don't point the problem out to the child * at the time . . .]

W: [178(*Interrupting.*)] Did I say I didn't? [179 I never said that I didn't.] (*Voice quavering increasingly.*) Just because I took the . . . about one half minute to tell you what I told you and it's gone on to something of a half an hour * . . . [180 and you presume a whole lot of nothing.]

H: [181This has gone on for years and years and years.]

W: Ya, well all right. [182You just presume your whole lot of nothing.]

H: [183Well, I don't *_presume that I'm going to be doing any punishment of the children.]

W: [184(*Interrupting.*)] (*Exasperated.*) I'm not asking you to! And I never have.

H: [185 Okay. All right.]

W: So therefore, [186 you're right back when you started] [187 that I can't tell you then.]

H: [188 We're agreed * on that] but [189 what I would like . . .]

W: [190(*Interrupting.*)] [191 I always . . .] [192 we don't have to agree on it because we always did.]

H: [193 All I'm asking from you in _addition_, all I'm asking from you, in addition, * is what you did about . . .]

W: [194(*Interrupting.*)] [195Well, if I just can't tell you something for conversation or you know, forget it.]

H: [196 I don't want to hear the conversation.]

W: [197No, that's what I told you.] *___

H: [198 If you can't give me the complete sentence, don't start it.]

W: [199 I gave you a complete sentence.] [200You don't want to hear it, that's the meat of the whole thing. *]

H: [201Well, okay, it's like sitting down to a meal and you tantalize me with a little bit of information and then you don't finish the meal.]

W: [₂₀₂ I'm not doling out a little bit of information. I'm just, you know . . .] *___

H: [₂₀₃ But you get overly emotional about it.]

W: [₂₀₄ No, I don't.] Did I get emotional about it when I told you? [₂₀₅ I'm mad at *you,* that's what I'm mad at.] (*With strong feeling.*)

H: [₂₀₆ I know you're mad at me . . .]

W: (*Voice quavering.*) [₂₀₇ Well, all right.]

H: [₂₀₈ I understand that,] but [₂₀₉ the fact that you're mad at me * is the fact that you are also mad at yourself . . .]

W: [₂₁₀ No, I'm not mad at myself.]

H: [₂₁₁ . . . Mad at yourself because you don't have the children's respect.]

W: [₂₁₂ I'm not mad.] [₂₁₃ What are you talking about respect for?] * (*Silence.*) What I was talking about had nothing to do with respect whatsoever.

H: [₂₁₄ I feel that you do not have the children's respect.]

W: Well, you're going off what we're talking about now.

H: [₂₁₅ This is a great deal of the problem that you are now * at the moment experiencing. You're facing with them the fact that] [₂₁₆ they have not been dealt with properly by you . . .]

W: [₂₁₇ (*Interrupting.*)] [₂₁₈ In the first place who said it was a problem? I didn't.]

H: I did.

W: You did?

H: I did. *

W: [₂₁₉ Oh, all right.]

H: [₂₂₀ I recognize it as a problem.] (*Silence.*) [₂₂₁ Now, have we agreed to disagree or are we agreed * that something else should be done about it . . .]

W: [₂₂₂ (*Interrupting.*)] [₂₂₃ No, I just don't agree.] [₂₂₄ I'm not going to bother telling you any more, that's all.]

H: [₂₂₅ That's not bother.]

W: (*Whining, loudly.*) [₂₂₆ Well, it is.]

H: [₂₂₇ (*Silence.*) Well, I'm . . . (*Sighing.*)]

W: [₂₂₈ I just won't . . .]

H: I'm not going to repeat myself. * I think I've told you perfectly well right there and then what I think the situation should be done.

W: [₂₂₉ No,] because you see, [₂₃₀ you don't know how to discuss anything.]

H: [₂₃₁ That's a generality.]

W: [₂₃₂ No, it isn't. *] It's just as plain as the paper on the wall. [₂₃₃ You don't.] (*Silence.*)

H: [₂₃₄ I think we recognized the problem.] I think that we discussed the problem . . .

W: [₂₃₅ (*Interrupting.*)] [₂₃₆ I didn't have a problem.]

H: [₂₃₇ . . . and we have no * solution to it.]

W: [₂₃₈ I didn't have a problem.]

H: You don't have a problem. I see . . . [239 well, I'm telling you do have a problem.]

W: [240 All right. I do then.]

H: [241 You're not prepared, then, to recognize it * nor are you prepared to do anything about it.]

W: [242 That's right. Nor am I prepared to tell you either. (*Silence.*)] * [243 You want me to take the whole thing as a complaint.]

H: (*Silence.*) (*Sighing.*) Well, * . . . [244 I suppose I'll hear about it by other devious means then,] and I won't know what the heck to do about it.

W: [245 Hear about what?]

H: [246 It's too late, nine times out of ten, too late to deal with . . .]

W: [247 (*Interrupting, angrily.*)] [248 I'm not asking you to do * anything about it.]

H: [249 If a situation takes place whereby you are being injured and you don't know that you're being injured and you don't take . . .]

W: [250 Well, if I don't know it, I can't be injured, can I?]

H: [251 Yes, * you can.]

W: [252 No, I can't.] (*Peeved.*) Not in that instance.

H: [253 Mary, if you don't have the respect of your children, they don't have respect for themselves.]

W: [254 You are the one that's talking of respect. I'm not. * It had nothing to do with respect, about what I was talking about.]

H: [255 Well, they don't swear at me.]

W: [256 Well, did I say they swore at me?]

H: [257 Yup.]

W: Oh.

H: You told me quite a few times they swore at you.

W: [258 (*Interrupting.*)] [259 I'm not telling you about quite * a few times, I'm telling you about the one instance.]

H: They wouldn't dare swear at me and [260 they know damned well they wouldn't.]

W: [261 I'm talking about the one incident.]

H: Well . . .

W: So, anyway.

H: One particular * incident isn't going to help when you've got so many children in twenty years of experience with them.

W: [262 Yah, well then we don't have to tell you it, do we?] [263 So we won't.]

H: Well, * that brings us right back to the other serious bone of contention then in the marriage is the fact that [264 you are not prepared to come to grips with the situation of child . . .]

W: [265 (*Interrupting.*)] [266 That's right.]

H: . . . management. *

W: [267 I didn't say that.]

H: [268 Well, you just gave me twenty minutes of it.]

W: [269 No, I haven't.] I never said I didn't come to grips with it. *

H: [270 What's your solution then?]

W: I don't want a solution at the moment. I didn't ask for a solution.

H: [271 Well, I'd like a solution.]

W: To what? *___

H: [272 To the children's lack of respect of you.]

W: [273 Well, you're . . . because] [274 you're going off on a tangent on that.]

H: [275 I'm not going to pound it into them because you can't pound respect into somebody. You can't * buy respect, you have to earn it.]

W: (*Peeved, in monotone.*) [276 Well, how do you earn it?]

H: [277 By not letting them get away with the dickens.] Like I told you before, the boys are going *_to_ test you. They test me. Just give them so much rope . . .

W: [278 Well, you can certainly recognize it because in your mind everybody's testing you, so * of course they are.]

H: [279 No, they're not.]

W: [280 Yes, they are.]

H: [281 No, they're not.]

W: I don't go around thinking that everybody's testing me all day long.

H: (*Silence.*) (*Resigned tone.*) [282 Well, that ends that one. *]

Code for Instances of Verbal Categories, Couple E

EACH NUMBER REFERS to a segment of partner verbal behavior given in the foregoing transcript. The categories of verbal behavior referred to here are those presented in Chapter 2.

The segments are given for illustrative purposes to familiarize the reader further with the categories. It is important to realize that the segments marked are not all those that could be identified, that one segment may illustrate more than one category of verbal behavior, and that the segments are definitely not adequate code units for purposes of research or systematic evaluation.

1. Other content shifting.
2. Negative talk surfeit in the form of faulting.
3. Obtrusion.
4. Agreement.
5. Rapid latency.
6. Obtrusion.
7. Agreement.
8. Disagreement and quibbling.
9. Other content persistence and faulting.
10. Obtrusion.
11. Faulting and overgeneralization.
12. Disagreement and quibbling.
13. Disagreement and quibbling.
14. Faulting.
15. Obtrusion.
16. Illogical comment considering that W just said she didn't know why.
17. Redundant information.
18. Possibly overgeneralization.
19. Obtrusion.
20. Overresponsiveness.
21. Redundant information.
22. Obtrusion.
23. Obtrusion.
24. Poor referent specification.
25. Questionable referent specification.
26. Overgeneralization.
27. Agreement.
28. Obtrusion.
29. Improved referent specification.
30. Faulting, quibbling, and illogical inasmuch as W had earlier

asked for more information about how H knew that the boy was showing off the car to people.

31. Improved referent specification.
32. Dogmatic statement.
33. Obtrusion.
34. Topic shifting.
35. Obtrusion and topic content persistence.
36. Disagreement.
37. Presumptive attribution.
38. Cueing.
39. Obtrusion.
40. Faulting.
41. Disagreement.
42. Cueing.
43. Obtrusion.
44. Dogmatic statement and possibly redundant information.
45. Dogmatic statement.
46. Faulting.
47. Possibly overgeneralization.
48. Dogmatic statement.
49. Pedantry.
50. Presumptive attribution and, considering all that H just said, topic content persistence and overresponsiveness.
51. Obtrusion.
52. Disagreement and, possibly, presumptive attribution.
53. Content persistence, dogmatic assertion, and overresponsiveness.
54. Content persistence, dogmatic assertion, and overresponsiveness.
55. Presumptive attribution.
56. Pedantry.
57. Quibbling.
58. Quibbling.
59. Obtrusion.
60. Disagreement and quibbling.
61. Pedantic statements.
62. Poor referent specification.
63. Pedantry.
64. Pedantry.
65. Presumptive attribution.
66. Obtrusion.
67. Acknowledgment.
68. Better referent specification.
69. Redundant information.
70. Fault.
71. Lack of positive talk.
72. Temporal remoteness, in this case, a hypothetical case involving the past.
73. Obtrusion.
74. Agreement.
75. Some disagreement and quibbling.
76. Faulting.
77. Agreement.
78. Illogical statement.
79. Disagreement.
80. Obtrusion.
81. Presumptive attribution and, possibly, illogical statement, in view of what W just said.
82. Agreement.
83. Fault.
84. Illogical statement.
85. Illogical statement.
86. Illogical statement.
87. Disagreement.
88. Illogical statement.
89. Illogical statement.
90. Obtrusion.
91. Presumptive attribution.
92. Disagreement.
93. Cueing.
94. Content persistence.
95. Cueing.
96. Content persistence and overresponsiveness.
97. Obtrusion.
98. Disagreement.
99. Possibly some faulting.
100. Possibly presumptive attribution.

101. Obtrusion.
102. Disagreement.
103. Content persistence.
104. Obtrusion.
105. Cueing.
106. Faulting.
107. Obtrusion.
108. Illogical statement and affective talk.
109. Threat and affective talk.
110. Disagreement.
111. Disagreement and affective talk.
112. Obtrusion.
113. Disagreement and affective talk.
114. Content persistence.
115. Illogical statement.
116. Content persistence.
117. Affective talk.
118. Illogical statement.
119. Disagreement.
120. Threat.
121. Fault.
122. Disagreement and affective talk.
123. Cueing.
124. Content persistence.
125. Content persistence.
126. Disagreement, affective talk, and quibbling.
127. Redundant information.
128. Presumptive attribution and illogical statement.
129. Disagreement.
130. Disagreement.
131. Content persistence.
132. Obtrusion.
133. Illogical statement.
134. Cueing.
135. Cueing.
136. Fault.
137. Affective talk and fault.
138. Cueing and content persistence.
139. Disagreement.
140. Obtrusion.
141. Cueing and content persistence.
142. Disagreement and affective talk.
143. Agreement with statement 141, but illogical in view of statement 142 and the next statement.
144. Fault and illogical statement.
145. Redundant statement.
146. Fault.
147. Disagreement.
148. Disagreement.
149. Threat and illogical statement.
150. Fault.
151. Obtrusion.
152. Disagreement.
153. Misrepresentation.
154. Obtrusion.
155. Disagreement.
156. Redundant information.
157. Disagreement and affective talk.
158. Disagreement.
159. Disagreement.
160. Content persistence.
161. Disagreement.
162. Threat and content avoidance.
163. Obtrusion.
164. Content persistence.
165. Overgeneralization and fault.
166. Disagreement and affective talk.
167. Fault.
168. Threat and content avoidance.
169. Possible fault and content persistence.
170. Fault.
171. Possible fault.
172. Possible presumptive attribution.
173. Redundant information and fault.
174. Fault.

175. Dogmatic statement, fault, and redundant information.
176. Dogmatic statement.
177. Fault.
178. Obtrusion.
179. Disagreement and affective talk.
180. Fault.
181. Fault.
182. Redundant information and possible fault.
183. Content persistence and overgeneralization.
184. Obtrusion.
185. Acknowledgment.
186. Fault and content persistence.
187. Illogical statement, given H's earlier disavowals.
188. Agreement.
189. Cueing.
190. Obtrusion.
191. Detached utterance.
192. Illogical statement.
193. Content persistence.
194. Obtrusion.
195. Detached utterance and ambiguous message.
196. Cueing and content avoidance.
197. Ambiguous message.
198. Fault.
199. Disagreement.
200. Content persistence and fault.
201. Content persistence.
202. Quibbling.
203. Fault.
204. Disagreement.
205. Affective talk.
206. Acknowledgment.
207. Affective talk.
208. Acknowledgment.
209. Illogical talk and presumptive attribution.
210. Disagreement.
211. Content persistence, redundant information, and presumptive attribution.
212. Disagreement.
213. Cueing.
214. Fault.
215. Content persistence.
216. Fault.
217. Obtrusion.
218. Content persistence and disagreement.
219. Agreement.
220. Content persistence.
221. Cueing and misrepresentation of prior discussion.
222. Obtrusion.
223. Disagreement.
224. Threat.
225. Quibbling and disagreement.
226. Affective talk.
227. Possibly content avoidance.
228. Detached utterance.
229. Disagreement.
230. Fault and overgeneralization.
231. Implied fault.
232. Disagreement.
233. Detached utterance.
234. Misrepresentation of prior discussion.
235. Obtrusion.
236. Content persistence, disagreement, and quibbling.
237. Dogmatic statement.
238. Content persistence, redundant information, and disagreement.
239. Disagreement, content persistence, redundant information, and fault.
240. Agreement and implication of content avoidance.
241. Fault and content persistence.
242. Content avoidance.
243. Content persistence.
244. Implied fault and poor referent specification.
245. Cueing.
246. Poor referent specification.
247. Obtrusion.

248. Affective talk.
249. Temporal remoteness.
250. Illogical statement.
251. Disagreement.
252. Disagreement and affective talk.
253. Content persistence, dogmatic statement, and illogical statement.
254. Disagreement and content persistence.
255. Content persistence.
256. Cueing.
257. Acknowledgment.
258. Obtrusion.
259. Illogical statement.
260. Presumptive attribution.
261. Content persistence.
262. Illogical statement.
263. Threat.
264. Fault.

265. Obtrusion.
266. Agreement.
267. Disagreement.
268. Fault and misrepresentation of prior discussion.
269. Disagreement.
270. Content persistence.
271. Content persistence.
272. Content persistence and fault.
273. Detached utterance.
274. Fault.
275. Content persistence and redundant information.
276. Monotone speech.
277. Content persistence and redundant information.
278. Fault and overgeneralization.
279. Disagreement.
280. Disagreement.
281. Disagreement.
282. Content avoidance.

APPENDIX C

Assessment Analysis of Transcript 1, Couple E

SOME OF THE contributions that the analysis of one response display of marital communication may make to assessment are presented here, using Transcript 1, with which the reader should now be familiar. Transcript 1 was only one of several sources of data in the assessment for this couple and hence should be considered as only a segment of the assessment process. The topics covered below are the results of scanning and rating of the partners' verbal behavior using the Verbal Problem Checklist.

Results of Scanning

Scanning should indicate that among the communication difficulties for the husband are overgeneralization, topic content persistence, opinion surfeit, misrepresentation, provision of redundant information, and a large surfeit of negative talk consisting of faulting the wife. Among the communication problems for the wife are affective talk, quibbling, topic content avoidance, and illogical talk. Furthermore, both partners indicate positive talk deficit, acknowledgment deficit, obtrusions, and excessive disagreement. (Ratings of possible verbal problems for each partner are given in the following section.) Taken together, the partners exhibit clear-cut communication difficulties.

The response display also provides important leads concerning possible sources of these difficulties. First, there is little to suggest that the difficulties were the result of repertoire deficits, as these were defined earlier, or of structural deficits. No setting events were clearly indicated, although the display suggested that it might be worthwhile for the practitioner to follow up on unfavorable setting events such as sexual deprivation or anger for one or both of the marital partners that might be contributing to the difficulties. However, a major source of difficulty was indicated: namely, the referent condition of child management.

The couple was asked first to discuss the concerns they had in handling their children because information obtained earlier suggested that this referent condition might have given rise to the communication defects. In the display, the couple referred to difficulties in handling the four-year-old, who evidently disrupted the family activities; the way the father related to the oldest child; car privileges for and the driving behavior of "child number 2"; the need to discipline the fourteen-year-old, according to the husband; the children's lack of "respect" of the wife, alleged by the husband; disagreement of the spouses concerning what a child-management problem is; and the practices of the partners in regard to backing each other up in child management; among others.

To the extent that the communication difficulties are occasioned by child-management problems, detailed examination of the roles of partner interaction as a source of the communication difficulties is not required. Even so, the display suggested that the partners' interaction was itself a source of communication difficulties. For instance, each tended to respond to the misrepresentations, inaccuracies, and illogical talk of the other. Such responding very likely served to cue further responding along similar lines and may have functioned simultaneously to reinforce those responses of the partner, if only negatively by presenting aversiveness that the partner could reduce by speaking in reply. Each partner also tended to respond to the quibbling and off-topic talk of the other, again cueing more of the same and also possibly reinforcing it. Moreover, each of the partners failed to reinforce the accurate, on-topic, and problem-solving verbal behavior of the other.

The display failed to turn up any evidence of an *Alpha* problem or preeminent decision-making difficulty.

At this point we can find two "source hypotheses." One is that the communication difficulties of the partners arise at least in part from the child-management difficulties; the second is that there are also maintaining conditions for the difficulties deriving from the way partners interact with each other. Through postdiscussion inquiry, the practitioner would pursue additional information bearing upon these hypotheses. For instance, the helping person would want to know the ways in which this response display was typical or atypical, and whether the partners talked this way only when discussing child management or when they discussed other subjects as well.

If postdiscussion inquiry and subsequent assessment provided support for what was learned in this response display, modification would then be planned so that attention would be directed first toward alteration of any referent conditions, such as child management and, then, if necessary, to change partner interaction.

Rating Using the VPC

Following the Response Display, problems and strengths of marital communication were rated using the VPC. The ratings for the husband and wife are given below for forty-eight categories of the VPC.

The Verbal Problem Checklist[1]

Couple: E   Practitioner:_____   Discussion Topic: "The Concerns You Have in Handling Your Children"   Date:_____

RESPONSE CATEGORY	AMOUNT RATING*		COMMENTS
	H	**W**	
1. Overtalk	3	0	
2. Undertalk	0	2	
3. Fast talk	0	0	
4. Slow talk	0	0	
5. Loud talk	0	1	
6. Quiet talk	0	0	
7. Singsong speech	0	0	

* Amount rating key: 0 = not at all; 1 = a slight amount; 2 = a moderate amount; 3 = a large amount.

[1] The form is from Edwin J. Thomas, Claude L. Walter, and Kevin O'Flaherty, "A Verbal Problem Checklist for Use in Assessing Family Verbal Behavior," *Behavior Therapy* (1974), 5, 235–246.

The Verbal Problem Checklist (*cont.*)

RESPONSE CATEGORY	AMOUNT RATING*		COMMENTS
	H	W	
8. Monotone speech	1	0	
9. Rapid latency	1	1	
10. Slow latency	1	0	
11. Affective talk	0	3	
12. Unaffective talk	2	0	
13. Obtrusions	2	3	
14. Quibbling	1	3	
15. Overresponsiveness	3	0	
16. Underresponsiveness	0	2	
17. Excessive question asking	0	0	
18. Pedantry	2	0	
19. Dogmatic statement	3	0	
20. Overgeneralization†	3	2	
21. Excessive cueing	0	0	
22. Incorrect autoclitic	0	0	
23. Presumptive attribution	2	1	
24. Misrepresentation of fact or evaluation	3	0	

† Embraces "undergeneralization" also; see Chapter 2.

The Verbal Problem Checklist (*cont.*)

RESPONSE CATEGORY	AMOUNT RATING*		COMMENTS
	H	**W**	
25. Topic content avoidance	0	3	
26. Other content avoidance	3	0	
27. Topic content shifting	0	2	
28. Other content shifting	2	0	
29. Topic content persistence	3	0	
30. Other content persistence	0	2	
31. Poor referent specification	1	1	
32. Temporal remoteness	2	1	
33. Detached utterance	0	1	
34. Positive talk deficit	3	3	
35. Positive talk surfeit	0	0	
36. Acknowledgment deficit	3	3	
37. Acknowledgment surfeit	0	0	
38. Opinion deficit	0	0	
39. Opinion surfeit	3	2	
40. Excessive agreement	0	0	
41. Excessive disagreement	3	3	
42. Dysfluent talk	0	0	

The Verbal Problem Checklist (*cont.*)

RESPONSE CATEGORY	AMOUNT RATING*		COMMENTS
	H	W	
43. Too little information given	0	0	
44. Redundant information given	3	3	
45. Too much information given	0	0	
46. Negative talk surfeit	3	3	In the form of faulting
47. Negative talk deficit	0	0	
48. Illogical talk	2	3	

Patterning

Recommended areas for modification

APPENDIX D

Examples of Coding

THIS APPENDIX GIVES examples of coding to illustrate three commonly used measures for verbal behavior—namely, duration, frequency (and rates), and time-interval coding (TIC coding). Brief attention is also given to reliability. The data used here are based upon the transcript presented in Appendix A.

Duration is illustrated by measures of the amount of time that Mr. and Mrs. E talked for Transcript 1. A coder used an electric stopwatch activated to record time cumulatively in hundredths of a second each time the spouse in question talked. (An ordinary stopwatch would be adequate here.) The duration of the husband's talking was 13 minutes, or 55 percent of the total talk time of 23 minutes, 48 seconds. The figures for the wife were 6.30 minutes, or 26 percent of the total time. (For the remaining 19 percent, neither partner talked; this is slightly less "dead time" than is generally found in discussions such as these.) Thus, the husband talked approximately twice as much as the wife.

The coding of frequency is illustrated in the counting of faults for the husband and wife in Transcript 1. The response category of faults was the same as that defined for that category in Chapter 2. The number of faults was counted for each spouse, using the instances of faults identified in Appendix B, where examples of verbal categories are given. Although the coding there was done only to illustrate response categories, it serves our present purposes adequately inasmuch as it provides a frequency count of faults for husband and wife. There were 30 such faults for the husband and 9 for the wife. These frequencies are more adequately expressed as rates of faulting for the duration of time talked by each partner. Converted in this way, the rate of faulting for the husband was 2.3 per minute and that for the wife was 1.4. Thus, the husband faulted the wife almost twice as often as she faulted him, given the amount of time each talked.

TIC coding is restricted to time intervals during which at least one instance of a given behavior occurs. Thus, if the interval for coding is twelve seconds and the behavior of interest is faulting by marital partners, the procedure consists of counting all twelve-second intervals in which there was at least one fault for a given partner. This type of coding was done for illustrative purposes in Transcript 1, where all twelve-second intervals are identified by an asterisk and those containing a fault of one or both partners are marked by an asterisk with a short dash beneath and to the right of it. For Transcript 1, there were 119 twelve-second intervals, of which 34 included at least one fault by one or both partners (34/119, or 29 percent faulting). In 26 such intervals the husband alone faulted (26/119 or 21 percent); in 7 intervals the wife alone faulted (7/119 or 6 percent). Although TIC coding is generally somewhat less exact than pure durational or frequency coding, it has the advantage of being somewhat easier and faster inasmuch as the coder needs to discriminate only whether or not at least one instance of the coded event occurred in a given interval of time, thus eliminating the additional discriminations of detecting the onset and the offset of the events.

Reliability of coding is illustrated by considering the degree of agreement of coders A and B in TIC coding of faults for the husband in Transcript 1. Coder A found 26 twelve-second intervals in which there was a fault for the husband whereas coder B found 27. In 23 intervals the coders agreed in identifying faulting by the husband. A useful measure of reliability is based upon the number of agreements times 2 divided by the total number of judgments. In this case it is $(23 \times 2)/(26+27)$ or 86 percent.

Couple J: "I Don't Think I Expect You to Do Too Many Things"

THIS TRANSCRIPT derives from a response display for a childless couple in their mid-twenties who were requested, as part of the assessment of their communication, to discuss "The Expectations You Have of Each Other as Husband or Wife." Although by no means exemplary of excellent marital communication, the transcript illustrates relatively good communication as compared with that of most couples who complain of communication difficulties, and certainly as compared with that shown by couple E. There are certain communication shortcomings, which are very different from those of couple E. The transcript also illustrates the type of content evoked by this topic as well as how this display served to provide assessment information particularly relevant for this couple. These and related matters are taken up more fully in the discussion section that follows the transcript.

H: I guess I'll start. My expectations are things concerning the house. The money responsibility I think . . . ah . . . we've decided pretty well . . . that it will be taken care of by you because of the time, time factor. I wouldn't have time to take care of the banking and you have a little more time to . . . oh . . . write the bills and ah . . . and so forth. (*Long silence.*)

Sometimes, I think you would . . . I would like you to take a little more responsibility as far as planning certain things because, generally, we both like to do the—both enjoy doing the same things. So, sometimes it's—I hate to make a decision because it's . . . ah . . . I guess I'm afraid that you might not like to do it. Even if you preferred to do something else I don't think you would always say that you wanted to . . . and . . . ah, I would like to hear more what you would like to do—

199

things that you would like to do and . . . (*Silence.*) I always don't like to make the decision—what to do for some things.

W: Like what things?

H: Well, like . . . like free weekends where we haven't given it too much thought. Generally, it doesn't matter, you know, where we go or anything . . . and . . . and ah . . . I don't think you want to make the . . . ah . . . decision because you think it's . . . ah . . . you know, my time. . . .

W: That's right, that is the way I feel. You don't have a weekend very often. I want to do what you want to do and so I don't suggest things or I may not suggest things because I don't want to influence you. I'm afraid you'll say that it's okay for us to do that when maybe you really don't want to do it. But it's not really what you want to do . . . So I want you to decide what we should do and you want me to decide what we should do.

H: Right.

W: (*Laughs.*) Why don't you want to decide? (*Silence.*)

H: Well, because . . . ah . . . I just feel it's easier for you to make the planning . . . timewise, because I just can't break away and ah . . . while you're the one that always writes the letters, the letters, you know, for going home or something and . . . ah . . . it's . . .

W: Um-hm.

H: I just think it's simpler that way.

W: Well, sometimes I get the feeling that you don't like the things I suggest we do.

H: No, I don't think that's—I don't think that's true. I think I would say something, I would say something in a situation if I didn't want to go to a particular place or I just don't; I would say something. You know, if you suggested . . . you know, I'd like to know what we're doing or what you would like to do.

W: Um-hm.

H: You know, I'd like to say "Yes, that sounds good" or "No, I don't want to do that." (*Long silence.*) Now, what about other responsibilities? Or do you want to talk about that more?

W: Well, I don't know. I don't think that's really settled. Maybe that's something that _____ [*the therapist*] can help us with because neither of us seems to want to suggest things to do. (*Silence.*) And, we don't know what to do about it, right?

H: Right.

W: Well, maybe we can go on to something else?

H: Okay, because I feel that . . . ah . . . you should have a choice, too, about what you would like to do.

W: Um-hm. That's true. Quite often I like to see things that you do, you want to do, too.

W: Okay, well let's . . . ah . . . move on to something else, then. What else do you expect of me as a wife besides taking care of the financial things?

H: (*Long silence.*) Well, ah . . . the house in general, I don't know . . . maybe that's the same category as taking care of the . . . you know, I think that is, you know, that's done quite well. And you know, I don't mind helping doing different things. I think that's my responsibility, too. (*Long silence.*) I guess that's it. (*Long silence.*) What do you expect of me?

W: (*Silence.*) What do you think I expect from you?

H: (*Silence.*) Well, that ah . . . probably that I share more of my feelings on matters and . . . ah . . . and ah . . . let you know about certain things . . . and ah . . . tell you about different things that have happened.

W: Um-hm.

H: Just in general, let you know what things have changed.

W: Um-hm. . . . Ya, I expect you to share . . . just about everything with me. I realize that there are some things that . . . that are, that you just don't share. We don't have to say everything, everything that you think or feel. I feel, I expect you to make a pretty good effort to share important things with me. (*Long silence.*) And I expect you to do something about McGregor [*their dog*].

H: (*Long silence.*) Well, I don't know what really could be done with him but I guess just take him for a walk more and see that he gets his exercise.

W: (*Silence.*) I can't help but feel that more could be done to eliminate some of his bad behaviors. I mean, just seeing that he gets enough exercise isn't going to stop him from barking and stop him from jumping up on the door and jumping up on people and running in and out. (*Silence.*) Like the lady at the kennel, today, told me, you know, I told her about the barking. And I asked her if there is anything that we could do to stop the barking and she said "Well, when the weather gets nice you can keep a half a bucket of water out there, outside, with a couple capfuls of ammonia in it and when he barks, you throw that in his face and say 'No,' " and she said, "after two or three times, he'll stop barking." So other people think, seem to think, that there are things that could be done to eliminate some of his bad behaviors. And I just can't believe that there's nothing we can do to change his behavior and yet I don't feel it's my responsibility.

H: (*Long silence.*) Well, I agree with this. It's my responsibility, maybe. I can start looking into different things that I, that I can do and try to get started right away because I know it's bothered you quite a bit more lately . . . his behavior . . . ah . . . Sometimes I don't realize how bad it is because you're with him more than I am.

W: That's right.

H: (*Long silence.*) Anything else?

W: (*Silence.*) Nothing else I expect of you as a husband. Oh, I expect you to take care of certain things around the house, too. Like the yard, you take care of that real good . . . And, I expect you to take care of the car, as far as cleaning the car and everything. Well, I took care of that for a long, long time but I just decided that I had enough other things to take care of around the house and that I'm not going to take care of the car anymore. (*Long silence.*) Did you know that?

H: No. I don't mind taking care of the car. I sort of enjoy that kind of work anyway. That's okay with me.

W: And I expect you to do certain things, certain other things—like fixing certain things; like fixing that drain so our basement doesn't flood every time it rains and mopping up the water when it comes into the basement. (*Long silence.*) I don't think I expect you to do too many things. I don't think I make too many demands on you as far as doing things around the house. . . . I don't expect you to do any of the housework or I don't expect you even to help with the dishes or do anything with the laundry. I don't expect you to do most of the painting—just the big jobs, like the walls and the outside of the house. But I don't expect you to do the small parts, like the doors and trim and the windows and things like that because I can do those, but I can't do the big jobs so I expect you to do that. (*Silence.*) And when you don't do the things that I expect you to do around the house I get pretty upset about it.

Discussion

Responses to the topic "The Expectations You Have of Each Other as Husband or Wife" suggested that each partner, especially the wife, might have some unmet expectations in the marriage. The discussion did turn up several unmet expectations involving behaviors and provided useful additional information concerning the couple's decision making and marital communication. The reader may have noted that the discussion was rather commonplace and unexciting, which is characteristic of many but not all response displays of marital partners who do not have serious communication difficulties.

The picture in regard to communication is mainly one of strengths because of the relative absence of some of the major difficulties, such as faulting, overgeneralization, and excessive disagreement. The couple managed to stay on topic rather well, they agreed with each other at several important points when requests were made for a partner to change, each partner generally responded to what the other said, and each was generally responsive to efforts of the partner to guide the conversation.

However, both mates displayed several shortcomings. The husband had very slow latency in speaking, spoke very slowly when he did speak, specified referents poorly (although the wife seemed to understand what he was talking about), did not give a great deal of information, and, at some points, underresponded to what appeared to be called for in the discussion. The wife, for her part, displayed slow latency and had a tendency to shift content, in this case, from the topic of their mutual expectations to decision making and an endeavor to persuade her husband to change aspects of his behavior.

The response display was also informative in other ways in regard to the couple's communication. One of their initial complaints was that they talked very little, and this discussion indicated that although their interchanges were slow and dull, at least to an outsider, they were capable of having a reasonable interchange when requested to do so. The wife also made it clear in the display that she wanted her husband to discuss personal matters more fully with her. Altogether, it appears that the partners have relatively few difficulties in carrying on verbal interchange, once it is initiated, and that a major difficulty might be to have the partners carry out a verbal interchange and, especially, to have the husband discuss topics that would be pleasurable to his wife.

Although not necessarily intended to yield particular information about decision making, the response display indicated that the partners did not make decisions to their satisfaction in regard to how their weekends should be spent. Evidently each partner failed to make his or her preferences known, and it was suggested (and confirmed by later inquiry) that this was one of several areas requiring joint decision for which decisions were not made properly in advance. At several points the partners departed from the assigned topic of partner expectations and endeavored actually to make some decisions. For instance, in the discussion about the dog, we learned that the wife was capable of making her preferences explicit. In this instance, the husband agreed that he should take more responsibility in caring for the dog. The husband also indicated that he would be willing to take care of the car, and, in fact, would enjoy doing so, when informed that his wife no longer considered this her responsibility. Although not necessarily models of excellence, several strengths were revealed in these brief excursions into decision making. Information from the postdiscussion inquiry indicated that a major difficulty was failure of one or both partners to make decisions in advance.

Considering now the referents of a response display not already mentioned, the most important consideration would appear to be the relative absence of referent conditions that could give rise to communication difficulty. Judging from this response display, the communication difficulties of these partners cannot be readily attributed to any referent condition. The matter of the care of the dog was a referent problem that did come up, but discussion of it did not even lead to expression of disagreement; rather, when the wife brought up the need for the husband to take more responsibility for the dog, he readily agreed that he should do so. Later, in postdiscussion inquiry, it was learned that the couple did argue about the care of the dog. This referent condition, then, was discovered to be a source of communication difficulty. More important, however, was what has been called a structural deficit, in this case the absence of proper times and places for talking on desired subjects.

Although the objective here is to illustrate some features of assessment, aspects of the intervention are relevant. The intervention plan was formulated in conformity with the priorities for behavioral objectives presented in Chapter 3. The decision making, although not by any means serious, was addressed first, following more detailed assessment in that area. Part of the intervention plan here was to have the couple set aside agreed-upon times in advance to make decisions involving such matters as upcoming activities. Once this plan was set in motion, the two sources of communication difficulty were taken on. In one portion of the intervention here, the referent condition of care of the dog was resolved by agreements the couple made concerning exactly what the husband's and wife's responsibilities were. The structural deficit was handled by setting aside regular agreed-upon Talk Times during which such topics as "personal matters" were discussed. Although the communication difficulties were minor, several tailor-made interaction rules were formulated and followed by the partners during their frequently scheduled Talk Sessions.

Couple G:
"You Have to Eat"

THE G'S WERE CHILDLESS young marrieds in their early twenties, among whose initial concerns was the adequacy of their decision making. As part of the assessment for the decision making, a response display was obtained by asking the couple to try to make a real decision in the area of how much to spend on groceries, one of the several areas in which they said they had disagreement. No assistance was provided by the practitioner in the form of coaching or other intervention. The transcript illustrates how a couple may reach a mutually satisfactory decision by means of having one or both partners concede on one or more points. Although the couple did not follow a stepwise pattern in which each relevant topic was taken up in order, they managed nonetheless to give attention at various points to what needed to be discussed to reach the decision.

W: The problem we have in buying food is that every time I go to the grocery store to spend money for food, we have a hard time deciding on how much money we should spend, and I think that $25 a week is not a lot of money to spend on food. Some weeks I'll skip a week and it's going to be two weeks before I go, so I'm supposed to be able to spend $50. Well, if I'm at the store and spend $50 you would have a fit. You don't think it's necessary to have food in the house, and I do because when we have friends over, I do not like to have nothing to offer them when they come over; and I think it's terrible that I can't have food in the house.

H: (*Pause.*) All right. I don't think you should have to spend $50 because I'm going to manage my eating habits. I just like to munch, eat sandwiches.

W: Silly.

H: We work different shifts; we're not at home the same time; there's no real meals cooked, and to me $25 or $30 a week is too much just for munching on lunch meat and pop.

W: Well, you cannot survive on lunch meat and pop, and if I had some food to cook you would have some meals to eat; and $25 is nothing the way food prices are in the store, for a couple to eat, and I don't even spend that sometimes. I'm just saying $25 as an average figure. We don't even spend that. Sometimes I spend $40 every two weeks, $35 every two weeks, with a little bit in between running to the store for bread and milk. Don't you think that you should be able to eat properly? One of my problems is that I don't eat right.

H: Well, I don't starve to death. I don't get sick. I always get enough food to eat.

W: So, what do you think would be a good, ah, good compromise . . . like . . . $13 a week?

H: $20 a week at the most.

W: At the most, $20 a week? And how about when you enter . . .

H: Because with the two of us. Like when you entertain, that's different. Go to the store that day and buy what you plan on serving.

W: No, no.

H: Like I do when I cook a meal. I go to the store and buy just what I need and cook it.

W: No, no. I don't agree. If somebody comes unexpectedly, I don't feel like running to the store and buying what I need and leaving the company. I think we should have it there so I won't have to leave the house.

H: Well, when people come over unexpectedly how many times do they eat? You just drink some beer or something—make a few drinks.

W: (*Sighing.*) I'm still—that's not the point. I just don't think that we can survive on $20.00 a week—and that's $20—that means cigarettes, everything. Food, cigarettes, everything! Twenty dollars a week. Cigarettes are almost $4 a carton, so that leaves you $16 almost.

H: Now, how often do you buy cigarettes in a carton?

W: Why, I can't because I can't afford to because you won't let me spend the money. You can argue when we come home about this. Last time we were in the grocery store we had a big fight because I was going to go grocery shopping and you had a fit because I . . .

H: Yeah, but you remember that day you wanted to write a check for it and the money wasn't in the account. It wasn't going to be in the account until the next day.

W: Well, that wasn't the point. The point was that you didn't want me going anyway.

H: No, I told you to go the next day.

W: But you didn't want me spending that much money, did you? As much as I spent.

H: I don't even recall how much you spent that time.

W: I spent $37.

H: Doesn't seem like to me when you spend that much, there isn't that much in the refrigerator. Two days later it's gone.

W: (*Sighing.*)

H: That's what gets me upset more than anything, to see one day a refrigerator full of food and the next day it's gone.

W: Well, I . . .

H: That's why it seems to me you waste the money buying crazy things.

W: What is it you don't like? You don't like the idea of spending the money for food, or would you rather spend it on something else? Is that your problem?

H: Maybe, I don't know.

W: I think your problem is that you think the money can be used elsewhere instead of being spent for food when food is a necessity. Is that what— what you think?

H: No, I don't mind spending money on food if it's worth it.

W: What do you mean, if it's worth it? If it's something that can stay in the refrigerator for a week . . .

H: The prices—the prices they want for food now I ain't going to pay what they want.

W: (*Exasperated.*) Well, you *have* to.

H: I'm not gonna pay.

W: You have to eat.

H: I'll just eat something else.

W: No, no, no. What can you eat? You have to eat. That's not making any sense.

H: I'll eat but I'll just substitute other things.

W: Like what are you going to substitute?

H: A can of soup instead of steak.

W: I don't buy many steaks.

H: No, but expensive hamburger, at $1.25 a pound. Crazy!

W: What are you going to eat if you don't eat hamburger?

H: Eat soup. It's cheaper.

W: Soup? I'm sorry. I can't survive on soup all week. I mean, if I was really poor or something . . .

H: I can't see how you eat anyway. You might fill your plate with food and then you leave half of it there—throw it away.

W: Listen—so we have to make a decision.

H: And that's another thing that gets me upset. Leftovers stay in the refrigerator two and three weeks and finally you just got to throw them away because they're no good. Use the leftovers.

W: Okay.

H: Make something with them.

W: Okay, I agree, I'll . . .

H: Make stew with the vegetables.

W: Okay, I'll have to use the leftovers.

H: Potatoes you can cook for breakfast.

W: We're going to have to make a decision now on how much we should spend, on what we should eat, what we should buy to eat, okay?

H: Okay.

W: Now, I think $25 to $30—$25 a week I should be able to spend on food, and that includes cigarettes.

H: Well, I'll agree with that if you're buying cigarettes and pop.

W: That's $25 a week and that means if I don't go to the grocery store for a week the next time I go I am able to spend $50 without you getting upset. That would upset you, wouldn't it? It would, wouldn't it, if I spent $50 instead of spending . . .

H: It might, if we're short of money or something.

W: So you'd much rather me go once a week.

H: I'd rather you go once a week, yeah.

W: Instead of waiting?

H: Say you go every Friday night or have me . . . you make a list down and have me go for you Saturday morning since I'm off.

W: I see it's just the idea of $50 all at once. If I go every week and spend $15 or $20 and $25 you won't get upset.

H: Right.

W: But if I miss a week and have to spend $50 . . .

H: I'd rather just go every week because if you miss a week and then keep the money out, you end up buying something else with it.

W: Okay.

H: Then you got twice the burden the next week.

W: What happens if I do miss a week? You're gonna get upset?

H: There's no reason to miss a week.

W: Well, I said, "What happens if I do?"

H: No, I won't . . . get upset but there's no reason to miss and I'm off on Saturdays, I can go.

W: Okay, there'd be no reason for you to . . .

H: I can even go Friday mornings.

W: But what happens if there's a week missed? I'm just saying.

H: Okay.

W: You won't like it, though, you'd much rather me go once a week.

H: Right.

W: Okay. But you won't get upset if I don't. If something did come up, you wouldn't get upset.

H: Right.

W: Okay. I think our decision is to spend between $20 and $25 a week, once a week instead of waiting two or three weeks to go shopping, right?

H: Right.

W: Okay.

Therapist Feedback

Therapist feedback in this case was immediate because the other assessment tasks had been completed, the couple had done a good job, and the therapist wanted to give the partners the benefit of immediate positive feedback. Ordinarily, in carrying out assessment, therapist feedback would not be provided until the assessment had been completed and the therapist could endeavor to be neutral so as to reduce unwanted bias in collecting information.

T: Are you satisfied with your decision?
W: Yes. Now I won't have to argue with him the next time I go to the grocery store.
T: (*Turning to the husband.*) How about you?
H: Yes.
W: We'll go once a week.
T: That's excellent. Let me give you some feedback now while the tape is on.
W: Okay.
T: You did several things that are good. First, you made the decision, which was something of a compromise—to spend $20 to $25 a week.
W: Um-hm.
T: Second, the idea was brought up that you should shop every week rather than every two weeks or more. That was agreed to, and that's important. Third, the idea was brought up that leftovers should be used and not wasted, and that was agreed to.
W: Um-hm.
T: So, altogether, I think you did a super job.[1]
W: Good.
H: Thank you.

---

[1] This judgment is based on the fact that the couple had made a mutually satisfactory decision and, in so doing, each had conceded on critical points, and all this was done without bitterness, obstinacy, irrelevant faulting, or escalation.

Training Procedures for Rating Verbal Behavior

SELECTED MATERIAL in the book provides a basis for training in the use of the Verbal Problem Checklist (VPC). Readers interested in acquiring greater facility in rating with this schedule may follow the steps given here.

Orientation
1. Familiarize yourself with the rating categories by carefully reviewing the categories of verbal behavior and examples in Chapter 2.
2. Read the transcript in Appendix A, which contains examples of a large variety of categories of verbal behavior.
3. Identify at least one applicable verbal-behavior category for each marked segment of the transcript in Appendix A. Then check Appendix B to see if your identification matches the one given there.
4. Practice identifying segments of a tape-recorded response display by playing a portion of the tape, stopping the tape recorder, naming the verbal behavior category (or categories) most appropriate, and then turning the machine on again and repeating the process.
5. Read the material on the rating procedure for the VPC in Chapter 3, pp. 67–68.

Rating Practice with Transcripts and Tapes
6. Rate couple E on the VPC using a schedule such as the one given in Appendix C.
7. Compare your VPC ratings with those in Appendix C.

8. Read the transcript for couple J, given in Appendix E.
9. Identify categories of verbal behavior in this transcript.
10. Rate couple E on the VPC.

Rating Response Displays

In using the VPC to rate verbal behavior of marital partners in actual response displays, the procedures for obtaining response displays described in Chapter 3 should be followed. The VPC should be completed immediately after the response display. It is helpful to have two practitioners listen to the response display discussion as it transpires and complete postsession ratings independently. This makes it possible for the two to confer later, compare differences, and thereby sharpen discriminations. For additional information concerning the VPC, read a research report on this schedule by Thomas, Walter, and O'Flaherty (1974a).

Training Modules for Special Coaching Problems

IF A COACHING session fails to enable partners to produce the target behavior requisite for any step, special alternatives and training modules may be employed to increase the likelihood of evoking the behavior. The special problems, steps of the coaching procedure where they are likely to be encountered, and procedural alternatives are summarized in Table 7-3. This appendix takes up the Alternative Generation Procedure, Information Display Procedure, Preference Display Procedure, and Disagreement Resolution Procedure.

Alternative Generation Procedure

When partners have not generated an adequate number of solution alternatives in Step 3, the coach may use this procedure as a special subroutine. The coach first stops the partners, explains that they will need to generate more alternatives in order to progress satisfactorily to the next stage, and that a special procedure will help them to do so. To begin, the coach suggests that they pretend that they are outside experts and that their job is to help a couple like themselves think of possible solutions for a decision issue like this one. They are reminded that, in so doing, they should not judge the alternatives but should think freely, openly, and creatively without regard to whether the alternatives are good and bad. In effect, they should "hang loose" and brainstorm possibilities. The couple is then requested to go ahead and try again to generate additional alternatives.

If the couple still has trouble, the coach prompts additional alternatives with suggestions such as "Have you thought of Y?" Then, after affirming with the couple that the suggested alternative is indeed legitimate, the coach prompts again, if necessary. The session is continued until a reasonably rich set of options has been generated that contains one or more feasible solution alternatives. The coach then returns to Step 4 of the main coaching procedure.

Information Display Procedure

The Information Display Procedure is appropriate for partners who have failed to provide sufficient information about the positive and negative aspects of the proposed solution alternatives. Learning how to exchange relevant information is important in the process of selecting an alternative because the information can identify previously unrecognized consequences associated with the possible solution alternatives. Information display thus helps to bring the behavior of selecting a solution response under the control of information about the consequences, were that solution to be followed. The procedure given below is a modification of a related procedure described by O'Flaherty (1974), which in turn derives from research on coaching by the author and his associates.[1]

1. The partners together list the main solution alternatives generated in Step 3.

2. A number is assigned to each of these alternatives for purposes of identification.

3. Each partner is given an Information Display Form, shown in Table H-1, on which each writes the number or other identification for these solution alternatives (if more than four alternatives are required, additional forms are used). Table H-1 gives a display of information for a husband for three vacation alternatives (Alternative 1, go to Bear Lake; Alternative 2, visit Grandma; and Alternative 3, stay at home). An analogous display would be obtained for the wife.

4. Partners are instructed to write out all positive and negative aspects of each alternative, with special focus on these aspects of the consequences, were the alternative to be carried out. The husband

[1] Conducted on the Socio-behavioral Research Project at the University of Michigan from 1969 to 1975.

TABLE H-1. Information Display Form

Husband _____
Wife _____

INFORMATION	SOLUTION ALTERNATIVES			
	Number 1	*Number 2*	*Number 3*	*Number 4*
Positive Aspects of the Alternative	Wife and kids want to go; can boat, swim, picnic, and cook out.	Should see Grandma; kids like Grandma; Grandma's house needs repairs I can make; not as expensive as the lake.	Easy, inexpensive, restful; I have jobs I want to finish at home.	
Negative Aspects of the Alternative	Rent is costly; it's a long distance; the car may not make it without breaking down; family on a tight budget.	Little privacy; the seventeen-year-old won't go this time; wife argues with Grandma.	Wife and kids prefer to go to lake; I might get bored and might not rest enough at home.	

and wife are encouraged to respond as fully as possible for alternatives they like as well as for those they do not.

5. Each partner completes the form working individually.

6. Each partner reads aloud what he or she has written.

7. The coach asks the partners to see if they can now reach agreement by combining the information each has provided, considering that information as it applies to each of the alternatives. If agreement is reached, and it generally is, the coach returns to Step 5 of the coaching procedure. If not, the Preference Display Procedure or Disagreement Resolution Procedure is followed.

Preference Display Procedure

The Preference Display Procedure is helpful when the partners have fairly full information concerning the alternatives but their preferences are not crystallized, are unexpressed, or, if expressed, have been ignored by the partner. The procedure described below is also a modification of one described by O'Flaherty (1974), which, in turn, was developed by the author and his associates in research on coaching.[2]

1. The coach lists the various solution alternatives.

2. For each alternative, he obtains the strength of preference for each partner on a scale ranging from +3, for most preferred, to −3, for least preferred, with 0 indicating indifference.

3. After this display of preferences, the coach asks the partners to discuss which alternative is best in view of this information. Meanwhile the coach calculates the algebraic sum of the preferences for each alternative to determine which choice yields the highest value. (For example, if alternative A is rated by the husband as +3, by the wife as −1, the sum is +2; this would be preferred to alternative B if the husband gave it a rating of −2, the wife +3, with a resulting sum of +1.) The coach then indicates which alternative (or alternatives) received the highest sum. If the partners now reach agreement on an alternative, and they generally do, coaching is resumed at Step 5. If an alternative is not selected at this point, the coach then can stop, if time alone might help to crystallize preferences further, or he can turn to the Disagreement Resolution Procedure.

[2] Again, from the Socio-behavioral Research Project at the University of Michigan.

Disagreement Resolution Procedure

Although coaching itself is in fact a method by which disagreements are generally resolved, there are occasions when no resolution is achieved in the step in which a solution alternative is to be chosen (Step 4). In these cases, it is appropriate to use the Disagreement Resolution Procedure.[3] It is presupposed here that the partners already have the requisite information regarding alternatives and that the preferences of partners are clear and known, either through prior discussion or through the use of the Information Display or Preference Display Procedure.

The steps follow.

1. Coaching is stopped, usually at Step 4, when the partners have demonstrated clearly that they disagree concerning the preferred alternatives and have not resolved the disagreement.

2. The coach reaffirms the desire of the partners to make this decision together and their willingness to continue to work on this decision issue. (This failing, the coach stops the session and carries out coaching on another decision issue in this or at the next session.)

3. In the orientation to the procedure, the coach indicates that their disagreement can be resolved and that it is valuable for partners to learn new ways to resolve disagreements such as these so that they will then be better able to resolve issues that may arise in the future. He suggests that they try to resolve their disagreement here, using a special method, as part of their training in marital decision making. The coach then indicates that he will illustrate resolution options for a hypothetical example, the partners will apply these options to their own particular disagreement, and they will then try to work out a mutually satisfactory resolution.

4. To illustrate resolution options, we use an example of disagreement between marital partners concerning when to buy a car. The wife wants to buy a new car right away whereas the husband wants to wait three years. Among the resolution options for this couple are the following: (1) the car may be purchased now, as the wife prefers, or three years later, as desired by the husband (resolution by compliance of a partner); (2) they may agree to buy the car sometime

---

[3] Related procedures that address fewer resolution alternatives than are taken up here are the Frequency Fulfillment Technique, used for compromising differences (Azrin, Naster, and Jones, 1973), the somewhat more general Simulations-Options-Consequences-Simulation (S.O.C.S.) model (Kifer, Lewis, Green, and Phillips, 1974), and the general Parent Effectiveness Training (P.E.T.) approach (Gordon, 1970).

between now and three years hence, say in about a year and a half (compromise); (3) they may decide that a new car will be purchased now, in accordance with the wife's preference, and the husband will get the opportunity to select where the couple will go for their vacation (trade); (4) the partners may delay making a decision, letting the time to purchase the car be determined by other factors, such as possible changes in income and the condition of their present car (default); (5) they may agree to allow a third party, such as the coach, help them to reach an agreement (mediation); (6) they may agree to follow the advice of a third party, such as a trusted relative (arbitration); or (7) they may agree that this decision will henceforth be delegated to the wife exclusively (delegation). (These options are summarized for the reader in Table H-2.) The coach then hands the partners a written description of the disagreement resolution options, just described verbally.

TABLE H-2.   Classes of Options in Marital Disagreement

RESOLUTION	NONRESOLUTION
1. Compliance with partner	9. Continued negotiation
2. Compromise	10. Negotiation moratorium
3. Trade	11. No negotiation, continued disagreement
4. Default	12. Uncertain status
5. Delegation of decision	
6. Mediation	
7. Arbitration	
8. Forced resolution	

5. The partners are requested to generate as many resolution options as possible that apply to their particular disagreement. One partner is asked to write down options along with the coach, who also does so. The generation of resolution options in the Disagreement Resolution Procedure is, in effect, a counterpart to Step 3 of Coaching, where solution alternatives are generated. However, Step 3 of coaching involves generation of possible solutions to a decision issue whereas, here, options for disagreement resolution are also generated.[4] The coaching activity remains the same in that the coach monitors on-topic and off-topic talk, providing positive feedback for the former and negative for the latter, and gives intervening instructions as necessary. The coach allows the partners to discuss resolution options until they have stopped.

---

[4] The resolution options are clearly more extensive than the ordinary solution alternatives generated in Step 3 by coaching.

6. The partners are requested to review their list of resolution options for completeness, and the coach does the same. Then, after noting any additional options suggested by the partners, the coach may say, "Have you thought of X?" as a way of including options that were omitted. When the list is complete with at least one plausible example for each resolution alternative, the coach moves on to the next step.

7. The following guidelines for resolving disagreements are suggested to the partners:

    a. Accept your partner's preferences as relevant information, even if you disagree with them. He or she has a right to his or her opinion just as you have to yours.

    b. Avoid early commitment to one alternative, because this may blind you to other options that would be more acceptable to both of you.

    c. Be prepared to change and make some concessions. If you are flexible, it will be easier for your partner to work with you in resolving the disagreement, and the resolution will almost certainly have benefits for the marital relationship as a whole.

    d. If your partner gives a little, be sure that you do the same.

    e. You may find that one good concession opens the door to resolution, but, if not, don't hesitate to move further.

    f. Try to reach a resolution in this session by moving forward quickly. You'll have limited time; I can't tell you how much now.[5]

    g. Be sure that the option you finally agree to is one you will really carry out. Having once agreed, it is important that you stick to the understanding so that the resolution can in fact be carried out and so that your partner will trust your word in the future.

8. Partners are instructed to begin their negotiation. Again, the coach monitors on-topic and off-topic verbal behavior, using procedures described before. (This is Step 4 now applied to selection of a disagreement-resolution alternative.) When an option has been chosen, the coach asks that the partners summarize it.

If resolution is not reached, the coach tries to have the partners at least reach some understanding concerning the lack of resolution.

---

[5] Research by Hammer (1974) has shown that when people work within time limits or deadlines, they tend to reach mutually satisfactory agreements more rapidly than when they do not face any time demands.

As rationale, he indicates that even though the disagreement has not been resolved, the partners should come to an understanding about how they are going to handle the matter so that undesirable side effects can be minimized. The following alternatives are suggested (see Table H-2):

    a. Continue negotiation. This is often desirable if mates will abide by what they have learned about decision making in recent modification.

    b. Call a moratorium on negotiation until there is additional information indicating the desirability of returning to negotiation. During the moratorium there would be no arguments or conflict about the disagreement.

    c. Discontinue negotiation and continue to disagree. This is suitable only if the partners can contain and tolerate the disagreement and not escalate conflict.

    d. Leave the status uncertain concerning how to proceed from that point. This is appropriate when partners are very uncertain about what to do.

The partners are instructed to select one of these alternatives.

9. The final step is deciding action (Step 5 of coaching proper), and this is carried out in the same way as with the main coaching procedure.

If any of the special training modules described above fails to produce the desired behaviors, the practitioner may employ assisted coaching with very simple and narrow decision issues before returning again to a coaching regimen.

References

ALDOUS, J. A framework for the analysis of family problem solving. In J. Aldous, T. Condon, R. Hill, M. Straus, and I. Tallman (Eds.), *Family problem solving: A symposium on theoretical methodological, and substantive concerns.* Hinsdale, Ill.: Dryden, 1971.

ALKIRE, A. A., and BRUNSE, A. J. Impact and possible causality from videotape feedback in marital therapy. *Journal of Consulting and Clinical Psychology,* 1974, *42,* 203–210.

ALVORD, J. *Home token economy.* Champaign, Ill.: Research Press, 1973.

ATTHOWE, J. N., and KRASNER, L. Preliminary report on the application of contingent reinforcement procedures (token economy) on a "chronic" psychiatric ward. *Journal of Abnormal Psychology,* 1968, *73,* 37–43.

AYLLON, T. and AZRIN, N. H. Reinforcement and instructions with mental patients. *Journal of the Experimental Analysis of Behavior,* 1964, *7,* 327–331.

————. *The token economy: A motivational system for therapy and rehabilitation.* New York: Appleton-Century-Crofts, 1968.

AZRIN, N. H., NASTER, B. J., and JONES, R. Reciprocity counseling: A rapid learning-based procedure for marital counseling. *Behavior Research and Therapy,* 1973, *11,* 365–383.

BACH, G. R., and WYDEN, P. *The intimate enemy.* New York: William Morrow, 1968.

BANDURA, A. *Principles of behavior modification.* New York: Holt, Rinehart and Winston, 1969.

BATESON, G., JACKSON, D. D., HALEY, J., and WEAKLAND, J. Toward a theory of schizophrenia. *Behavioral Science,* 1956, *1,* 251–264.

BAVELAS, A., HASTORF, A. H., GROSS, A. E., and KITE, W. R. Experiments on the alteration of group structure. *Journal of Experimental Social Psychology,* 1965, *1,* 55–71.

BENNETT, T. S., and MALEY, R. F. Modification of interactant behaviors in chronic mental patients. *Journal of Applied Behavior Analysis,* 1973, *6,* 609–620.

BIJOU, S. W., and BAER, D. M. Operant methods in child behavior and development. In W. K. Honig (Ed.), *Operant behavior: Areas of research and application.* New York: Appleton-Century-Crofts, 1966.

BIJOU, S. W., PETERSON, R. F., HARRIS, F. R., ALLEN, K. E., and JOHNSTON, M. S. Methodology for experimental studies of young children in natural settings. *Psychological Record,* 1969, *19,* 177–210.

BIRCHLER, G. R. Differential patterns of instrumental affiliative behavior as a function of degree of marital distress and level of intimacy. Ph.D. dissertation, University of Oregon, 1972. *Dissertation Abstracts International,* 1973, *33,* 14499 D-4500B. University Microfilms No. 73-7865,102.

BIRCHLER, G. R., WEISS, R. L., and VINCENT, J. B. A multi-method analysis of social reinforcement exchange between maritally distressed and non-distressed spouse and stranger dyads. *Journal of Personality and Social Psychology,* 1975, *31,* 349–360.

BRISCOE, R. B., HOFFMAN, D. B., and BAILEY, J. S. Behavioral community psychology: Training a community board to problem solve. *Journal of Applied Behavior Analysis,* 1975, *8,* 157–169.

BROWNING, R. M., and STOVER, D. O. *Behavior modification and child treatment.* Chicago: Aldine-Atherton, 1971.

BUTTERFIELD, W. H., THOMAS, E. J., and SOBERG, R. J. A device for simultaneous feedback of verbal and signal data. *Behavior Therapy,* 1970, *1,* 385–401.

CANTRELL, R. P., CANTRELL, M. L., HUDDLESTON, C. M., and WOOLDRIDGE, R. L. Contingency contracting with school problems. *Journal of Applied Behavior Analysis,* 1969, *2,* 215–220.

CARTER, R. D., and THOMAS, E. J. A case application of a signaling system (SAM) to the assessment and modification of selected problems of marital communication. *Behavior Therapy,* 1973, *4,* 629–645. (a)

————. Modification of problematic marital communication using corrective feedback and instruction. *Behavior Therapy,* 1973, *4,* 100–109. (b)

CHAPPLE, E. D. The interaction chronograph: Its evolution and present application. *Personnel,* 1949, *25,* 295–307.

COMMORATO, A. J., and BRIEGER, J. A. Agency application of a communication procedure. Unpublished manuscript, 1973.

CORSINI, R. J. *Role playing in psychotherapy.* Chicago: Aldine, 1966.

COSSAIRT, A., HALL, R. V., and HOPKINS, B. L. The effects of experimenter's instructions, feedback and praise on teacher praise and student attending behavior. *Journal of Applied Behavior Analysis,* 1973, *6,* 89–100.

DAS, J. P. *Verbal conditioning and behaviour.* London: Pergamon Press, 1969.

DERISI, W. J., and BUTZ, G. *Writing behavioral contracts: A case simulation practice manual.* Champaign, Ill.: Research Press, 1975.

DULANY, D. E., and O'CONNELL, D. C. Does partial reinforcement dissociate verbal rules and the behavior they might be presumed to control? *Journal of Verbal Learning and Verbal Behavior,* 1963, *2,* 361–372.

D'ZURILLA, T. J., and GOLDFRIED, M. R. Problem solving and behavior modification, *Journal of Abnormal Psychology,* 1971, *78,* 107–126.

EISLER, R. M., HERSEN, M., and AGRAS, W. S. Effects of videotape and instructional feedback on non-verbal marital interaction: An analog study. *Behavior Therapy,* 1973, *4,* 551–558.

ELLIS, A. *Reason and emotion in psychotherapy.* New York: Lyle Stuart, 1962.

FAVELL, J. E. Reduction of staff tardiness by a feedback procedure. *Proceedings of the 81st Annual Convention of the American Psychological Association,* Montreal, Canada, 1973, *8,* 899–900.

GAMBRILL, E. D., THOMAS, E. J., and CARTER, R. D. Procedure for sociobehavioral practice in open settings. *Social Work,* 1971, *16,* 51–62.

GARCIA, E. The training and generalization of a conversational speech form in non-verbal retardates. *Journal of Applied Behavior Analysis,* 1974, *7,* 137–149.

GOODMAN, D. S., and MAULTSBY, M. C. *Emotional well-being through rational behavior training.* Springfield, Ill.: Charles C. Thomas, 1974.

GORDON, T. *P.E.T. Parent effectiveness method: The tested new way to raise responsible children.* New York: Peter H. Wyden, 1970.

HAMNER, W. C. Effects of bargaining strategy and pressure to reach agreement in a stalemated negotiation. *Journal of Personality and Social Psychology,* 1974, *30,* 458–467.

HOLZ, W. C., and AZRIN, N. H. Conditioning human verbal behavior. In W. K. Honig (Ed.), *Operant behavior: Areas of research and application.* New York: Appleton-Century-Crofts, 1966.

HOMME, L., CSANYI, A. P., GONZALES, M. A., and RECHS, J. R. *How to use contingency contracting in the classroom.* Champaign, Ill.: Research Press, 1969.

HONIG, W. K. (Ed.). *Operant behavior: Areas of research and application.* New York: Appleton-Century-Crofts, 1966.

HOPS, H., WILLS, T., WEISS, R. L., and PATTERSON, G. Marital interaction coding system. Unpublished manuscript, Department of Psychology, University of Oregon, 1971.

HURSH, D. E., SCHUMAKER, J. B., FAWCETT, S. B., and SHERMAN, J. A. Training behavior modifiers: A comparison of written and direct instructional methods. Paper presented at the 81st Annual Convention of the American Psychological Association, Montreal, Canada, 1973.

JACKSON, D. D. The study of the family. *Family Process,* 1965, *4,* 1–20.

JACOBSON, N. S., and MARTIN, B. Behavioral marriage therapy: Current status. *Psychological Bulletin,* 1976, *83,* 540–557.

JAFFE, J. and FELDSTEIN, S. *Rhythms of dialogue.* New York: Academic Press, 1970.

JOHNSON, S. M., and BOLSTAD, O. D. Methodological issues in naturalistic observation: Some problems and solutions for field research. In L. A. Hamerlynck, L. C. Handy, and E. J. Mash (Eds.), *Behavior change: Methodology, concepts, and practice;* 4th Banff International Conference on Behavior Modification. Champaign, Ill.: Research Press, 1973.

JOHNSTON, J. H., and JOHNSTON, G. T. Modification of consonant speech-sound articulation in young children. *Journal of Applied Behavior Analysis,* 1972, *5,* 233–247.

KANFER, F. H. Verbal conditioning: A review of its current status. In T. R. Dickson and D. L. Horton (Eds.), *Verbal behavior and general behavior theory.* Englewood Cliffs, N.J.: Prentice-Hall, 1968.

KANFER, F. H., and PHILLIPS, J. S. A survey of current behavior therapies and a proposal for classification. In C. M. Franks (Ed.), *Behavior therapy: Appraisal and status.* New York: McGraw-Hill, 1969.

KATZ, D. An automated system for eliciting and recording self observations during dyadic communication. *Behavior Therapy,* 1974, *5,* 689–698.

————. Televised self confrontation and recalled affect: A new look at videotape feedback. Paper presented at the American Psychological Association, 1974.

————. Videotape programming for social agencies. *Social Casework,* 1975, *56,* 44–52.

KAZDIN, A. E. Role of instructions and reinforcement in behavior changes in token reinforcement program. *Journal of Educational Psychology,* 1973, *64,* 63–71.

KAZDIN, A. E., and BOOTZIN, R. R. The token economy: An evaluative review. *Journal of Applied Behavior Analysis,* 1972, *5,* 343–372.

KIFER, R. E., LEWIS, M. A., GREEN, D. R., and PHILLIPS, E. L. Training pre-delinquent youths and their parents to negotiate conflict situations. *Journal of Applied Behavior Analysis,* 1974, *7,* 357–365.

KRASNER, L. Studies of the conditioning of verbal behavior. *Psychological Bulletin,* 1958, *55,* 148–171.

LAUVER, P. J., KELLEY, J. D., and FROEHLE, T. C. Client reaction time and counselor verbal behavior in an interview setting. *Journal of Counseling Psychology,* 1971, *18,* 26–31.

LAZARUS, A. A. Behavior rehearsal versus nondirective therapy versus advice in effecting behavior change. *Behavior Research and Therapy,* 1966, *4,* 209–212.

LEDERER, W. J., and JACKSON, D. B. *The mirages of marriage.* New York: Norton, 1968.

LEITENBERG, H. Positive reinforcement and extinction procedures. In W. S. Agras (Ed.), *Behavior modification: Principles and clinical applications.* Boston: Little, Brown, 1972.

LEITENBERG, H., WINCZE, J. P., BUTZ, R. A., CALLAHAN, E. J., and AGRAS, W. S. Comparison of the effects of instructions and reinforcement in the treatment of a neurotic avoidance response: A single-case experiment. *Journal of Behavior Therapy and Experimental Psychiatry,* 1970, *1,* 53–58.

LEVENGER, G., and SENN, D. J. Disclosure of feelings in marriage. *Merrill-Palmer Quarterly,* 1967, *13,* 237–249.

LINDSLEY, O. R. Direct behavioral analysis of psychotherapy sessions by conjugately programmed closed circuit television. *Psychotherapy: Theory, research and practice,* 1969, *6,* 71–81.

MATARAZZO, J. D., and WIENS, A. N. *The interview: Research on its anatomy and structure.* Chicago: Aldine-Atherton, 1972.

MCFALL, R. M., and LILLESAND, D. B. Behavioral rehearsal with modeling and coaching in assertion training. *Journal of Abnormal Psychology,* 1971, *77,* 313–323.

MEHRABIAN, A., and FERRIS, S. R. Inference of attitudes from non-verbal communication in two channels. *Journal of Consulting Psychology,* 1967, *31,* 248–252.

MERBAUM, M., and LUKENS, H. C. Effects of instructions, elicitations, and reinforcements in the manipulation of affective verbal behavior. *Journal of Abnormal Psychology,* 1968, *73,* 376–380.

MOWRER, O. H. *Learning theory and behavior.* New York: Wiley, 1960.

NATHAN, P. E. "Transmitting" and "receiving" in psychotherapy and supervision. *American Journal of Orthopsychiatry,* 1965, *35,* 937–952.

NATHAN, P. E., SMITH, S., and ROSSI, A. M. Experimental analysis of a brief psychotherapy relationship. *American Journal of Orthopsychiatry,* 1968, *38,* 482–492.

NAVRAN, L. Communication and adjustment in marriage. *Family Process,* 1967, *6,* 173–184.

O'FLAHERTY, K. W. *Evaluation of a coaching procedure for marital decision making.* Ph.D. dissertation, University of Michigan, 1974.

O'LEARY, K. D., and DRABMAN, R. Token reinforcement programs in the classroom: A review. *Psychological Bulletin,* 1971, *75,* 379–398.

PATTERSON, G. R. An application of conditioning techniques to the control of a hyperactive child. In L. T. Ullmann and L. Krasner (Eds.), *Case studies in behavior modification.* New York: Holt, Rinehart and Winston, 1964.

PATTERSON, G. R., and HOPS, H. Coercion, a game for two: Intervention techniques for marital conflict. In R. E. Ulrich and T. Mountjoy (Eds.), *The experimental analysis of social behavior.* New York: Appleton-Century-Crofts, 1972 .

PATTERSON, G. R., and REID, J. B. Reciprocity and coercion: Two facets of social systems. In C. Neuringer and J. L. Michael (Eds.), *Behavior modification and clinical psychology.* New York: Appleton-Century-Crofts, 1970.

PIAGET, G. W. Training patients to communicate. In A. A. Lazarus (Ed.), *Clinical behavior therapy.* New York: Brunner/Mazel, 1972.

PRUITT, D. G., and JOHNSON, D. F. Mediation as an aid to face saving in negotiation. *Journal of Personality and Social Psychology,* 1970, *14,* 239–247.

RAMP, E., ULRICH, R., and DULANEY, S. Delayed time out as a procedure for reducing disruptive classroom behavior: A case study. *Journal of Applied Behavior Analysis,* 1971, *4,* 235–239.

RAUSH, H. L., BARRY, W. A., HERTEL, R. K., and SWAIN, N. A. *Communication, conflict and marriage.* San Francisco: Jossey-Bass, 1974.

RIMM, D. C., and MASTERS, J. C. *Behavior therapy: Techniques and empirical findings.* New York: Academic Press, 1974.

SALZINGER, K. The problem of response class in verbal behavior. In K. Salzinger and S. Salzinger (Eds.), *Research in verbal behavior and some neurophysiological implications.* New York: Academic Press, 1967.

SALZINGER, K., PORTNOY, S., and FELDMAN, R. S. Experimental manipulation of continuous speech in schizophrenic patients. *Journal of Abnormal and Social Psychology,* 1964, *68,* 508–516.

SHERMAN, J. A. Reinstatement of verbal behavior in a psychotic by reinforcement methods. *Journal of Speech and Hearing Disorders,* 1963, *28,* 398–401.

SHNEIDMAN, E. S. Logical content and analysis: An explication of styles of "concludifying." In G. Gerbner, O. R. Holsti, K. Krippendorff, W. J. Paisley, and P. J. Stone (Eds.), *The analysis of communication content: Developments in scientific theories and computer techniques.* New York: Wiley, 1969.

SIMKINS, L., and WEST, J. Reinforcement of duration of talking in triad groups. *Psychological Reports,* 1966, *18,* 231–236.

SKINNER, B. F. An operant analysis of problem solving. In B. Kleinmuntz (Ed.), *Problem solving: Research, method and theory.* New York: Wiley, 1966.

———. *Verbal behavior.* New York: Appleton-Century-Crofts, 1957.

STAATS, A. W., *Learning, language, and cognition.* New York: Holt, Rinehart and Winston, 1968.

STAATS, A. W., MINKE, K. A., FINLEY, J. R., WOLF, M. M., and BROOKS, L. O. A reinforcer system and experimental procedure for the laboratory study of reading acquisition. *Child Development,* 1964, *35,* 209–231.

STAATS, A. W., and STAATS, C. K. *Complex human behavior: A systematic extension of learning principles.* New York: Holt, Rinehart and Winston, 1963.

STRAUGHAN, J. H., POTTER, W. K., and HAMILTON, S. H. The behavioral treatment of an elective mute. *Journal of Child Psychology and Psychiatry,* 1965, *6,* 125–130.

STUART, R. B. Behavioral contracting within the families of delinquents. *Journal of Behavior Therapy and Experimental Psychiatry,* 1971, *2,* 1–11.

———. Operant interpersonal treatment for martial discord. *Journal of Consulting and Clinical Psychology,* 1969, *33,* 675–682.

THOMAS, E. J. Uses of research methods in interpersonal practice. In N. A. Polansky (Ed.), *Social work research: Methods for the helping professions* (Rev. ed.). Chicago: University of Chicago Press, 1975.

THOMAS, E. J., and CARTER, R. D. Instigative modification with a multi-problem family. *Social Casework,* 1971, *52,* 444–455.

THOMAS, E. J., CARTER, R. D., and GAMBRILL, E. D. Some possibilities of behavioral modification with marital problems using "SAM" (signal system for the assessment and modification of behavior). In R. D. Rubin, H. Fensterheim, A. A. Lazarus, and C. M. Franks (Eds.), *Advances in behavior therapy.* New York: Academic Press, 1971.

————. (Eds.), *Utilization and appraisal of socio-behavioral techniques in social welfare—pilot phase.* Final report on research supported by the Department of Health, Education and Welfare, Social Rehabilitation Service, SRS-CRD Grant No. 425-CL-9. Ann Arbor, Michigan: University of Michigan School of Social Work, 1970.

THOMAS, E. J., CARTER, R. D., GAMBRILL, E. D., and BUTTERFIELD, W. H. A signal system for the assessment and modification of behavior (SAM). *Behavior Therapy,* 1970, *1,* 252–259.

THOMAS, E. J., O'FLAHERTY, K., and BORKIN, J. Coaching marital partners in family decision making. In J. D. Krumboltz and C. E. Thoresen (Eds.), *Counseling Methods.* New York: Holt, Rinehart and Winston, 1976.

THOMAS, E. J., and WALTER, C. L. Guidelines for behavioral practice in the open community agency: Procedure and evaluation. *Behavior Research and Therapy,* 1973, *11,* 193–205.

THOMAS, E. J., WALTER, C. L., and CARTER, R. D. *Socio-behavioral techniques for open welfare settings.* Progress report for research supported by the Department of Health, Education and Welfare, Social and Rehabilitation Service, Grant 10-T-56023 / 5-01. Ann Arbor: University of Michigan School of Social Work, 1971.

————. *Socio-behavioral techniques for open welfare settings.* Final report on research supported by the Department of Health, Education and Welfare, Social and Rehabilitation Service, Grant 10-T-56023 / 5-02. Ann Arbor: University of Michigan School of Social Work, 1972.

THOMAS, E. J., WALTER, C., and O'FLAHERTY, K. A verbal problem checklist for use in assessing family verbal behavior. *Behavior Therapy,* 1974, *5,* 235–246. (a)

————. Computer-assisted assessment and modification: Possibilities and illustrative data. *Social Service Review,* 1974, *48,* 170–183. (b)

THOMSON, N., FRASER, D., and McDOUGALL, A. The reinstatement of speech in near-mute chronic schizophrenics by instructions, imitative prompts and reinforcement. *Journal of Behavior Therapy and Experimental Psychiatry,* 1974, *5,* 83–91.

TRACEY, D. A., BRIDELL, D. W., and WILSON, G. T. Generalization of verbal conditioning to verbal and non-verbal behavior: Group therapy with chronic psychiatric patients. *Journal of Applied Behavior Analysis,* 1974, *7,* 391–403.

WALKER, H. M., and BUCKLEY, N. K. Programming generalization and maintenance of treatment effects across time and across settings. *Journal of Applied Behavior Analysis,* 1972, *5*, 209–225.

WALTON, R. E., and McKERSIE, R. B. Bargaining dilemmas in mixed-motive decision making. *Behavioral Science,* 1966, *11*, 370–385.

WATZLAWICK, P., BEAVIN, J. H., and JACKSON, D. D. *Pragmatics of human communication.* New York: W. W. Norton, 1967.

WEICK, K. E. Group process, family processes, and problem solving. In J. Aldous, T. Condon, R. Hill, M. Straus, and I. Tallman (Eds.), *Family problem solving: A symposium on theoretical, methodological, and substantive concerns.* Hinsdale, Ill.: Dryden, 1971.

WEISS, R. F., LOMBARDO, J. P., WARREN, D. R., and KELLEY, K. A. Reinforcing effects of speaking in reply. *Journal of Personality and Social Psychology,* 1971, *20*, 186–199.

WEISS, R. L., HOPS, H., and PATTERSON, G. R. A framework for conceptualizing marital conflict: A technology for altering it, some data for evaluating it. In L. A. Hamerlynck, L. C. Handy, and E. J. Mash (Eds.), *Behavior change: Methodology, concepts, and practice;* 4th Banff International Conference on Behavior Modification. Champaign, Ill.: Research Press, 1973.

WIEMAN, R. J., SHOULDERS, D. I., and FARR, J. H. Reciprocal reinforcement in marital therapy. *Journal of Behavior Therapy and Experimental Psychiatry,* 1974, *5*, 291–297.

WILLS, T. A., WEISS, R. L., and PATTERSON, G. R. A behavioral analysis of the determinants of marital satisfaction. *Journal of Consulting and Clinical Psychology,* 1974, *42*, 802–811.

WINCZE, J. P., LEITENBERG, H., and AGRAS, W. S. The effects of token reinforcement and feedback on the delusional verbal behavior of chronic paranoid schizophrenics. *Journal of Applied Behavior Analysis,* 1972, *5*, 247–263.

WOLPE, J. *The practice of behavior therapy.* New York: Pergamon Press, 1969.

INDEXES

Name Index

Subject Index

A

Alternative generation procedure, 212–213

Assessment, *see* Assessment of marital communication, Assessment of marital decision making

Assessment feedback, 66–67

Assessment of marital communication, 44–77
and analysis of verbatim transcript, 191–196
and assessment feedback, 66–67
and assessment probe, 65–66
and baselining, 64–65
basic steps of, 45–54
and categories of verbal strengths and problems, 24–42
coding in, 69–72
and commitment to cooperate, 47
and contract for target area of, 46–47
and electromechanical devices, 73–76
and home assessment, 72–73
and identification of probable sources of difficulty, 47–61
initial inquiry in, 51–52
and inventory of problem areas, 46
and nonverbal behavior, 53–54, 56*t*.
other steps in, 64–67
perspective for communication problems, 43–44
and referent conditions, 53–54, 55*t*.

respecification of problem contract in, 64
response display transcript, 174–184
response specification, 47–61
and setting events, 54, 56*t*.
specialized procedures in, 67–76
and specification of behavioral objectives, 61–64
tasks of, 44–45
and Verbal Problem Checklist, 67–68

Assessment of marital decision making, 129–137
and behavioral and environmental resources, 135
and behavioral objectives, 135–136
identification of probable controlling conditions in, 131–134
inventory of problem areas, 130
other steps of, 136–137
overview of basic steps, 129–130
preliminary steps in, 130–131
and respecification of problem contract, 136
and Response Display Procedure, 133–134
response specification in, 131–134
selection of and contract for target area, 130–131
verbatim transcript of response display, 205–209

Assessment probe, 65–66

Assisted decision-making procedure, 172–173